David Livingstone

David Livingstone

Meriel Buxton

palgrave

First published 2001 by
PALGRAVE
Houndmills, Basingstoke, Hampshire RG21 6XS and
175 Fifth Avenue, New York, N. Y. 10010
Companies and representatives throughout the world

PALGRAVE is the new global academic imprint of
St. Martin's Press LLC Scholarly and Reference Division and
Palgrave Publishers Ltd (formerly Macmillan Press Ltd).

ISBN 0–333–74041–6

This book is printed on paper suitable for recycling and made from fully managed and sustained forest sources.

A catalogue record for this book is available from the British Library.

Library of Congress Cataloging-in-Publication Data
Buxton, Meriel.
    David Livingstone / Meriel Buxton.
       p. cm.
    Includes bibliographical references (p.) and index.
    ISBN 0–333–74041–6
       1. Livingstone, David, 1813–1873. 2. Explorers—Africa,
    Southern—Biography. 3. Explorers—Scotland—Biography.
    4. Africa, Southern—Discovery and exploration. I. Title.

DT1110.L58 B89 2001
916.704'23'092—dc21
[B]
                                                    00–065218

10   9   8   7   6   5   4   3   2   1
10 09 08 07 06 05 04 03 02 01

Printed and bound in Great Britain by
Antony Rowe Ltd, Chippenham, Wiltshire

To Jack
without whom this book would never have been written

Contents

List of Plates

All plates most generously provided by the David Livingstone Centre at Blantyre.

List of Maps

Foreword

David Livingstone has not lacked biographers throughout the century and a quarter since his death! The earlier biographies relied on his published works supplemented by recollections of some who knew or had worked with him. They portrayed the Victorian hero who inspired succeeding generations. Then in the mid-1900s came a number of scholarly studies by historians with different interests exploring various aspects of his life or particular journeys, as well as a series of expertly annotated collections of his correspondence and journals. These additional sources have in the last 25 years been used to analyse his life and character against the background of his times. Frequently such biographies have exposed and publicized his failures or character failings. So the Victorian hero acclaimed as a missionary, explorer and liberator has also been branded a failure. Of course he had his strengths and weaknesses, his failures as well as his successes.

I worked for several years as a medical missionary living not far from one of my great-grandfather's routes and more recently followed his last journey from his meeting with Stanley. Livingstone wanted the world to appreciate Africans as human beings whose potential could only be fulfilled through Christianity, commerce and civilization. He is far from forgotten in the countries he traversed and is especially remembered in Zambia where he died, not merely as a historical figure, but as the one who brought the Christian Gospel to their land. Even today in his own country people who may recall little about him are still interested in him.

For the twenty-first century Meriel Buxton has undertaken a new biography – quite a daunting task. She has researched her subject thoroughly and ably guides the reader through Livingstone's life story: the missionary who, unusually for his time, became deeply interested in the way of life and language of the Kwena tribe with whom he lived and worked, but then felt compelled to become a traveller and explorer through ten countries of modern Africa, and played a significant role in exposing the evils of the slave trade.

Hers is an engrossing story of Livingstone who was neither a saint nor a failure – and paradoxically that is a positive, not a negative view.

David Livingstone Wilson
Auchterarder
March 2000

Acknowledgements

I would like to thank Dr David Livingstone Wilson, great-grandson of David Livingstone, for all the help he has given me by reading and commenting on the typescript and especially by writing the Foreword. He is a fund of information on every aspect of Livingstone's life.

Everyone at the David Livingstone Centre at Blantyre has gone out of their way to be helpful and encouraging. The Centre is a remarkable place, quite unlike any other museum, with an enthusiastic team and a friendly atmosphere which cannot fail to engender an interest in Livingstone and his early life in the building now devoted to his memory. In particular, Karen Carruthers, the Property Manager, has arranged to provide all the illustrations for this book and has helped in innumerable different ways. The Centre was managed by the Scottish National Memorial to David Livingstone Trust, founded in 1926, until 1999, when management passed to the Scottish National Trust.

Professor Jack Spence has been my mentor and guide throughout the writing of this book: without his sound advice, knowledge and encouragement it would never have been started, much less completed.

I am also grateful to Anthony and Merrill Dawson Paul and to Jane Stanley for their help, to my son Hugh for all his technical assistance with the word processing, and to my daughter Rose and especially my husband James for all their encouragement, interest and support.

A note on spelling

While Livingstone's own spelling is far from consistent, I have attempted to adhere to the form most commonly used by him throughout. Many of the names are different from their modern equivalents. The Livingstone family, as mentioned in the text, spelt their own name without the final 'e' until 1855 when David Livingstone's father Neil asked all his children to revert to the original spelling with an 'e'. I have used this form throughout except for quotations from letters.

Chronology

1813   19 March born Blantyre, Lanarkshire.
1823   Started work as a cotton piecer.
1826   The only boy at the mills to continue learning Latin.
1832   Promoted to spinner.
1833   Abolition of slavery throughout British Empire.
1834   Read Karl Gutzlaff pamphlet concerning medical missionaries in China.
1836   Anderson's College, Glasgow.
1838–9 Probationer of London Missionary Society at Chipping Ongar.
1840   Qualified in medicine. Ordained. Sailed to Africa.
1841   Kuruman. Bechuanaland with Edwards.
1842   Travelled.
1843   Founded mission at Mabotsa. Travelled with Captain Steele. Attacked by lion.
1844   Engaged to Mary Moffat.
1845   2 January married. Moved to Chonuane.
1846   Robert born.
1847   Moved to Kolobeng. Agnes born.
1848   Sechele's conversion.
1849   Thomas born. To Lake Ngami with Oswell.
1850   Expedition with Mary and children. Elizabeth born and died. Mary had stroke.
1851   Visited Sebitoane. Oswell (Zouga) born.
1852   Cape Town. Mary and children sailed to England. Sack of Kolobeng. Kuruman.
1853   Returned to Makololo: Sekeletu now chief. Started for West coast.
1854   To Loanda then started back.
1855   To Sekeletu. Saw the Victoria Falls.
1856   To Quilimane. Sailed to England.
1857   *Missionary Researches and Travels in South Africa* published.
1858   Start of Zambesi Expedition. Anna Mary born at Kuruman. Bedingfeld left.

1859	Shire River and Lakes Shirwa and Nyassa. Baines and Thornton dismissed.
1860	Linyanti and back to deliver Makololo. Heard fate of Helmore mission.
1861	*Pioneer* arrived. Mackenzie's mission to Shire Highlands. Explored Lake Nyassa.
1862	Arrival of Mary, missionary ladies and *Lady Nyassa*. Deaths of Mackenzie, Burrup and Mary. To Rovuma.
1863	*Lady Nysassa* launched. Thornton returned then died. Kirk and Charles left. Expedition recalled. DL walked 700 miles by Lake Nyassa. Tozer withdrew mission.
1864	Sailed *Lady Nyassa* to Bombay. Sailed to England. Death of Robert.
1865	Newstead. Completed *Zambesi* book. Mother died. To Bombay.
1866	Zanzibar. Expedition started from Mikidani along the Rovuma. False report of DL's murder.
1867	Medicines stolen. Seriously ill and much delayed. To Lake Moero.
1868	Lake Bangweolo.
1869	Seriously ill. To Lake Tanganyika by litter. Reached Ujiji.
1870	Long stay at Bambarre.
1871	To Nyangwe. 15 July massacre. To Ujiji. Arrival of Stanley. Journey north.
1872	18 February Unyanyembe. 14 March Stanley left. August left Unyanyembe for Lake Tanganyika.
1873	1 May died in Ilala at Chitambo's village. Body carried back to Zanzibar.
1874	18 April state funeral in Westminster Abbey.

1
Blantyre: the Boy

Fourteen hours is a long working day which few would choose to extend. For children of ten, allowed just half an hour for breakfast and an hour for lunch between six in the morning and eight in the evening, it seems inconceivable that any should follow this with a further four hours of voluntary study. Yet some boys at the mill at Blantyre, near Glasgow, in 1823 did attend school from 8 until 10 p.m. One then continued to read until midnight if his mother did not forcibly intervene. David Livingstone was always different from other people.

The Livingstone family were originally crofters on the island of Ulva, west of Mull. David's great-grandfather was killed at the Battle of Culloden. His grandfather, Neil, finding his croft too small to support his large family, showed the initiative, ambition and drive which were to be so characteristic of his grandson. In 1792 Neil Livingstone left the austere, isolated life of the island for the very different, though equally hard, environment of the newly created industrial suburbs of Glasgow. He took with him few material objects but, in addition to his family, he had one invaluable possession, his reputation for integrity, evidenced by a written reference from the minister. This stated that he 'has always maintained an unblemished moral character and is known for a man of piety and religion'.[1]

His qualities did not go unrecognized in the world to which he had moved. Neil's grandson was to write years later that he was 'highly esteemed for his unflinching honesty, was employed in the conveyance of large sums of money from Glasgow to the works and in old age was, according to the custom of that company, pensioned off so as to spend his declining years in ease and comfort'.[2]

So successful was the older Neil that, although his son and name-sake, a child of four at the time of the move, started work in the mills, he was subsequently apprenticed to a tailor. The younger Neil's integrity was as unchallenged as his father's, but he was of a more pious less practical nature. He soon abandoned tailoring in favour of selling tea, which combined well with handing out religious tracts, his real enthusiasm. Before this change he married the tailor's daughter, Agnes Hunter. They lived for a time in Glasgow, but returned to Blantyre before the birth of their second son on the 19 March 1813. The baby was christened David.

While conditions in the mills at Blantyre seem inhuman to twentieth-century eyes, with young children being required to work 14 hour shifts and earning a pittance, this was not how it appeared to contemporaries. When Blantyre was first developed in 1785 it was at the forefront of social and industrial development. The company supported its own poor, there were sickness and funeral funds controlled by the workers and the firm provided a number of services: watchmen, scavengers to clean up the village, a library, public wash houses, bleaching greens and gardens; half the minister's salary was also paid. Provisions were available at low prices, unlike many factories where, on the contrary, employees were compelled to spend part of their meagre earnings on low quality goods at inflated prices under what was known as the 'truck system'.

Housing too belonged to the company. The Livingstone family was one of 24 sharing a three-storied tenement building. Each family had its own 'single kitchen', a room just 14 feet by 10, in which Neil and Agnes, their three sons, John, David and Charles (two further sons died in infancy), and two daughters Janet and Agnes all slept, ate, cooked and spent such spare time as was available to them. Two alcoves housed the beds, with additional truckle beds stacked underneath, to be pulled out at night. Small wonder that David's habit of reading late into the night found little favour with his mother: no doubt it was in the interests of the rest of the family as well as of the boy himself that she frequently took the book from him.

When John and David were in their teens (there was a six-year gap, caused by the deaths in infancy of two more boys between David and his next sister Janet) they moved out to board with their grandparents in the comparative luxury of a nearby cottage. David adored both his grandparents, later recalling the old man's 'never-ending stock of stories, many of which were wonderfully like those I have since heard while sitting by the African evening fires',[3] the same stories as those on which Sir Walter Scott was brought up and which formed the basis of many of his novels. David's grandmother too inspired him with her singing of Gaelic songs.

At the comparatively late age of ten (some children went into mills before they were six, and most before they were eight years old) David started work in the factory as a 'piecer'. Piecers were responsible for joining broken threads on the spinning machines, a job which was supposed to demand quick eyes and constant attention as well as speed and agility in making the necessary repairs before it was too late. How David achieved this remains a mystery, for he invested that part of his first week's wages which he was allowed to keep for himself in *Rudiments of Latin*. He propped this book up against the spinning jenny and soon learnt to concentrate on the words undisturbed by the overpowering noise of the machinery, an ability which stood him in good stead for the rest of his life.

If he avoided constant beatings for inattention to his duties, it must indicate that the atmosphere at Blantyre was considerably more relaxed than that in most of the mills at that time. A 13-year-old boy named Charlie Burns gave evidence to the Select Committee of Factory Children's Labour in 1831–2 about conditions in the four different mills where he had worked. He testified that 'if we looked off our work, or spoke to one another, we were beaten . . . if we let the machine stop half a minute we should have been beaten'. No such rules can have existed at Blantyre, for the other boys, unimpressed by such devotion to education, would take pot shots with their bobbins at the carefully balanced book. The young Livingstone, characteristically even then preferring to adopt the moral high ground rather than be 'one of the lads', later wrote 'the fellows used to try to turn me off from the path I had chosen, and always began with "I think you ought etc.", till I snapped them up with a mild "You think! I can think and act for myself; don't need anyone to think for me."'[4] Indeed he did not, even if his approach was not calculated to increase his popularity.

If the Blantyre mills were unusual in permitting the boys to talk and even indulge in some horseplay, the physical conditions under which the spinning was carried out were inevitably uncomfortable and unhealthy, as the Select Committee of Factory Children's Labour was informed by a witness:

'Is it not likewise, in what is called hot-water spinning, extremely hot in these mills?'
'Yes, very hot.'
'Is not the place full of steam?'
'Yes, and the machinery throws off water perpetually; so that we are wet to the skin by the hot water.'
'Then your clothes are entirely wet?'
'Yes, and as soon as we get home our clothes are quite stiff with the frost in the winter-time'
'Had you a cough with inhaling that dust?'
'Yes, I had a cough, and spit blood.'

This witness, who was almost 14 and working from 6 a.m. until 7 (not 8) p.m., also confirmed that he became extremely tired and as soon as he went home and sat down by the fire, he fell asleep directly.

The company at Blantyre was ahead of its time also in providing schooling for the boys in the evenings: this did not become compulsory until 1833 and even then observance of the law was frequently cursory. The schoolmaster was paid in part by the company and in part by his pupils, but at such a low rate that any boy wishing for education could afford it. For this reason, and because the master took trouble and was kind, many of the boys at Blantyre obtained a basic education. Before David even started work, he was fortunate that his father had taught him to read and write: more than 90 per cent of factory boys throughout Britain never even became literate. His Latin was soon of a sufficiently high standard to enable him to study all the classical texts he could lay his hands on. He was a voracious and omnivorous reader: only novels failed to attract him. A farmer who occasionally employed him to herd his cattle was not impressed: 'I didna' think muckle o' that David Livingstone when he worked wi' me. He was aye lyin' on his belly readin' a book.'[5]

'Scientific works and books of travel were my especial delight,'[6] he wrote later, and he pursued his enthusiasm for natural history in a more practical way whenever he had a free day, heading off into the hills and woods with his brothers to explore, walking until little Charles cried with exhaustion, 'yet we discovered to us so many new and interesting things that he was always as eager to join us next time as he was the last.'[7]

David was forever asking questions which those around him were often incapable of answering. One day he was intrigued by the discovery of shells in a quarry he was exploring. 'A quarry man, seeing a little boy so engaged, looked with the pitying eye which the benevolent assume when viewing the insane. Addressing him with "However did these shells come into these rocks?" "When God made the rocks, He made the shells in them" was the damping reply.'[8]

In the absence of anyone to teach him about all that interested him in the world around, and with the resources of the library no doubt limited, he made full use of such books as he did possess. He came to know every word of his first medical book, 'that extraordinary old work on astrological medicine, Culpeper's "Herbal"', and, aided by another book on the plants of Lanarkshire, spent much time 'collecting simples'.[9] In this way he developed not only a basic understanding of the medicinal properties of herbs but also a deep interest in every aspect of the natural world. Throughout his life he was constantly observing, sketching and compiling detailed notes on everything he saw, building up a remarkable knowledge of botany, zoology, geology and astronomy. At this time, his eager brain was led by Culpeper into the study of astrology too, half frightened and half attracted by what, with greater maturity, he defined as 'that abyss of fantasies'.

Some of his adventures with his brothers showed less precocious erudition. No doubt most of his contemporaries devoted some of their precious free time in the country to the attempt to poach a salmon. It is reassuring to know that even David was not above such behaviour, and, after one such successful fishing trip, he hid his prize down his little brother Charles's trouser leg. The catch was evidently a worthwhile one, for Charles was offered much misguided sympathy on the way home for his horribly swollen, presumably painful, leg.

Perhaps the boys were lucky that their mother did not refuse to accept their catch, despite her perpetual struggle to make both ends meet. She was noted for her fierce independence as well as for adhering to what seemed to others to be absurdly high standards. On Sundays the boys were dressed up with frills and ribbons before walking the three miles to the little chapel they attended. Here they, and others coming from a distance, were offered a most hospitable welcome, but Mrs Livingstone always insisted on bringing lunch for all her family with her, accepting only boiling water to make the tea and chairs to sit down. After lunch she would enjoy her only indulgence, smoking her clay 'cutty' pipe.

Her husband was almost fanatical in his approach to religion. A strict Calvinist, his conviction that redemption depended upon God alone and that nothing a man did or attempted to do could lead to his salvation was not one likely to appeal to his son. David Livingstone's whole life was a demonstration of what a man could achieve by sheer determination, persistence and hard work against all the odds. In a time when many lives were made wretched by the dread of Hell fire, his fear that he was not among the Elect of God and, much worse, that there was nothing which he could do to rectify the position, weighed heavily on the sensitive, intelligent boy.

The gulf between the approach of father and son to religious issues went even deeper during the boy's adolescence and compounded his feelings of guilt. His passion for scientific investigation was not only outside his father's interest and understanding, but something which the older man actively deplored, 'believing', as David later wrote, 'with many of his time who ought to have known better, that [scientific works] were inimical to religion.'[10] The boy in his turn resisted all attempts to make him spend precious time on what he considered 'dry doctrinal reading'. This difference of opinion eventually culminated in open warfare between the two. David later recalled that his refusal to read Wilberforce's 'Practical Christianity' was the reason for the last beating he received from his father.

Then in 1832, when David was 19, different influences caused both him and his father to alter their respective positions and move much closer together. The younger man discovered the writings of Dr Thomas Dick, an author who shared his conviction that religion and science were not hostile to each other. To find this conviction endorsed by a reputable writer lifted an overwhelming burden of guilt, anxiety, incomprehension and perhaps even terror from his shoulders. Indeed so deep was the impression made on the young man that he travelled some eighty miles to meet Dr Dick and discuss the matter face to face.

In the same year, Neil Livingstone's views too underwent a metamorphosis. In an age when religion really was the most important element in most people's lives, indeed their only concern beyond the daily struggle to stay alive, and the opportunity to hear controversial views openly expressed was rare indeed, itinerant preachers could attract huge audiences. Somewhat surprisingly in view of his narrow-minded outlook, Neil Livingstone allowed himself to be taken to such a lecture at the independent church at Hamilton. The young preacher must have possessed a remarkable power of oratory. His blistering attack on the way in which the Established Kirk was run as well as on its approach to certain theological issues might have been expected to shock and antagonize the pious, unbending Calvinist and lifelong devotee of that Established Kirk. Instead Neil Livingstone underwent a conversion more sudden and absolute than any which his son was to bring about in more than thirty years' preaching in Africa. He joined the independent church at Hamilton and began to play an active part in the new liberalizing movement, not long afterwards becoming a deacon of that church. Soon father and son were together attending lectures advocating reform and supporting the Congregational Union, which upheld the rights of church congregations to elect their own leaders and take their own independent decisions.

This spirit of increasing democracy in religious matters was but a small manifestation of the spirit of the age. The year 1832 was not only that in which the Livingstones, father and son, reconciled their differences. It was also the year in which the Reform Bill was passed by Parliament. A year later Parliament took an even more momentous step, and one which was to have a profound influence on the life of David Livingstone. Slavery was declared illegal throughout the British Empire.

2
Glasgow, Chipping Ongar and London: the Student

At the time of his twenty-first birthday, Livingstone was working in the mill as a spinner, promotion which had come two years earlier. He described the work, which was better paid than his previous occupation, as 'excessively severe on a slim, loose-jointed lad',[1] a harsh criticism from one who virtually never complained of physical hardship. But its routine nature left him free to make plans and to dream. His desire to travel to remote corners of the globe must have been inspired originally by books, for he knew no one with personal experience of distant lands. But, if any of the accounts written by the great African explorers of the time reached him, they failed to fire his imagination. His thoughts were all of China, teeming with so many millions of souls destined to be lost eternally unless someone could reach them in time to tell them the good news of the Christian gospel.

He thought too of all that he was learning of the world around him, its trees and rocks and plants. He was discovering much about the properties of herbs, their healing powers and the ways in which they could be used to relieve suffering, heal wounds and cure diseases. Other aspects of medicine interested him as well though the science was then in its infancy. Parliament passed a statute in 1832 as significant in its way as the Reform Act the same year and the Act for the Abolition of Slavery a year later. For the first time the sale of bodies for dissection was legalized, wiping out the trade of the body snatchers and grave robbers. The need for doctors to learn by scientific observation and practice was at last acknowledged.

Medicine as a profession appealed to Livingstone at two levels. He had a keen academic interest in it, backed by a reasoned, logical approach which today is inculcated into everyone wishing to study any scientific subject as a matter of course but was rare in the 1830s. Not so many years before, the physician had been closely allied to the magician, compensating for a lack of any true understanding of the workings of the human body by claims to mystical powers. Livingstone believed only in what could be objectively proved, and sought to extend the limits of his knowledge by experiment and observation.

He also had an intense desire to alleviate human suffering, to improve the plight of mankind. Ever a practical man, he saw physical health as the other side of the coin of spiritual welfare and strove to bring both to those in need. Yet he could also be the cause of physical hardship to those whom he loved or esteemed. He was later to expose his wife and children unnecessarily to excessively harsh living conditions and was oblivious to the risks incurred by other Europeans, members of his Zambesi expedition or the missionaries led by Bishop Mackenzie, for example. None of us live up to our ideals, but for Livingstone the apparent inconsistency had a deeper basis. The demands he made of others were never greater than those he imposed upon himself. While the impression received by the rest of the world was very different, Livingstone himself, without clearly articulating the idea, probably deemed it a compliment to consider others worthy to face the same suffering and dangers as he himself willingly embraced for the causes he held so dear. In the same way, when the rigours of boyhood excursions into the country reduced his small brother to tears, he noted that the child, still keen to come on the next occasion, would have been insulted had he been left behind.

When the young man first expressed an interest in studying medicine, there was no reason to query his determination, as he wrote subsequently, 'to devote my life to the alleviation of human misery'.[2] Yet his father, more concerned with questions of the soul than the body, later wrote: 'I was much opposed to it, until he informed me that it was not to gain a livelihood he thought of doing so, his anxious wish was to be enabled to spend his life in the service of the Redeemer among the heathen, I no longer felt inclined to oppose his design but felt thankful that such a thought was in his heart.'[3]

The spiritual motivation was quite as strong in Livingstone as his desire to confer material benefit on humanity. The brevity of his reference to it in the introduction to his first book indicates the intensity of feeling. 'I shall not again refer to the inner spiritual life which I believe then began, nor do I intend to specify with any prominence the evangelistic labours to which the love of Christ has since impelled me.'[4] Yet, strangely, he, like his father, at first saw the two ambitions as contradictory rather than complementary.

Then, a few weeks after his twenty-first birthday, Livingstone read a pamphlet which bound all his hopes and dreams into a single track. At this stage the track seemed to be leading towards China, for the pamphlet had been published in Canton the previous year by a Dutchman named Karl Gutzlaff. It introduced the idea, a new and revolutionary one to Livingstone and most of his contemporaries, of the medical missionary.

This was the key to all his dreams. A way was opened for combining all his interests in a single profession, and, in the short term more important still, the pamphlet enabled him to convince his father of the desirability of training as a doctor. At least now he had family support. Even so, neighbours and friends in Blantyre no doubt shook their heads in disbelief at the strange boy who had grown up among them. An ambitious boy in that environment was one who dreamed of providing himself, his wife and his children with sufficient food, sufficient clothes and sufficient rest. To wish to go away from home to study medicine and obtain qualifications was extraordinary indeed. Had they known the full extent of his dreams, they would have been convinced that he was insane.

David was busy doing his sums. Anderson's College in Glasgow (now the University of Strathclyde) charged fees of £12 a session. He had been unable to save anything for himself until he was nearly 19, when he was promoted to cotton spinning. Even so, when earning around four shillings a week, £12 represented more than a year's wages without making any allowance for living expenses, either while working or when at the college, where lodgings would also have to be paid for. However, his brother John as well as his father felt that the boy deserved such financial support as they were able to offer. College sessions filled the winter months, and in summer he would be able to return to Blantyre and his job at the mill. Even this he could not count upon: towards the end of his time at college the drunken factory manager told him that 'if he went to Glasgow any more, following after education, he must lose his work as he would not keep it any longer for him.'[5] But by the late autumn of 1836, when he was 23, enough money had been put together to enable him to enrol as a student.

Father and son walked the eight miles into Glasgow on a bitterly cold day with snow lying. They searched all day in increasing desperation for lodgings which he could afford, but it was evening before they found a room in Rotten Row going for two shillings a week. David soon learnt why it was so cheap: the landlady supplemented the rent by helping herself to the tenant's sugar and tea. He decided that a rather better room in the High Street with a more honest landlady was worth an additional sixpence a week.

On Saturday afternoons, he would walk the eight miles home every weekend, as well as three miles each way to the service at Hamilton on Sundays. On Monday mornings a kindly rich draper named Fergus Ferguson, who knew the family through the church at Hamilton, offered to drive him back to Glasgow in his gig. But by the time Mr Ferguson reached Glasgow David would have missed one complete lecture and part of the second. He therefore preferred to get up at five and walk, regardless of the weather, to make sure that he arrived between eight and nine in the morning.

In addition to his medical studies, he also attended theology lectures given by Dr Ralph Wardlaw, the Principal of the Congregational Seminary, who was a campaigner for the abolition of slavery, and studied Greek. Academic competition may not have been strong, for the college was open to anyone capable of paying the fees, but Livingstone's background and approach must have made him stand out. At all events, he attracted the attention of the lecturers, for he became a close personal friend of Dr Andrew Buchanan, the Professor of Medicine, later one of his Trustees, and was also friendly with the Professor of Chemistry, Thomas Graham. Other topics which he studied included Anatomy and Surgery, but none of these sciences bore much resemblance to their modern equivalents. There were no biochemical or pathological laboratories to aid in diagnosis, and causes of diseases were not understood at all. There was no comprehension of the relevance of nutrition. In surgery, the most important skill was speed for there was no form of anaesthesia. Antiseptics too were not discovered for another quarter of a century. The tools available for doctors to use to help their patients were extremely limited. Medical students were learning, together with such accurate knowledge as was available, a number of positively harmful techniques, for example dependence on blood letting for the relief of pain and treatment of intestinal problems. However, Livingstone continued to develop the scientific approach which was to stand him in such good stead, experimenting, double checking his results and making careful observations. He was also, characteristically, always keen to learn about any new developments and follow them up. Thus he eagerly devoured any copies of *The Lancet* which reached him in Africa, through them learning about chloroform, which he immediately longed to use to help his wife in childbirth.

A number of Livingstone's contemporaries and friends did go on to achieve success and fame in various scientific fields. Outstanding among them was James 'Paraffin' Young, at this time assistant to the Professor of Chemistry. His invention of paraffin earned him a fortune, which he used wisely and generously. His many scientific and charitable projects included support for Livingstone at several critical moments in the explorer's life, as well as paying for Livingstone's two most faithful Africans, Chuma and Susi, to be brought to Britain after their master's death to tell all that they knew of his last years. Young described Livingstone as 'the best man I ever knew'.[6] Livingstone returned the compliment in 1866 when he wrote of Young as a 'fine, straightforward good man'.

At the end of his second session at the university, Livingstone returned to Blantyre, starting work in the mill once more the following morning, despite his father's suggestion that he would benefit from a few days' holiday. He had already planned his next move. The London Missionary Society not only sent missionaries out to every corner of the globe. It also, unlike other such societies, believed in freedom of worship, accepting missionaries of different Christian persuasions.

'It "sends neither episcopacy, nor presbyterianism, nor independency, but the Gospel of Christ to the heathen." This exactly agreed with my ideas of what a Missionary Society ought to do,' Livingstone wrote, adding characteristically 'but it was not without a pang that I offered myself, for it was not quite agreeable to one accustomed to work his own way to become in a measure dependent on others. And I would not have been much put about if my offer had been rejected.'[7]

He had more than a year to wait from the time of his decision to apply until his provisional acceptance. The first letter to the Society on his behalf was written in August 1837, the start of his second year at the Andersonian College, by the Reverend John Moir, the Hamilton pastor. Livingstone sent in his own application a month later. Early in the new year he received a booklet containing 17 questions which he answered in his customary forthright style. To a question on marriage he replied:

Unmarried; under no engagement relating to marriage, never made proposals of marriage, nor conducted myself so to any woman as to cause her to suspect that I intended anything relating to marriage; and so far as my present wishes are concerned, I should prefer going out unmarried, that I might be without that care which the concerns of a family necessarily induce, and give myself wholly to the work.[8]

Still there was no decision. Even for one who would not be much put about by rejection, uncertainty is wearing. In the spring, at the end of his second university session, his father, without telling David, who, Neil informed the Directors of the Society, would certainly have disapproved, wrote a testimonial for him in an attempt to persuade those Directors to make him an offer. In it he told most movingly of the young man's determination, of his rejection of Fergus Ferguson's lift on Monday mornings, of how he had also turned down a chance to become a teacher and of the possibility that he would lose his job at the mill. This letter was at least read and considered: it remains to this day in the archives of the London Missionary Society. David was invited to London for an interview on 13 August 1838, followed by a second interview a week later. This time he accepted an offer from Fergus Ferguson and the lace manufacturer Henry Drummond of the money to pay his fare to London.

At last an offer was made to him. He should spend a three-month probationary period, together with half a dozen other young would-be missionaries, at Chipping Ongar in Essex studying classics, Hebrew and theology with an elderly clergyman named Richard Cecil. If he passed this stage satisfactorily, he would go on to theological college and then return to medical school, this time in London. At least he was going into the academic stream: the majority of prospective missionaries were given only a basic theological training combined with a more practical apprenticeship in such skills as carpentry and bricklaying.

But Richard Cecil was not used to students from a background such as Livingstone's and had no conception of the academic difficulties faced by one who was almost entirely self-taught. The Scotsman's broad accent, rough manner, restricted knowledge and general lack of polish did little to endear him to the prim, scholastic old man.

Unfortunately the one practical skill required of him was not one at which he excelled either. He never enjoyed preaching, partly because of a physical problem with an excessively large uvula in the back of his throat, which made his speech thick and difficult to understand, and partly because standing up in public, the centre of attention, accentuated his awkward, somewhat uncouth, manner. All this was evident from the start in the practice sermons regularly demanded of the students. Consciousness of his own limitations led to stage fright. When the clergyman in an adjacent village was ill one Sunday and Livingstone was sent to preach in his stead, he was overcome by nerves, forgot all that he had planned to say, muttered an explanation to this effect to the congregation and fled from the church.

Richard Cecil felt unable to give him a satisfactory report at this stage, although he later indicated a few redeeming features: '. . . but he has sense and quiet vigour; his temper is good and his character substantial, so that I do not like the thought of his being rejected.'[9] Meanwhile the Board of the Society decided to compromise. One member, despite describing him as 'ungainly in movement, slow and indistinct in speech', felt that he should be given a second chance. His probationary time at Chipping Ongar was extended.

Somewhat surprisingly, he appears to have been more popular with his contemporaries than with the authorities. One of the students who arrived at Chipping Ongar at the same time (and, like Livingstone, was required to stay for longer than the customary term) was Joseph Moore, who became a lifelong friend and was subsequently a missionary in Tahiti. Moore was admittedly writing with the benefit of hindsight, at a time when he could marvel that the boy with whom he had first wandered round Westminster Abbey would eventually be buried there.

'I grew daily more attached to him,' Moore recorded. 'If I were asked why, I should be rather at a loss to reply. There was a truly indescribable charm about him which, with all his rather ungainly ways and by no means winning face, attracted almost everyone.' Moore continued: 'He won those who came near him by a kind of spell. There happened to be in the boarding house at that time a young MD, a saddler from Hants., and a bookseller from Scotland. To this hour they all speak of him in rapturous terms.'[10] Moore related also a characteristic tale of David's efforts on behalf of his older brother, whose generosity had enabled the younger man to attend university. John was now working for a Hamilton lace dealer. David once got up at 3 a.m. on a foggy November day to walk the

27 miles to London so that he could visit lace shops and merchants on his brother's behalf. On the way he fell in a ditch, but went on chilled, soaked and dirty to complete his errands before starting to walk home. His return journey was quite as eventful: he found an unconscious lady who had been thrown from a gig. By the time he had helped to carry her to a house, examined her and summoned a doctor, then walked on, inevitably becoming lost in the woods and marshes, it was well past midnight before he reached home.

Another student wrote: 'I never recollect of him relaxing into the abandon of youthful frolic or play. I would by no means imply sourness of temper. It was the strength of a resolute man of work.'

Serious minded though he was, the young man enjoyed some relaxation. The group of young people centred on the trainee missionaries at Ongar included a middle-class girl named Catherine Ridley. Perhaps for the first time, Livingstone showed some interest in a girl. But his background and social inadequacies destroyed his self-confidence in her company. As he wrote to her, he was 'not very well acquainted with the feelings of those who have been ladies all their lives'. His feelings at this time seem to have blended romanticism with religion: he gave Catherine a book of sentimental religious verse which she must have received with enthusiasm for he then sent another copy to his sister Janet extolling its merits. But when Janet later sent him a volume in similar vein his mood had changed and he wrote mockingly of 'poetastresses who would have been far more usefully employed darning their grannies' stockings than clinking words together, cruelly murdering the English language in the attempt'.[11] For by then Catherine had declared her preference for another student, Thomas Lomas Prentice, whom she eventually married.

This rejection was a serious blow to Livingstone. It is less clear whether he was more deeply affected in his heart or in his pride. He remained on ostensibly good terms with the couple, writing them long letters from Africa, but he also made a number of bitter, sometimes contradictory, comments about them. He suggested that Prentice had misled Catherine by becoming a corn merchant rather than a missionary, a decision actually reached on grounds of health, while indicating that Catherine would not have made a suitable missionary's wife. He was strengthened in this opinion five years later when Catherine, apparently very unhappy, joined the Plymouth Brethren. Thirty years after their rift, he had perhaps even convinced himself that it was he not she who had decided to break off their relationship. Whether or not he truly believed this, the episode was still niggling in his mind, for he wrote an account stating this to his son Thomas.

The end of 1839 was a dispiriting time for Livingstone. Another dream, longer held than that of marrying Catherine, was finally shattered. Anticipating the September outbreak of the Opium War between Britain and China, the London Missionary Society determined to send no more missionaries to China. In July they proposed instead that Livingstone should go to the West Indies. He was appalled and wrote immediately to point out that a half-trained doctor would be of little use in an area which was already well served by numerous fully qualified, experienced doctors. Service there would, he wrote, be too 'like the ministry at home'. He did not add that such an area, subject for many years to Western influence and geographically restricted, offered none of the challenges which he sought. Nor did he attempt to put into words, even to himself, the essence of his vision. The words were supplied for him a few months later: 'The smoke of a thousand villages where no missionary had ever been.'[12] The speaker was Robert Moffat.

Moffat was one of the most successful missionaries of his generation (he was in fact only 18 years older than Livingstone himself), held up by the London Missionary Society as an example of all that the young trainee missionaries should aim to become. A tall, strong, impressive looking Scotsman with his bushy eyebrows and massive white beard, Moffat had been working in Africa for 23 years. A man of diverse talents, he translated the whole of the Bible and *Pilgrim's Progress* into Sechuana as well as using his practical skills (his first job had been as a gardener and he was also a capable builder, carpenter, smith and farmer) to establish a settlement and family home at Kuruman. When Livingstone first visited Kuruman he was bitterly disappointed: he had visualized a large, thriving Christian community. He found a small village. While there was a congregation of 350, less than 40 of these were communicants. Later experience of missionary life in Africa was to teach him that Moffat's achievements were indeed impressive. In London, Moffat inspired and encouraged him. When he nervously asked whether he would 'do for Africa', Moffat replied that he would. Thus he first gained the approval of his future father-in-law.

Livingstone met Moffat at Mrs Sewell's Aldersgate boarding house for young missionaries where he stayed from early January 1840 to continue his medical training, which was now financed by the London Missionary Society. He was fortunate at this time in the people with whom he had dealings. Mrs Sewell was as different from his first, sugar-stealing, landlady in Glasgow as it was possible to be and he kept up a correspondence with her for many years. He regularly attended the Silver Street Chapel in Falcon Square, where the minister was an outstanding preacher named Dr Bennett. He introduced Livingstone to his son, a brilliant young doctor who subsequently became Sir Risdon Bennett, President of the Royal College of Surgeons, another man whose friendship with Livingstone was to continue for the rest of their lives. Sir Risdon was immediately impressed with Livingstone's character and ability. Finding that the young man's theoretical knowledge of medicine was greater than his practical experience, Bennett arranged admission for him to all the hospitals with which he was connected. Livingstone was thus able to attend the Aldersgate Street Dispensary (where Bennett was at that time physician), Moorfields Ophthalmic Hospital and the Charing Cross Hospital, where Bennett lectured on the practice of medicine. The experience he thus gained stood him in good stead throughout his career.

Another academic who singled him out from his other students was Professor Owen, who was lecturing on comparative anatomy at the Hunterian Museum. The two men shared a deep interest in natural history, and Livingstone promised that if he came across any particularly interesting specimen during his travels he would bring it home for Owen. Owen's delight and gratitude knew no bounds when, years later, his former pupil returned to a hero's welcome in England, bearing with him an elephant's tusk with a spiral curve in fulfilment of his promise. The professor was particularly appreciative of the fact that his specimen was so big, heavy and inconvenient to transport and yet had reached him despite everything.

The young Livingstone provoked a wide range of different reactions from his acquaintances, as he has continued to do from those who have studied him ever since. A childhood contemporary commented that he 'was no thocht to be a by-ordinar laddie; just a sulky, quiet, feckless sort o' boy'.[13] This does not accord with most of the other descriptions which remain: 'by-ordinar', meaning extraordinary or unusual, is precisely the quality which impressed most of those who knew him, though to some this was a recommendation and to others the reverse.

Walter Inglis, who knew him in England and Africa, wrote: 'I have to admit he was "no bonny". His face wore at all times the strongly marked lines of potent will.'[14] He goes on to tell of Livingstone hitting a patient's boil hard with a book as a 'practical joke'. Richard Cecil wrote 'He is too heavy and has too little of the agreeable about him.' He also described him as 'worthy but remote from brilliant'.[15] Modern commentators have been equally dismissive. Tim Jeal visualizes him as 'an awkward, sullen young man'. C. S. Nicholls, while allowing that 'his reserve was misinterpreted as sullenness and his undoubted application and seriousness as lack of humour. His looks were also to his disadvantage', concludes that 'he appeared to be a man whose spirit was as gloomy and dark as his hair and eyes. He was obsessed with his bowel movements, an interest he was to retain throughout his life.'

Yet his friend Joseph Moore at Ongar was not the only one to notice his 'truly indescribable charm'.[16] Another of the students, J. S. Cook, wrote 'He was so kind and gentle in word and deed to all about him that all loved him. He had always words of sympathy at command, and was ready to perform acts of sympathy for those who were suffering.'[17] Benjamin and Elizabeth Pyne continued to correspond with him for many years, and his daughter who died in infancy was named after Elizabeth. Isaac Taylor also knew him at that time:

> I well remember as a boy taking country rambles with Livingstone when he was staying at Ongar. Mr. Cecil had several missionary students, but Livingstone was the only one whose personality made any impression on my boyish imagination. I might sum up my impression of him in two words – Simplicity and Resolution. Now, after nearly forty years, I remember his step, the characteristic forward tread, firm, simple, resolute, neither fast nor slow, no hurry and no dawdle, but which evidently meant – getting there.[18]

This quality was also noted by Alexander Macmillan, the future publisher: 'I have heard it said of him, "Fire, water, stonewall – would not stop Livingstone in the fulfilment of any recognised duty."'[19]

Certainly at this time, in Glasgow, Chipping Ongar and London alike, he made many friends both among his contemporaries and among those lecturers and teachers from whom he was so keen to learn so much. A number of these friendships were to last a lifetime. Perhaps friendships are easier to maintain, provided that both parties are good correspondents, when thousands of miles separate those involved from the pressures of day-to-day communications and the increasing fame of the distant traveller makes the connection a matter of pride. But all these men and women must have had a liking, respect or admiration for Livingstone before he ever left the shores of Britain.

On 1 June 1840 Livingstone attended a public meeting, which had a profound influence on his thinking for the rest of his life. The meeting was held in Exeter Hall in the Strand and was attended by a vast crowd, for it was the first public engagement to be performed in England by Prince Albert following his marriage to Queen Victoria. It was not the words of the Prince Consort which so enthralled Livingstone, however, but those of Sir Thomas Fowell Buxton of the Society for the Extinction of the Slave Trade and for the Civilization of Africa. Buxton had taken over the leadership of the Anti-Slavery movement after the death of William Wilberforce, shepherding the Bill for the abolition of slavery in the British colonies through Parliament. He was an excellent public speaker and at Exeter Hall he was expounding his own convictions which opened up a whole new avenue of thought for Livingstone.

Buxton was a passionate believer that the only way to resolve the problem of slave trading in Africa was to open up the continent to trade in other commodities which grew or could be produced there. In this way the Africans would be able to acquire the paraphernalia of the Western world which they so craved: guns and cloth as well as trinkets and beads. They would not have to offer in return their own people nor members of neighbouring tribes whom they conquered. Buxton longed to bring to Africa the three great Cs: Christianity, Commerce and Civilization. He saw a great future for Europeans in introducing Africans to all the blessings of Western life, helping them to develop products which would be attractive to Europeans, to establish transport systems and benefit from medical advances. As a first step, Buxton proposed, and the meeting endorsed, the setting up of a large expedition of technical experts travelling up the Niger River.

These ideas struck Livingstone like a blinding light. His conversion was as dramatic as that of St Paul on the road to Damascus. Henceforward for the rest of his life he never wavered in his conviction that this was indeed the way forward for Africa. Even when a year later he learnt of the tragic and absolute failure of the Niger

Expedition, he never doubted that, whatever the outcome of individual efforts, these were the right principles for solving the problems of the slave trade and of the inevitable meeting of two diverse worlds. The approach appealed both to his intellect and to his inclinations. Livingstone always favoured a broader perspective. In this outlook lay the seeds of his success but also of his failures. Why struggle to scrape a living as a factory hand when you could be the first to cross a distant continent? Why devote a lifetime to the attempt to convert a handful of villagers when you could be starting to bring Christianity, Commerce and Civilization to the whole of Africa? In a vision which encompasses a fifth of the globe, the visionary's own small family are easily overlooked.

Not everyone reacted to Buxton's philosophy with the same enthusiasm. It was widely held that charity should start at home: so many people were living in appalling conditions in Britain at the time that any available money should be spent on their welfare rather than being sent abroad. Even Charles Dickens, with all his determination to improve the lot of the downtrodden, satirized Buxton's approach in *Bleak House*. Mrs Jellyby is portrayed as a mother who neglects her children, a wife who impoverishes her husband, in her determination to devote every second of her time and every farthing of her money to 'the African project'. There were other criticisms. Few missionaries would have been willing to be associated in any way with commercial activities. The convictions shared by Buxton and Livingstone did not accord well with the spirit of their age.

Not long after this meeting, Livingstone became ill. He diagnosed his own complaint as congestion of the liver and lungs, attributing it to 'Too much effluvia of sick chambers, dissecting rooms etc.'[20] So serious was the illness that he was sent home to Scotland to stay with his family: 'in accompanying him to the steamer, Mr. Moore found him so weak that he could scarcely walk on board. He parted from him in tears, fearing that he had but a few days to live.' This was, however, but the first of many occasions when he was to make a remarkable recovery.

He had resigned himself to leaving Britain without a medical diploma as he could not afford the cost of the examination. However, the London Missionary Society solved this problem by paying for him to qualify in Glasgow, where it was cheaper. Disaster nearly struck for a characteristic reason. Livingstone's final thesis involved reference to the use of the stethoscope.

I unwittingly procured for myself an examination rather more severe and prolonged than usual among examining bodies. The reason was, that between me and the examiners a slight difference of opinion existed as to whether this instrument could do what was asserted. The wiser plan would have been to have had no opinion of my own. However, I was admitted a Licentiate of Faculty of Physicians and Surgeons.[21]

This was on 15 November 1840 and there was just time for a farewell visit to his family before returning to London. They talked and talked. Indeed, David proposed that they should not go to bed at all, but his mother for a final time insisted, as she had done so often before when he was reluctant to put down his book, that they should all sleep. Next morning she made coffee for them at five and David read aloud the 121st and the 135th psalms, praying for himself at the start of his great enterprise, 'I will lift up mine eyes unto the hills, from whence cometh my help', for his family at home, 'The Lord shall preserve thy going out and thy coming in from this time forth, and even for evermore'; then perhaps turning his thoughts to the work ahead: 'The idols of the heathen are silver and gold, the work of men's hands.' Then his father walked with him into Glasgow to catch the steamer. It was the last time they ever saw each other.

There was one more formality to be completed before he sailed for Africa, and remarkably Livingstone viewed it simply as a formality. His ordination took place on 20 November at the Albion Chapel, London Wall, 'a ceremony which would be recognised by all Non-conformist denominations although not by the Anglican and Catholic churches'. He afterwards wrote 'I do not attach any importance to ordination'. This reaction was in marked contrast to his comment on his qualification five days before: 'It was with unfeigned delight I became a member of a profession which is pre-eminently devoted to practical benevolence, and which with unwearied energy pursues from age to age its endeavours to lessen human woe.'[22] Perhaps this was a point of principle. However, three elements of the service may have coloured his judgement. Firstly, it was Presbyterian. Secondly, one of the two ministers conducting it was his pedantic old teacher from Ongar, Richard Cecil. Thirdly, his co-ordinand was William Ross, a recently married former schoolmaster some 11 years older than Livingstone who was to travel with him to the Cape, and whom he already disliked. His certificate of Ordination was signed by Arthur Tidman, foreign secretary of the London Missionary Society, with whom he was subsequently to have much correspondence.

On 8 December, in company with William Ross and his wife, he embarked on the *George* for the voyage to South Africa.

3
Kuruman and Mabotsa: the Newcomer

Livingstone made use of his time on board ship to acquire new skills. As well as starting to study the Sechuanan language, he was befriended by the captain. Livingstone found him 'very obliging to me and gave me all the information respecting the use of the quadrant in his power, frequently sitting up till twelve o'clock at night for the purpose of taking lunar observations with me.'[1]

The young missionary was also more homesick than he would have been prepared to admit. His letters from the barque *George*, like many of his later letters from Africa, are full of complaints to the recipients about their failure to write to him. 'You have returned from the celebration of Christmas and settled down quietly to your studies for some time now. But have you remembered your promise to write your humble servant when you had done so?'[2] he wrote indignantly to Thomas Prentice, revealing a line later that his real wish is to hear news of Catherine Ridley. His regular correspondence at this time with Catherine, occasionally directly but more often through her fiancé, shows how much she remained in his thoughts. Some six weeks later he attempts to cover this up with naive clumsiness: 'I don't know why I feel so much interest in your good lady, perhaps selfishness, the prospect of having both as fellow labourers.'[3] The feeling that, had Catherine agreed to become his wife, she would now be at his side, increased his irritation with Mr and Mrs William Ross. The couple seemed to him to epitomize a smug, cosy 'togetherness' which he constantly mocked. When both suffered badly from seasickness, he wrote (to Prentice, inappropriately) saying that Ross had been quoting the text 'Two are better than one' to him. 'The only cruelty I was guilty of was quoting the same text to him when both he and his spouse were turning their stomachs inside out into one basin.' Bickering between the two missionaries seems to have been constant. When Livingstone tried to use his medical skills to help Mrs Ross, her husband's jealousy was aroused. This was too much for Livingstone, who 'told a friend indignantly that he would rather have flirted with his grandmother than with Ross's "blooming bride of 34 or 5"'.[4] They continued in similar vein long after their arrival in Africa.

The foremast of the *George* was split in a storm, so the captain decided to make an unscheduled stop at Rio de Janeiro. Livingstone, alone of the ship's company, decided despite the heat to walk six or seven miles into the Brazilian forest for his first fascinated sight of a foreign land. He enjoyed taking a shower under a waterfall, unaware of the dangers in that area from runaway slaves. 'A man and his wife having gone to the same place a few days before; he was stript of everything he had not even excepting his wife. (Let us hope she was not an over good one),'[5] he later wrote sardonically to Prentice. He also received a hospitable welcome from a friendly Brazilian family, restricted only by the language barrier. Although he spoke not a word of Portuguese, his knowledge of Latin at least enabled him to reject their offers of alcohol and ask for a drink of water.

This caused some surprise for English and American seamen had an appalling reputation for drunkenness, borne out by Livingstone's own observations in the back streets of Rio and indeed of the crew of the *George*. He could only watch helplessly, frustrated by lack of materials and time in his burning missionary zeal to reform all those with whom he came in contact.

On the day when the *George* docked in Rio, 28 January 1841, a 19-year-old housemaid in North Wales gave birth to a baby allegedly fathered by the village drunk. The child was registered as John Rowlands, Bastard. He later adopted the name of Henry Morton Stanley.

In mid-March, after a journey of 14 weeks, the *George* landed at Simon's Bay close to Cape Town. Cape Town was originally intended to be simply a calling station for ships of the Dutch East India Company, a settlement where much of the manpower soon came to be supplied by imported slave labour. The Boers, or farmers, refused to continue to farm in the immediate vicinity: the Dutch East India Company officials had intended their labours to be devoted entirely to the servicing of passing ships. Finding the rigorous control which the Company attempted to exercise over them irksome, the Boers started to trek inland, unaware at first of a mass movement of Bantu tribesmen migrating south towards them. Meanwhile control of the Cape Colony had passed from the Dutch to the British government early in the nineteenth century. If the Boers were on a physical collision course with tribesmen, they were on a moral one with the British missionaries.

As early as 1811, two years before Livingstone was born, evidence given by two members of the London Missionary Society resulted in the conviction of a number of Boers for brutality to their slaves and other Africans. The long struggle to obtain equal rights and security for Africans found a new leader in 1819 when John Philip, later to be Livingstone's host in Cape Town, was sent out by the London Missionary Society.

In other parts of Africa little attempt had been made to penetrate the interior. England and France each had a number of small trading posts on the West coast between Cape Verde and the Niger. The East coast had been inhabited by Arabs for hundreds of years, but they had made little effort to travel inland, trading instead in such goods, including slaves as well as gold and ivory, as the Africans chose to bring out to them. From the beginning of the sixteenth century, after Vasco da Gama had rounded the Cape of Good Hope, the Portuguese started to dominate the coastal regions and strove to push further inland. Eventually they learnt what the Arabs had realized for centuries: that it was not mere indolence which confined foreigners to the periphery of the continent. Further progress was almost impossible to achieve. None of the four great rivers of Africa, the Nile, the Zambesi, the Congo and the Niger, was navigable. Few men survived malaria, few horses or oxen the tsetse fly. Those who did often died of drought. When the rains did come, they nullified the invention of the wheel.

As soon as they reached Cape Town, Livingstone and Ross found themselves embroiled in all the ramifications of inter-missionary politics. It had been arranged that they should stay for the first month with Dr and Mrs Philip. John Philip and Robert Moffat were the two outstanding personalities in the African missionary field at this time and it was sad, though predictable, that neither had a good word to say of the other. Perhaps it was more remarkable that Livingstone, not in general a great admirer of Europeans in Africa, particularly those involved in the same work as himself, should eventually have developed a deep affection and profound admiration for both men.

This took time. Each of the two men in turn succeeded in prejudicing the young man against his rival. Livingstone was clearly anticipating spending his time in Cape Town in the company of a dictatorial ogre, and was both relieved and delighted to find the doctor 'a very amiable man . . . He does not . . . appear so bad to us as he is represented at home . . . I was always determined not to submit to any bishop, and am therefore happy to know that he does not wish to domineer.'⁶ For Livingstone shared not only the opinions held by the older man but also the forthright way in which Dr Philip upheld them. Whether Philip's former congregation opposed his forceful support of the Africans against Boer tyranny or only his equally strongly held views on the management of London Missionary Society affairs in Africa is unclear, but he was certainly so unpopular that he been compelled to resign. When his young visitor was invited to speak from the pulpit, he succeeded in alienating the congregation yet further. For a brief moment it seemed that Ross might agree to take on the ministry of the New Union Chapel and remain in the city, but to Livingstone's disappointment this was not to be.

In mid-April the two new missionaries and Mrs Ross embarked once more on the *George* for the short journey round the Cape to Algoa Bay, with Livingstone's mind now filled with thoughts of Moffat's alleged tendency to stir up trouble. The extent to which each of these two men succeeded in prejudicing him against the other is remarkable in one who had long ago declared: 'You think! I can think and act for myself; don't need anyone to think for me.' On the other hand as soon as he had the opportunity to judge for himself he did do precisely that. From Algoa Bay they travelled the remaining five or six hundred miles to Kuruman by ox wagon.

The journey delighted Livingstone, with the one reservation that he would have liked to be able to spend some time studying or reading. But the slow, steady pace of the oxen lumbering through the bush, covering some twenty miles a day, resting in the heat of the day, and stopping when and where they chose to light a fire and cook a meal made travelling a glorified picnic. He was mesmerized by the beauty of the country and the wildlife and vegetation around them. Owning his own wagon and team of 12 oxen was in itself a pleasure, and an expensive one as they cost him a large proportion of his first year's salary. He wrote home with superb self-mockery of the enjoyment of talking about '*my* 12 oxen, *my* waggon [*sic*], *my* people etc., and whistling *I am the monarch of all*

I survey'. The steepness of the hills and his own lack of experience spiced his travels with a pleasurable excitement. 'Crossing the Orange river I got my vehicle aground, and my oxen got out of order, some with their heads where their tails should be, and others with their heads twisted round in the yoke so far that they appeared bent on committing suicide, or overturning the wagon ... I like travelling very much indeed.'[7]

This journey gave Livingstone his first experience of life in the African bush, of working with the Africans in his own party and meeting and negotiating with those living in the country they passed through. It was a gentle introduction, for they were travelling a well-worn route regularly followed by many Europeans: there was no element of exploration or trail-breaking. This gave him not only an opportunity to learn about the practical aspects of travel but also time for reflection.

His parents, brothers and sisters were never far from his mind in his early days in Africa. He seems to have had little hope of ever seeing them again, but was much concerned with their welfare, financial, physical, mental and spiritual. He sent them what money he could with detailed explanations and apologies for shortfalls, and was keen that the whole family should emigrate to the United States, although in fact only his two brothers ever left Britain. His younger brother Charles was a particular source of anxiety to him, which was to have unfortunate consequences later on when he included him in the Zambesi expedition. To his parents and sisters he sent copious spiritual and medical advice, though the latter can have been of little practical value since letters took several months in each direction. He could also be scathing about comments and thoughts which they had put into their letters to him in a manner which they must sometimes have found hurtful. From the dictatorial tone of some of his letters they must sometimes have been relieved rather than saddened by the distance between them.

The journey lasted ten weeks, including visits to a number of mission stations: they stayed at Griqua Town a week. The arrival at Kuruman on 31 July was a bitter disappointment. This was the station portrayed in Britain as the jewel in the crown of missionary achievement in Africa. While conceding that the church was large and well built and the gardens excellent, particularly considering the barren nature of the surrounding countryside, professionally he was appalled. Referring to the reputation the place enjoyed in Britain as an outstanding success, he commented 'it is great but to one coming from England it is invisible or nearly so'. He does modify this by adding 'Those who had to deal with Bechuanas 20 years ago and those who have seen them far in the interior alone can appreciate the greatness of the change.'[8]

Everything was on such a small scale. China had originally appealed to him because the population was so large. Here it was minute, Kuruman itself a mere village, and the proportion of those few who were Christians minuscule. David Livingstone had no conception at this time that while he himself would one day become famous as a missionary as well as an explorer, it would also be truly pointed out that he only ever made one convert, and that one lapsed. Had the problems of converting Africa to Christianity been fully understood in England, funds to support the work of the missionaries would have dried up to a mere trickle. Only exaggerated tales of glorious success could stimulate the sort of support needed to keep the mission stations open at all.

While a faint inkling of this terrible truth penetrated his brain as soon as he saw Kuruman, he was at first more inclined to attribute the situation to the shortcomings of the individual missionaries. Everyone to whom he spoke talked of the local personalities, the petty jealousies and rivalries around which all their lives revolved, and of the advantages and disadvantages of the different methods adopted. He soon learned, for example, that at Griqua Town native teachers were trained and employed, whereas at Kuruman this practice was frowned upon. As the Griqua missionaries enthusiastically expounded their views to him and Robert Moffat was not at Kuruman to put the other side of the case, Livingstone was soon convinced that the Griqua approach must be right.

The absence of Robert Moffat was the cause of much of Livingstone's disappointment. As Jeal writes, 'The almost total paralysis [in Kuruman] had a simple cause: Moffat was the driving force and Moffat was not there.' Worse, local gossip was beginning to poison his mind against the man who had first inspired him to come to Africa. He was soon writing to tell Prentice that, while the missionaries were all excellent men, 'perhaps the one you have seen in England is not the most favourable specimen.'

To Livingstone's disgust, his superiors in London had no immediate plans for him and expected him to wait patiently for Moffat to return and tell him what to do next. This unimaginative and time-wasting approach was not calculated to bring out the best in the ambitious young man who had already developed strong and independent opinions on how he would start to change the world. Before he ever left Cape Town, he had written to his sisters using the phrase which was to become famous as exemplifying his approach. 'I would never build on another man's foundation,' he wrote. 'I shall preach the gospel *beyond every other man's line of things.*'

Livingstone was delighted when Rogers Edwards, Moffat's assistant at Kuruman, invited him to join him on an expedition to the north. Livingstone liked the older man, with whom he had been staying at Kuruman. Edwards longed to start his own mission station, independently of Moffat, and had obtained permission from the Directors in London to select a suitable site. The younger man, while showing his lack of African experience when writing with horror: 'Bows, arrows and assagais [*sic*] . . . look terrible weapons when bristling around the wild, restless, sparkling eye of the real savage, smeared all over with red paint',[9] was already finding Kuruman dull.

Soon the wide-eyed amazement of the tourist was replaced by the more blasé tone of the seasoned traveller. Tales of the toughness of rhino meat were only included because it was the sort of thing which his sister would want to know about. As he travelled north he was at last seeing things no European had ever seen before. The first tribe they visited on their journey north, the Bakhatla, honoured the two Europeans by allowing them to visit their primitive iron smelting works. They were first asked whether they had had sexual intercourse in recent weeks, since this would have a deleterious effect on the iron. To Livingstone's amazement, his indignant reply that he was not married did not seem to satisfy the tribesmen totally.

They then travelled further north to the country of the Bakwains where Livingstone first met the man who was to become famous as his only convert in a lifetime as a missionary. The Bakwain tribe at this time was divided in two and Sechele was ruler of one half.

On the way back to Kuruman, Livingstone played knight errant to a little orphan girl of 11 or 12. Finding that she was about to be sold, against her will, as a wife, she planned to run away to friends near Kuruman. Livingstone found her hiding near his wagon, prepared to walk behind them all the way. He befriended her and gave her some food, but soon afterwards heard her 'sobbing violently as if her heart would break'. Her enemy had appeared with a gun and was demanding her return. The young missionary hesitated, uncertain how to handle the situation, but fortunately Pomore, an African convert with him, was the son of a chief. A deal was soon struck whereby the jewellery worn by the child to raise her price in the marriage market was handed over and the little girl was allowed to remain with the missionaries. To make sure that the gunman did not renege on the agreement, Livingstone carefully hid the child for the rest of their journey. In less heroic mood, he used the story in his next letter home to show his mother and sisters how fortunate and privileged was the position of Victorian women in Britain.

He was amused at this time by the reaction of the Africans to such Western devices as watches and mirrors, and especially to his appearance. They were fascinated but repelled by his white skin, straight hair and relatively large nose. He was already wearing what he described soon afterwards as 'a common midshipman's cap'. His own approach to dress was inevitably entirely practical. 'Colour is nothing, & strength is everything,' he declared when attempting to obtain trousers strong enough not to be reduced to shreds by the thorns. Yet this style of cap, in its later manifestations, was to become his particular trademark.

After a brief rest at Kuruman, he set out again in February, accompanied by the native convert Pomore but no European companions, planning to immerse himself for six months in the local language. He stayed first at Lepelole where Bubi held sway over those of the Bakwain not ruled by Bubi's cousin Sechele. The Bakwain tribe had become divided after the assassination of Sechele's father. Livingstone found Bubi and his family friendly and welcoming. One of Bubi's wives in particular, whom Livingstone called 'sister', proved exceptionally kind.

He now began to develop his own system for working with African communities, a skill at which he excelled all his life. It was the custom for missionaries to beg for permission to work with the natives, teaching and preaching among them. Livingstone declared that they were privileged indeed to have him to help them and, at the slightest hint that they did not appreciate his presence, he would leave. Rainmaking was the most highly rated art, a secret skill allegedly possessed only by the doctor. The young man declared that he too could make rain, not by magic but by scientific methods of irrigation, and persuaded the community to combine to dig an irrigation channel. 'This, I believe,' he commented drily, 'is the first instance when Bechuanas have been got to work without wages.' Some visiting tribesmen from the Kuruman area urged them to down tools (some sharpened sticks and a single, broken spade) unless they were paid. Livingstone told them that he had been exceedingly kind in staying to show them how to organize irrigation but since they did not want his help he would go. They immediately surrounded him, begging him to stay. After a month he continued north, visiting three further tribes, the Bamangwato, the Bakaa and the Makalaka. Sekhomi, chief of the Bamangwato, welcomed his visitor enthusiastically: Livingstone was not yet aware how much chiefs valued the presence of a visiting missionary. He knew that he could offer them such technical benefits as irrigation techniques but naturally, if naively, felt his main contribution would be in bringing Christianity to them. He had not yet realized that for the Africans this was seen as a disadvantage, for this was the way in which white men strove to prevent them from having all the wives they desired and which under their culture were so important to them. Nor did Livingstone appreciate his worth in African eyes as a mender, and perhaps a giver, of guns, and as a valuable diplomatic tool in relations between one tribe and another, or black men and Boers.

Sekhomi himself was the great-great-grandfather of Sir Seretse Khama, the distinguished first president of Botswana, as their country became in 1966. In 1842 Sekhomi's town was the biggest Bechuanan settlement Livingstone had seen, including some 600 houses. The inhabitants were suffering from a serious lion problem, and Sekhomi insisted on supplying his distinguished visitor with a guard for the shortest of walks. Livingstone realized that this was a necessary precaution when a woman whose house he had frequently passed was eaten by a lion in her own garden.

In other ways the missionary did not find Sekhomi so easy to communicate with. The chief initially greeted some of his teaching with enthusiasm, and declared that he did indeed wish to have his heart changed as he was always proud and angry. But when Livingstone got out his Bible he stated that this was not what he wanted: he wished to take medicine which would instantly change his heart.

When Livingstone continued his journey Sekhomi sent some of his own men to accompany him. They did not realize how much of their language the Scotsman understood and he was not pleased to hear them speaking scathingly of his allegedly poor physique and weakness. Predictably, during the next few days he outwalked them all, thus winning their respect. Later in his travels he passed through areas which his native team were afraid to enter, for the country at this time was riven with tribal warfare. On these occasions he would sometimes leave them in charge of the wagon and continue alone, riding an ox. He told Sir Risdon Bennett that he travelled more than 400 miles in this uncomfortable fashion, doing his best to avoid the beast's long horns, carried dangerously close to his stomach.

The next tribe to receive him, the Bakaa, had a fearsome reputation. Their neighbours considered them treacherous and cruel, and no white man had yet returned alive from their territory. Two had previously entered the country. The first had died of fever, the more recent visitor, a trader named Gibson, had been poisoned together with two of his three men, and when the third man had survived the poison he had been hanged. The Bakaa had then burnt the wagons and eaten the oxen. Livingstone noted that they wore necklaces made with pieces of gunlocks and one had a headdress of sailcloth, all obviously trophies.

With nerves of iron, he presented a perfectly unconcerned front. The villagers, themselves unnerved, fled in terror. He was offered a bowl of porridge and coolly ate it without any indication of suspicion. A few natives slowly crept back into sight. Showing complete trust, he lay down and slept. At last relief flooded through the town and they all swarmed round him, remaining kind and considerate throughout his stay. 'I had more than ordinary pleasure in telling these murderers of the precious "blood which cleanseth from all sin".' Yet in his account of this visit in *Missionary Travels,* the book he wrote on his return to England, he mentions none of this, referring only to the European who had died of fever.

His final visit, a short one, was to the Makalaka tribe of the Mashona people. He observed that they had many things not otherwise seen in the villages he had visited, and that they fought 'with guns not Assagai. These they obtain from the Portuguese on the eastern coast, and from some circumstances which have come to my knowledge; I am inclined to believe they procure them in exchange for slaves . . .'[10]

Much of the country through which Livingstone was travelling at this time was suffering from tribal warfare. Treachery and violence marked all the dealings between neighbouring tribes. Mosilikatse with his Matabele was the most aggressive, terrible and dreaded of all the tribal warriors. Scourge of Africans and Europeans alike, he terrorized much of the continent with his vicious, destructive raids. Almost the only chance of escape lay in hiding in one of the vast networks of caves where local knowledge afforded protection against the invader.

By the end of June 1842 Livingstone was back at Kuruman. In a matter of weeks he longed to be on the road once more, but was unable to find men to drive and lead the oxen for him. 'Nobody will trust his precious black body where there is the least probability of it being scathed',[11] he wrote to his parents. During this enforced break from his travels Mrs Ross gave birth to a baby. Livingstone told his parents that only his timely arrival on the scene saved the infant's life, but that Mrs Ross gave him no credit for this. Fortunately for his reputation, Mrs Edwards witnessed the episode and told the women 'what a genius they have got among them'.

It was February 1843 before he once again set out from Kuruman. He stayed away until mid-June. His first visit was to Sebehwe, a chieftain whose courage and dignity he particularly admired, who had never been defeated by the Matabele, but had suffered terribly at the hands of neighbouring tribes after ignoring a friendly warning from Livingstone. The chief now explained that he had had no conception of the damage which could be done with guns.

Next he moved on to Sechele, who was later to become his close friend and only true convert. Relations between the two men had not been good the previous year when the missionary had spent much time with Sechele's enemy Bubi. But now Bubi was dead, killed in an accident with gunpowder. Sechele's son and one of his men were both ill and the doctor succeeded in helping them. 'Sechele did not seem able to speak a single angry word.' Less Christian was the reaction of the tribesmen to some of their own womenfolk who returned home at this time having escaped from the clutches of the Matabele. Being only women, their tales of sufferings were greeted with total indifference, except by Livingstone's own men, who were too terrified to continue towards the Matabele, forcing him to ride on alone on his ox.

In one place Livingstone saw a son of Conrad Buys, a vicious Boer with an evil reputation who had died some twenty years before. The unfortunate young man was being kept by the Africans in virtual slavery and Livingstone was unable to rescue him.

His second visit to the Bakaa, the tribe from whom no other white man had ever returned alive, was less successful than the first. Although on the first occasion Livingstone's courage and confidence had enabled him to break through the barriers of suspicion and guilt, one of his men had become ill while there. Livingstone knew that this was chance, and had been coming on before their arrival, but it unfortunately revived all the old tales of poisoning.

Accordingly this time the Bakaa refused to give him or any of his men any food at all to avoid all such accusations. After two days, Livingstone, faint with hunger, slipped on the rocks and broke his finger. Next night a lion attacked the little group. Livingstone managed to drive it off with a shot from his gun, but made his finger considerably worse in the process. He was unable to fire a shot to provide meat for the pot for some time, making the whole group more dependent than usual on local hospitality.

When travelling and when based at Kuruman, Livingstone was constantly observing and analysing the people around him from a medical point of view. He wrote detailed accounts to Risdon Bennett, putting forward his theories and asking for guidance and advice. His isolated position deprived him of the opportunity to discuss issues with professional colleagues, which he would have found particularly helpful since he was so frequently encountering situations outside the experience of doctors practising in Britain.

Yet something of his father's approach to medicine affected him. He did not see his skills as a wonderful gift, but almost as a hobby, like his interests in botany, zoology and astronomy, which he must not allow to take up too much time. He sets this out clearly in a letter quoted by Seaver (1957). Admittedly the letter is to Richard Cecil, whose connection with the London Missionary Society may have stirred Livingstone's conscience: no hint of this anxiety is betrayed in his correspondence with Risdon Bennett, for example. He wrote:

> I did not at first intend to give up all attention to medicine and the treatment of disease, but now I feel it to be my duty to have as little to do with it as possible. I shall attend to none but severe cases in future, and my reasons for this determination are I think good. The spiritual amelioration of the people is the object for which I came, but I cannot expect God to advance this by my instrumentality if much of my time is spent in mere temporal amelioration. And I know that if I gave much attention to medicine and medical studies, something like a sort of mania which seized me soon after I began the study of anatomy would increase, and I fear would gain so much power over me as to make me perhaps a very good doctor, but a useless drone of a missionary. I feel the self-denial this requires very much, but it is the only real sacrifice I have been called upon to make, and I shall try to make it willingly.

Although Livingstone was undoubtedly a deeply spiritual man, his priorities were imposed upon him by the Victorian world from which he sprang.

He found his African patients remarkably stoical, sitting quietly, talking and smiling as he performed painful operations without any form of anaesthesia. Their belief in, or fear of, the witch doctors often made them ignore his instructions, however. Sometimes he would use his scientific skills to show up the fraudulent tricks of these men, though on other occasions he preferred to work with them, encouraging them to use the powers they undoubtedly did possess for good not evil purposes.

By the time of his return to Kuruman he had been in Africa for two years and still the Moffat family had not come back. It was fortunate indeed that he had not followed his original instructions to do nothing save learn the language until Robert Moffat was there to advise and guide him. But if he had worried at all about the possible reaction of the Directors in London to his initiative, which he probably had not, any anxiety on that account was allayed by an enthusiastic letter from London. Arthur Tidman, Secretary to the LMS, showed enthusiasm for everything he had done.

Just two controversial issues were raised. The first was the question of establishing a local committee, which the Directors were convinced was the only way forward. Indeed, with letters taking six months to arrive from London, if any measure of control was to be exercised over individual missionaries and decisions reached fast enough for anything to be achieved, there was little alternative. But Livingstone had no wish to be controlled by anyone. He saw the slow communications as a positive advantage which in practice left him free to take his own decisions and act upon them. Further, as the autocratic side of his nature developed, he was becoming increasingly disillusioned with more and more of his fellow missionaries. He was influenced in part by local backbiting and gossip, for at this time Moffat, whom he had not seen since he left London, was the object of much of his criticism. In later years Moffat was to become the one exception to his universal condemnation of missionaries in Africa. He was also falling into the trap of feeling that he alone was always right.

The other issue was the employment of native agency. Tidman kept his options open on this question, leaving it to be decided by the proposed District Committee. But in this, before it was even set up, Livingstone had declared his lack of confidence: indeed he

wrote back specifically reserving to himself the power of withdraw-
ing from the Committee should he ever subsequently feel that to
be his duty. Livingstone had one trump card to play. He had already written to friends in Scotland and persuaded one to send
£12, sufficient to support one native preacher for a year, and was
hopeful that other donations would follow.

When word came that the Moffat family was once again delayed,
Livingstone's patience ran out. His general attitude was summed
up in a later letter to Tidman when he expressed himself ready to
'go anywhere provided it be forward'.[12] He and Edwards decided to
wait no longer but start to set up a new mission station at a place
they had selected named Mabotsa, 220 miles from Kuruman and
close to where Mafeking was later built. They left at the end of
August so that they could do much of the work before the hot
weather in October. By good fortune the Bakhatla had independently decided to move to the same area at the same time, and the
two missionaries bought the land they wished to build on from
the Bakhatla, a formality which they saw as more important than
did the tribesmen themselves.

They took with them to Mabotsa a young native convert named
Mebalwe, of whom Livingstone had high hopes. Ideally he would
have liked to send him to a different area from any European, in
the expectation that he would prove Livingstone's contention that
native converts would be quite as good as Europeans at spreading
the gospel. Mebalwe was being paid for with the £12 donated by
Mrs McRobert in Scotland. Her generosity in sponsoring the young
man was to have a momentous effect a few months later when he
saved Livingstone's life.

Three wealthy big game hunters, who had recently come to Africa
from India, accompanied them on their journey. Captain Steele was
a polished, educated officer in the Coldstream Guards, his two friends
were Mr Pringle from the East Indies and another unnamed son of
a planter in the West Indies. They were the first men from a totally different social background from himself with whom Livingstone
had ever spent much time. At first he was extremely scathing about
their extravagance, their lack of understanding of life in the bush,
their reasons for being there and some of their misadventures. He
stated his firm intention of parting with them in a day or so. They
for their part laughed sometimes at 'the little man', but were impressed by his courage, strength of mind, determination and
intelligence. Yet they would have been as surprised as Livingstone

had they known that thirty years later General Sir Thomas Steele would be proud to carry the little man's coffin into Westminster Abbey.

Livingstone and Edwards worked hard, building a hut 50 feet long by 18 feet, which they planned eventually to use as a church, on the land they had bought. They found the Bechuana men extremely idle, leaving everything to their womenfolk. Then word reached them that the Moffat family was at last genuinely close to home, and they hurried back to Kuruman.

Robert Moffat was finally returning to Kuruman from England. His wife Mary and two of his daughters, Mary and Ann, accompanied him. There were ten Moffat children of whom eight survived. Mary was 22 at the time. Mrs Moffat ran an extremely efficient household. Mary's first nurse was Sarah Robey, a little Bushman girl whom Mrs Moffat had rescued when she was about to be buried alive with her dead mother, so Mary was brought up speaking the clicking language of the Bushmen as well as Sechuana. Missionary families became used to long periods of separation. Mary was sent at the age of ten together with her younger sister to a school five weeks' journey from home. She stayed there for four years and during that time her mother visited her twice and her father not at all. After a few months at home helping while her mother was ill following the birth of another baby, she went with Ann and their brother Robert to school in Cape Town. When their parents finally appeared some three years later, the children expected to return home as a family. But the plan was instead to travel to England.

The journey, on a troop ship loaded with animals, was horrendous. All the family were seasick. Their mother was again pregnant and the baby was born during the voyage. The six-year-old contracted measles and died of it. In England their father was lionized and Sarah Robey became the star turn on missionary platforms throughout the country. The rest of the family were cold and depressed. When they eventually sailed once more for Africa, two of the children were left behind at school. Helen was 13 at the time. It was ten years before she and Mary saw each other again and Helen did not see her mother for 27 years.

Livingstone was not looking forward to his second meeting with Robert Moffat. He had listened to far too many tales told by other, frequently jealous, missionaries. However, he rode out to meet them all the way to the Vaal River, a week's travelling by ox wagon from Kuruman. Despite his misgivings, he was seized by excitement as he drew near and galloped 'across a wide plain under the burning sun as if "at Ascot or the Derby"'.[13]

As if both men had some presentiment of all that the future would bring, Moffat too was moved by the meeting. He later wrote: 'Few can conceive of the hallowed feeling his presence produced, direct from the station and people to whom all our fondest affections were bending.' Soon the two men were deep in conversation, with Livingstone at least amazed to find how much the older man represented everything that he most admired. All his old anxieties dissolved: public report had maligned Moffat just as it had earlier maligned Philip. Moffat was no bigoted opponent of native agency, nor was he an enthusiastic supporter of rule by Committee. Nor was he rooted to the home comforts of Kuruman, reluctant to venture into the interior. On the contrary he had twice visited the infamous Mosilikatse, dread leader of the Matabele and terror of African and European alike, in his homeland in what is now Zimbabwe. He had dared to criticize the tyrant: thousands had died for less. Yet Moffat had elicited only civility and, it was said, even a show of tears.

Where the attitudes of Moffat and Livingstone diverged was in their respective approaches to the African. Moffat, after years in Africa, persisted in seeing only stupidity and wickedness. Even in the short time he had spent in the continent, Livingstone had developed an understanding of the ways in which African culture differed from European, leading to behaviour and outlooks which were not indicative of moral or intellectual inferiority but of a different set of values inevitably created by varying social conditions. The prime example, which was to come to a head later in the case of Sechele, was the issue of polygamy.

By the time they reached Kuruman on 13 December 1843, Livingstone knew that he had met someone of a different calibre from all the other missionaries, with the possible exception of Philip. Moffat was a man with whom he would remain friends for life. Perhaps he had also already concluded that Moffat's daughter Mary would become his wife.

He was not a romantic man and viewed the prospect of choosing a wife in prosaic terms. Choice was extremely limited: having failed to bring a bride out with him from England, he had either to select one of the very few girls he met in Africa or, as he half jokingly once suggested, advertise in England. Mary was not the first single European girl whom he had met, however. One missionary couple were so disappointed with his lack of interest in their daughter that they even resorted to opening his post and spreading false rumours about his correspondence with his elderly widowed landlady in London. He himself not only wished to be married and have children but was aware of all the professional advantages of having a wife. She would help and support him, talk to the African women and children about subjects which their menfolk might resent them discussing with a man and stifle the inevitable gossip about young single men seeking consolation with native women. As he later wrote to the Directors, after he had 'made the necessary arrangements for union', 'various considerations connected with this new sphere of labour . . . [have] led me to the conclusion that it was my duty to enter into the marriage relation'.

For Mary too choice was limited, not only by the number of eligible young men whom she was likely to meet but also by the fact that she was unattractive and fat. But she was practical, a capable housewife with all the additional skills such as making soap and candles which were needed in distant mission stations, and no illusions about life in the bush. Her father was not only in a sense Livingstone's immediate boss, but also a man whom he admired and found congenial. Her mother's dictatorial nature ensured that she and her future son-in-law would frequently cross swords, but was also a reason for Mary's wish to leave home. Livingstone observed the whole family and concluded that Mary was 'the best spoke in the wheel'. He later wrote to a missionary friend summarizing what was needed: 'a plain common sense woman, not a romantic. Mine is a matter of fact lady, a little thick black haired girl, sturdy and all I want.' He did not, however, rate her intelligence as equal to his own and would not have wished to do so. Neither in marriage nor elsewhere did Livingstone ever form a partnership on equal terms. He later wrote to Mary's brother 'I have never found two agreeing unless one were a cypher' and, from his childhood relationships with the other boys in the mill to his treatment of Europeans working with him on expeditions, he adhered to this viewpoint, often with disastrous consequences. He would willingly learn from those with greater knowledge or experience of a particular subject, but, unless he conceded his own inferiority in a specific sphere, always expected to have the final word.

How many of his thoughts concerning Mary had crystallized during his first few weeks with the Moffat family is unclear. Certainly he felt that it was too early yet to propose. Soon after Christmas he returned to Mabotsa.

He had long been aware of the size of the lion population around Mabotsa. But, despite the death of the woman in her own garden in Sekhomi's village and the incident with the Bakaa when his finger was damaged, he had characteristically shown, and probably felt, little fear of the beasts. However, the Mabotsa lions were becoming exceptionally troublesome, attacking the cattle even in broad daylight. Since it was accepted that if one lion was killed the others would move away, Livingstone encouraged the people to kill one. Eventually, on either 7 or 14 February,[14] he noticed that a lion hunt was in progress and joined in. Although three lions were surrounded at one stage, and would normally have been speared as they attempted to break out of the armed ring, the Mabotsa men were less courageous than most tribesmen and seemed convinced that these lions were bewitched. The two men with guns, Livingstone and Mebalwe, dared not fire because of the encircling men. The circle was broken but soon afterwards a lion was seen sitting on a rock with a small bush in front of it. Livingstone told in his book how he fired both barrels into it, then shouted to the men to wait until he had reloaded.

When in the act of ramming down the bullets I heard a shout. Starting, and looking half round, I saw the lion just in the act of springing upon me. I was upon a little height; he caught my shoulder as he sprang, and we both came to the ground below together. Growling horribly close to my ear, he shook me as a terrier dog does a rat. The shock produced a stupor similar to that which seems to be felt by a mouse after the first shake of the cat. It caused a sort of dreaminess, in which there was no sense of pain nor feeling of terror, though quite conscious of all that was happening. It was like what patients partially under the influence of chloroform describe, who see all the operation but feel not the knife. This singular condition was not the result of any mental process. The shake annihilated fear, and allowed no sense of horror in looking round at the beast. This peculiar state is probably produced in all animals killed by the carnivora; and if so, is a merciful provision by our benevolent Creator for lessening the pain of death. Turning round to relieve myself of the weight, as he had one paw on the back of my head, I saw his eyes directed to Mebalwe, who was trying to shoot him at a distance of ten or fifteen yards. His gun, a flint one, missed fire in both barrels; the lion immediately left me, and, attacking Mebalwe, bit his thigh. Another man, whose life I had saved before, after he had been tossed by a buffalo, attempted to spear the lion while he was biting Mebalwe. He left Mebalwe and caught this man by the shoulder, but at that moment the bullets he had received took effect, and he fell down dead . . . Besides crunching the bone into splinters, he left eleven teeth wounds on the upper part of my arm.[15]

Thirty years later, after his death, Livingstone's body was identified by the state of that arm.

It is a brave man who can see such an attack upon himself in terms of an interesting scientific experiment. Livingstone the doctor continued to take a professional interest in his own recovery, being particularly impressed with the way in which his own wound made a better recovery than those suffered by the other two men. He attributed this to the sleeve of his thick tartan jacket, which he believed wiped the virus from the lion's teeth.

These were his reflections some years after the event. Sometimes, when constant questions about how he felt at the time were beginning to grate, he took to lightening the mood by replying 'I was wondering what part of me he would eat first!' His reactions in the days immediately following the attack were less scientific and less light hearted, though he still showed little concern for his own suffering. He was more worried that he would incur blame for the thoughtless way in which he had joined in the lion hunt. He wrote immediately to Moffat acknowledging that he had ignored all the usual rules for sensible behaviour and asking him to tell the Directors what had happened, which Moffat immediately did. Although it was his left arm, he was not finding writing easy and did not wish the Directors 'to hear from a less authentic source'. Ever the optimist, he also asked Moffat to send him some building tools so that he could continue work.

The effects of the attack were inevitably considerably worse than Livingstone implied. Risdon Bennett later gave an impartial professional opinion:

> The account which he gave me of his perilous encounter with the lion, and the means he adopted for the repair of the serious injuries which he received, excited the astonishment and admiration of all the medical friends to whom I related it, as evincing an amount of courage, sagacity, skill, and endurance that have scarcely been surpassed in the annals of heroism.[16]

He remained for some months at Mabotsa being nursed by Edwards, but by this time relations between the two missionaries were deteriorating fast. Never once does Livingstone acknowledge the constant care which the other man maintains he lavished on him. It must have been a great relief to both when Livingstone was finally fit enough to return to Kuruman for a convalescent break.

The peaceful atmosphere of Kuruman, with Mary helping in the nursing of the heroic invalid, produced the nearest approximation to a romantic setting that the young couple was likely to encounter. Livingstone 'screwed up . . . courage to put a question beneath one of the fruit trees in the garden'. Neither to his parents, his friends nor his employers did he show excitement or enthusiasm. The decision had needed taking and he was confident that he had reached the right conclusion. Soon after he returned to Mabotsa. (The name, taken from a nearby hill, means 'Marriage Feast'.) On his way back he wrote to Mary asking her to remind her father to obtain the marriage licence. 'If he forgets, then we shall make it legal ourselves. What right or portion has the state church in me? None whatever. If they don't grant it willingly, let them keep their licence. We shall licence ourselves.'[17]

At Mabotsa he built a home for himself and Mary. His next letters to her tell her about the house and various dramas in the building of it (both he and Edwards had accidents, Edwards having the tip of his finger crushed and Livingstone almost breaking his bad arm again). He also shows some enthusiasm for the school they had started. Mary's mother must have commented that the house was unnecessarily large. Livingstone justifies it as being necessary on account of the heat, adding 'If there are too many windows she can just let me know. I could build them all up in two days, and let the light come down the chimney, if that would please. I'll do anything for peace, except fighting for it.'

At the end of the year he returned to Kuruman, where the wedding took place on 2 January 1845.

4
Chonuane and Kolobeng: the Missionary

On their return to Mabotsa the young couple found that the honeymoon was indeed over. While the bridegroom's mind had been fully occupied during the preceding months, Rogers Edwards had had ample time to reflect on the relationship between himself and Livingstone. Their original friendship had crumbled long before. During the period of Livingstone's illness following his mauling by the lion, he had found the standard of nursing and care which Mr and Mrs Edwards offered him perfunctory, and the spirit in which it was offered grudging. They doubtless found their guest unappreciative and demanding.

In his delirium he imagined himself in the charge of Risdon Bennett, one of the top doctors in London. The reality when he awoke was inevitably depressing. Bennett himself would have found difficulty in treating a patient in a remote African settlement without medicines or even the most basic facilities. Edwards and his wife not only lacked all medical training. They were artisans, skilled only as manual labourers. Livingstone expected them to perform feats which would have taxed his own professional skills by following his instructions, probably issued in technical terminology which they did not understand, certainly in a tone sharp with impatience and with pain. Nor was Livingstone good at expressing appreciation for trouble taken if the desired results were not achieved. This is constantly illustrated in his letters to his family. When his mother tried to send him cakes she had baked especially, there is no hint of gratitude for an old woman's kindly impulse, only vitriolic scorn for her naivety. 'Mother's cakes were like wormwood to the taste, but I must not say so lest it should offend. Will cakes keep well at home for a twelvemonth? Ought they to be sent to a warm climate where they very soon become like [one word inde-cipherably obliterated]? I ask these questions only, I don't say send no more,' he wrote, to his parents, in December 1843.

When he returned to Mabotsa after his period of recuperation at Kuruman, he was engaged to Mary. Livingstone took it for granted that Edwards, the professional carpenter, would help him to build his new home. Unfortunately Edwards was unable to do so because of the accident to his finger. Livingstone had told Mary about this at the time, but, when he came to set out the details of the quarrel in a lengthy epistle to Arthur Tidman at the London Missionary Society, this detail escaped his memory. Edwards was becoming increasingly suspicious at the prospect of Moffat's daughter coming to live at Mabotsa. All the years he had spent in Africa had been passed at the beck and call of Moffat: Mabotsa represented for him the opportunity to find an independent life for himself. The last thing he wanted was to have a spy for Moffat watching his every movement.

Perhaps when he first invited Livingstone to travel with him in search of a suitable site, he had envisaged a situation where the younger man would become to him what he had for so long been to Moffat. If so, even without the force of Livingstone's character, this was an unrealistic dream. For a clear distinction was drawn in missionary circles between those like Moffat and his future son-in-law who were ordained, and those like Edwards himself who were mere artisans. 'The fact is, I unfortunately lodged in his house, and being an old fogey gent he thought all I had done was in subjection to his superiority,'[1] Livingstone wrote to a friend. It soon became apparent that the young missionary had no intention of playing second fiddle to anyone, least of all to a man whom he considered to be lacking in initiative and intelligence. An article appeared in the Missionary Chronicle in England, under a note stating that 'Our intrepid Missionary, Mr. Livingston, has made preparatory arrangements for the opening of a station among the tribe of the Bakhatla.'[2] Edwards is not mentioned at all.

Livingstone, from whose report the article was taken, was con-vinced that he was justified in this. At the time of their first journey together, the Mabotsa site had not been under consideration. Edwards originally preferred a different position at Mosega, some 30 miles away, only abandoning the idea when he found that the Africans were not prepared to live there, which would have rendered the proposition pointless. After the site was selected, Edwards had been unwilling to make a start until he was quite certain that he had full authority from the Directors to do so. Indeed he himself later wrote of his reluctance even to accept Moffat's word as sufficiently authoritative.

Thus for Edwards the dream was totally shattered. Mabotsa with Livingstone there would have all the worst features of Kuruman without its compensations. If he had longed to be independent of Moffat, how much more must he have dreaded a life of subordination to a man so much younger than himself, abrasive by nature and lacking the experience and reputation of the founder of Kuruman. All his pent-up emotion poured out as soon as Livingstone returned. 'Your conduct has been dishonest, dishonourable and mischievous; at least this is my opinion, and I don't believe there is another instance on record as bad' was his opening gambit.[3]

For his part Livingstone had decided long before his return that Mabotsa was too small to hold two European missionaries for long. The driving energy which made him forever wish to work beyond other men's lines, to go anywhere provided it be forward, meant that he would gladly leave Mabotsa to Edwards at the earliest opportunity. It was regrettable that he omitted to mention this fact to the older man.

The details of their quarrel, of who said what to whom, were irrelevant. When Livingstone's long tale of woe and self justification, written in response to a similar lengthy epistle by Edwards which the latter never in fact despatched, reached the Directors in London, they immediately realized this. They informed Livingstone that the story as they read it in his letter certainly seemed to indicate that he was in the right, but that they must reserve judgement since the case for the defence of Edwards had not reached them. However, they had no hesitation in commending Livingstone's decision to leave Mabotsa and set up a new base at a place called Chonuane. It was evident that the two men could never live and work together.

The whole issue was the subject of endless discussion among the other missionaries, both formally in the Committee and informally. Edwards' main ally was Walter Inglis, an old friend of Livingstone's from Chipping Ongar days, who had come out to Africa with Moffat. Before his arrival, Livingstone had suggested that Inglis would make a more suitable colleague for himself at Mabotsa than Edwards, but even before the two young men had renewed their acquaintance Livingstone had changed his mind. 'Inglis I suspect won't do for

Africa . . . I have not yet seen him . . . If he is not a blessing he will prove a curse.'[4] In this he was influenced entirely by Moffat's critical comments about Inglis.

On other occasions Moffat and Livingstone took opposing views. Just after his wedding, Livingstone proposed that a seminary should be set up for native teachers. Through the tactless manner in which he handled the issue, he succeeded in uniting all the other Europeans against him. The older men saw his comments as critical of the status quo rather than constructive. They were also suspicious that he wished to take charge of the proposed establishment, an improbable target for his pioneering spirit of ambition. He later realized how mistaken his approach had been, and regretted the way in which he had handled the matter.

Already the pattern was established. Throughout his life his achievements were to be corroded by this flaw in his character. He was incapable of dealing tactfully, sympathetically or diplomatically with the Europeans with whom he was working. Several facets of his nature and background combined to cause this. He expected others to attain to his own almost impossibly high standards of endurance and devotion to duty. He made no allowance for the fact that the strengths and weaknesses of others might be different from his own. He frequently behaved insensitively but was quick to take offence himself.

He had never learnt to work as part of a team. The whole of his life had been a successful but lone struggle against seemingly insuperable obstacles. Experience had not taught him that people worked together best when everyone's point of view was given consideration. He was at his worst with those whom he considered his inferiors, intellectually, morally, practically or in achievement. Unfortunately increasingly large numbers of his associates were relegated to this category. His letters home to his family in Scotland illustrate this only too clearly. He came to regard his parents and siblings alike in a manner more appropriate for a father to his young children. He wrote copious instructions for their physical, spiritual and practical welfare, apparently feeling that he was the best judge of all such issues and oblivious of the increasing extent to which he was inevitably losing touch with the realities of their existence. While generous in sending them money, he emphasized rather than glossed over the extent of the sacrifice. When they then failed to use the money as he recommended, his reproaches were unending. He sent money specifically to enable his parents and sisters to emigrate to the United States, but showed no trace of sympathy for their reluctance. He had no appreciation of the anxieties which would deter an elderly couple and their two spinster daughters from starting a new life at the other side of the world. He seemed oblivious to the fact that hitherto a visit to Glasgow had seemed a momentous undertaking.

Livingstone would also frequently tell his family that he never expected to see any of them again in this world and had no wish to return to Britain in order to do so. Enemies were rarely forgiven, even in death. When Mrs Ross died in 1847 he commented to a friend 'No loss certainly, not even to her own children.'

The Europeans with whom he had the best relationships were those whom he regarded as equals or even, in some respects at least, as superiors. Shared interests in a field where the other man was acknowledged to excel made a good basis for friendship with Livingstone. His best letters were written to men such as his father-in-law, the great missionary, Risdon Bennett, eminent man of medicine, and William Cotton Oswell, the experienced traveller.

With Moffat uniquely he had a long-term working partnership, which survived disagreements, as well as a close family relationship. He wrote to him, addressing him always as 'Father', of missionary business, of practical matters, to give him news of Mary and the children, often told with a delightfully light-hearted touch, or to discuss other family affairs. There was some concern at Kuruman over a suitor of Helen's, Mary's younger sister who was in England. Here Livingstone, positively but quite tactfully, took the side of the younger generation against the older: 'We [he and Mary] think the young man did right in speaking to Helen first, but it is a pity she was not at the time of age. I would not have come to you first for the world.'[5] When he did offer him medical advice, following an accident to Moffat's arm in a corn mill, for example, the tone had none of the condescension so evident in his letters to his own family.

With Africans the position was reversed. Here he personified patience, understanding and appreciation; here he was always ready to offer positive support, to create opportunities and show up endeavours in the most favourable light. More than any of his contemporaries he succeeded in seeing things through African eyes, making allowances and striving to compromise wherever possible. For their part, the best of the Africans with whom he came in contact venerated him throughout his life and indeed after his death.

The native teacher Mebalwe, who had saved Livingstone from the lion, begged to be allowed to accompany him on the move from Mabotsa to Chonuane. Mebalwe exemplified all the finest qualities of native teachers, as even the Directors in London came to appreciate from Livingstone's letters. They asked for full details of his life history and of his Scottish financial backer, realizing that the story would make excellent publicity material for the Society.

Life did not run quite so smoothly for the second native teacher, Paul. He and Livingstone spent some time in late 1846 and early 1847 travelling together in the country to the east of Chonuane, near the Limpopo, known to the local inhabitants as the 'mother of all rivers'. On the second journey they were accompanied by little Robert and his pregnant mother as well as Mebalwe. They had hoped to find somewhere for Paul to set up independently and met a number of friendly, welcoming chiefs. Paul might have found difficulties in some areas: one chief was just 20 years old with 48 wives and 20 children. However, the real problem was presented by the Boers who had taken all real power from the Africans, expecting them to supply free labour for their white masters in return for the right to continue to live on their own land, and frequently also abusing them in many other ways. The last thing the Boers wanted was to have a spy for a strong-minded British missionary watching and reporting on their every move.

Paul accordingly settled once more at Chonuane with his family. Some years later, after the missionary team had moved on again to Kolobeng, his son Isak caused considerable embarrassment by having an adulterous affair and making the woman pregnant.

In 1845, while Livingstone and his wife were still living at Mabotsa (for part of the time they had the place to themselves as Edwards made a journey to the Cape which lasted several months) they entertained a number of visitors. William Cotton Oswell was an attractive young Englishman who had served for some years with the East India Company. He was now enjoying big game hunting in Africa, a sport at which he excelled and which he could well afford. He was an exceptionally kind, generous, modest man, cultured, highly intelligent and well read. He had been educated at Rugby in the time of Thomas Arnold. He enjoyed staying at Kuruman in June and was encouraged by Robert Moffat to travel on with his friend Mungo Murray to visit Livingstone at Mabotsa. Having already been charmed by 'that grand old patriarch of missionaries, Mr. Moffat' it was praise indeed when he described Livingstone as

'the best, the most intelligent and most modest of the missionaries'.[6] This was the start of another of those remarkable friendships
of Livingstone's which were destined to last a lifetime.

By the autumn Livingstone was travelling regularly between Mabotsa
and Chonuane, while Mary remained at Mabotsa, for she was heavily
pregnant. She enjoyed a visit from her sister Ann, though Ann had
a terrifying encounter with a lion on her way home. In January
1846 Livingstone wrote home to Scotland to tell his family of the
birth of their son Robert. In July he went travelling with the
native teacher Paul in hostile country leaving Mary alone to cope
with all the strains of the new mission as well as with her tiny
baby. Mary's mother and three of the younger Moffat children paid
them all a visit in September for Mrs Moffat was justifiably worried
about Mary's health – she was again pregnant – and the hardships
she was having to face. Her concerns were to increase during the
coming years. No sooner did she leave than the family had more
visitors: Oswell returned, this time accompanied by Captain Frank
Vardon.

In March 1847 the family went down to Kuruman to enable
Livingstone to attend a Committee meeting, then stayed for the
birth of their second child, Agnes. 'Not a pretty name, but it is
that of my dear Mother,'[7] he wrote, to his mother.

Livingstone had selected Chonuane for his new base because
Sechele, chief of the Bakwena, was living there. The young missionary
had already noted Sechele's exceptional qualities. Unfortunately he
had been less discriminating in his choice of position. The site was
not well supplied with water and a dry year brought about conditions
of drought and near famine. When supplies had to be brought in
from Kuruman and people started to ask when they saw Mary whether
her husband was starving her, even Livingstone found this 'more
than [he] could well bear'. Sechele agreed to bring his tribe and
join them in another move to a position forty miles north-west on
the river Kolobeng.

Livingstone moved there with Mebalwe almost immediately after
their return from Kuruman, at first leaving Mary and the children
with Paul at Chonuane. Even her husband felt some sympathy for
her when she reported that lions had moved back into the now
almost deserted settlement. After a few weeks she joined him in
Kolobeng. Life in the new settlement was hard for the young woman,
living for the first year in a temporary hut with no protection from
the extremes of temperature nor from the flies. She strove to manage

her two young children as well as being what Livingstone himself described as a maid of all work, while he was a jack of all trades. They had difficulty in making time for anything beyond the essential practicalities of life. Houses had to be built; crops grown; shoes and clothes, candles and soap all made; wagons and guns maintained; woodwork and ironwork completed; cows milked and meals cooked: frogs and locusts both formed an important part of the diet. None of these practical duties could be delegated: 'We must be at the beginning, middle and end of everything everywhere. If not, matters invariably go wrong. Mebalwe is the only man I know who carries a piece of work right on to a termination without being looked after.'[8] Then Livingstone had still to fit in the care of the villagers, body and soul. He was doctor and preacher while Mary struggled to run a school. Sixty to eighty children attended: their mothers found it convenient. The birth of her third child Thomas in March 1849 forced her to abandon this enterprise.

The dangers presented by the wild animals were also only too real. While giraffe and eland made welcome additions to the diet, 'the rhinoceros is our frequent fare. Baba, a Kuruman convert was killed by one last week. Unprovoked, it rushed on him and ripped him up.'[9] Word did not reach Livingstone till late in the afternoon and he and Mebalwe galloped through the night, not then knowing that the man was already dead. 'The moon rose about one o' clock, and a rhinoceros at the same time disputed our path, standing snorting at us.'[10] Livingstone rarely showed, or apparently even felt, fear, but even he spent the rest of the ride convinced that every dark bush he passed was about to charge him. Eighteen months later he again told his father-in-law of an attack by a rhinoceros, this time a female with a new-born calf, and fortunately on a wagon not a person.

He expected Mary to be equally resilient. 'A big wolf came the night before last & took away a buffalo's skin from the door. Mary wanted me to go & see whether the room door were fastened, but in reference to a celebrated deed of brother John', he told his parents. 'I advised her to take a fork in her hand & go herself, as I was too comfortably situated to do anything of the sort.'[11]

Worst of all were the snakes. Livingstone admitted that in England he had had 'a great horror' of them but soon overcame this because there were so many about. Returning home one dark evening, a cobra gave him a nasty shock, and one snake they killed close to the house measured 8 feet 3 inches long: 'the clear poison dropped

from its two upper fangs for a long time after it was beheaded.'[12]
At Mabotsa, he recalled in *Travels*, 'Early one morning a man came
to call for some article I had promised. I at once went to the door
and, it being dark, trod on a serpent. The moment I felt the cold
scaly skin twine round a part of my leg ... I jumped up higher
than I ever did before ...'

Although the name Kolobeng meant haunt of the wild boar and
Livingstone commented that it seemed to have been the haunt of
everything wild, it was the nearest approach to a real home that
the Livingstone family was ever to know. It was also the place where
the famous missionary achieved his only true conversion. When
he first reached Africa he had been appalled by the low number of
conversions and interpreted this as evidence of failure by the missionaries. It remained a source of deep sorrow to him throughout his
life though experience made him look at the numbers question
rather differently. He felt that a high standard should be required
before conversions were accepted, even though this reduced numbers yet further. While his views fluctuated, sometimes he believed
that the missionaries were achieving much merely by introducing
their ideas, moral and practical, to the Africans, whether or not
these were accepted. His old belief in Commerce, Christianity and
Civilization persisted throughout his life, yet even here he wavered.
'If natives are not elevated by contact with Europeans they are sure
to be deteriorated. It is with pain I have observed that all the tribes
I have lately seen are undergoing the latter process',[13] he wrote to
Arthur Tidman in March 1847. Questions like these have no easy
answer, yet perhaps his own enduring reputation in Africa as a
force for good justifies his belief in the benefit of a good example
combined with such advantages as Western medicine. The behaviour of the Boers to the Africans they subjected to their control
was the other side of the coin. If Livingstone was eternally turning
the coin this way and that in his own mind, seeing first one side
then the other as uppermost, the world has done likewise for a
century and a half since then.

Arthur Tidman was sympathetic to his anxieties and generally
gave him excellent support and encouragement. Livingstone was
always in need of money though he managed to look at his difficulties with wry humour. He once wrote to his father-in-law: 'Wish
somebody would leave me a hundred or two. But nobody thinks
enough of me for that. None of my forefathers were worth their
breeches, else I might have had something. They wore kilts, poor

fellows.'[14] In another letter he jokingly suggests that Moffat should find out how much Mrs Moffat is leaving to her son-in-law in her will and, even if it is a much larger amount, cancel his current debts instead, then 'I shall no longer be wishing that she may cut her stick'.

Money was always in short supply for the Society also, but Tidman took the trouble, for example, to arrange for Risdon Bennett to make a selection of appropriate medicines and send them out at the expense of the Society. He expressed mild concern over the ill feeling with Edwards and over Livingstone's constant moves, writing 'we hope we may now regard you as permanently settled'. But he was not only supportive of Livingstone's own work but did his best to offer constructive comments over the missionary's wish to set up his brother Charles as a missionary also.

Livingstone wrote about Charles in late 1847, the time when his enthusiasm for his profession was probably at its height. Sechele was showing great promise as a pupil, justifying the missionary's conviction that he was a most exceptional man. Livingstone had no admiration for African chiefs as a class, indeed he once described them as hereditary asses, but Sechele demonstrated intelligence and sensitivity of an exceptional quality. He asked Livingstone to teach him to read, and learnt the alphabet in both capital and small case letters perfectly in just two days. Soon he was an avid reader, giving up his former love of hunting to devote more time to it (and putting on weight as a consequence). He loved to read aloud, particularly from the Bible, and took a deep interest. 'He was a fine man, that Isaiah; he knew how to speak,' he would declare.

All aspects of Western civilization interested Sechele. He was impressed with European ideas of dress and aspired to follow the fashion, wearing whatever items he could acquire in incongruous combinations. He would wear Mackintosh and boots in the blazing sun, animal skins made up into the style of an English suit or an ancient red coat and trousers both made for a smaller man. He was keen too to use soap and water. Passing Englishmen mocked at his farcical appearance, though his tribesmen were impressed. Livingstone was more sensitive to the desire to seek out the best in both civilizations and helped him by persuading his father-in-law to send shirts, handkerchiefs and a red cap from Kuruman. He too, however, could not resist a quiet smile when writing to a friend.

You would be amused to see his royal highness . . . a king standing up to his knees in water and two persons scrubbing his royal
person all over. As a preliminary to his washing his wardrobe
himself. It takes a whole day to wash an old red coat and a few
other duds the which if sold to a Jew in London would not
realise 5/-. His wives too are fond of European clothing.[15]

It was unfortunate that the aspects of his own civilization which
Sechele deemed superior to their Western equivalents were the very
ones which Livingstone was most keen for him to give up. And yet
Livingstone, as conscious as the chief that each of the two cultures
had much to offer the other, understood his reluctance only too
clearly.

African tribal culture was structured so differently from English
Victorian society that behaviour which was virtuous in one could
be positively anti-social in the other. Sechele once asked Livingstone
'if an individual acted justly, fairly avoided fighting, treated both
his own people and strangers kindly, killed witches, & prayed to
God, would he be saved?'[16] Realizing that Sechele considered the
killing of witches as something praiseworthy gave Livingstone an
entirely different perspective in their later discussions when a man
had indeed been put to death for witchcraft.

Sechele startled Livingstone early in their relationship by ques-
tioning why, if Livingstone's forebears had known about Christ for
many generations, no one had come before to save his own forefathers. This troubled the missionary, who muttered a reply about
the difficulties of reaching them but privately felt guilt for the whole
Christian world. However, the chief did not consider his subjects
as being in need of conversion. Admitting that he could do nothing with them without thrashing them, he offered to make them
all believe at once with the assistance of rhinoceros hide whips.
Similarly, Sechele's old enemy Bubi, always keen to please, would
happily declare that he loved the word of God. It was hard for
missionaries to be sure that any declaration of faith was made in
the spirit they desired.

The belief of the Africans in one thing was unfeigned and un-
shakeable. The most important person in every village was the
rainmaker. Without him there would be no rain and they would
all suffer and perhaps die. Sechele was himself noted for his skill in
that direction and believed in it implicitly. The people were all
convinced that white men had many skills which they lacked, but

that making rain was a skill which they possessed and white men did not. No test or experiment would convince them that the rain did not come as a result of their charms, just as men and animals could be cured of their diseases with medicine. Both, they argued, worked on some occasions but not on all.

Livingstone insisted that the only possible system was to live close to a good river and use it for irrigation. The first year by the Kolobeng illustrated this. Then there were three successive years of abnormal drought. Inevitably Livingstone was blamed. As he narrated in his book, Sechele's old uncle told him:

> We like you as well as if you had been born amongst us; you are the only white man we can become familiar with; but we wish you to give up that everlasting preaching and praying; we cannot become familiar with that at all. You see we never get rain, while those tribes who never pray as we do obtain abundance.

Livingstone accepted that this was a fact. More than anything else, this fact ensured that he never made any more converts amongst the Bakwain.

Sechele's empathy for Livingstone and his beliefs was clearly demonstrated when they first moved to Kolobeng. The chief insisted on building a school there at his own expense. He also requested regular family worship in his own home. But he noted that, while it was customary for members of a tribe to show enthusiasm for whatever interested their leader, be it hunting, dancing or drinking beer, no one followed his lead in embracing Christianity. All linked it to the problems of drought. As Sechele presciently remarked, 'Oh, I wish you had come to this country before I became entangled in the meshes of our customs!'

Livingstone had already confronted some moral issues with Sechele. Arming the tribesmen was controversial, for political as well as moral reasons. The Boers were opposed to any firearms reaching the Bakwain, and Livingstone maintained that they possessed even fewer than was in fact the case. 'Fire-arms render wars less frequent and less bloody,' he declared optimistically in *Missionary Travels*, but he intended them only to be used for defence and for hunting. He opposed Sechele's attack on Bubi's followers soon after Bubi's death, but since the attack was seen by the tribesmen as a triumph, support for the missionary was weakened.

One problem dwarfed all the others for missionaries in Africa.

This was the question of polygamy. No issue more clearly demonstrated the impossibility of bridging the gulf between the two cultures; nothing did more to ensure the unpopularity of Christianity. The accepted Christian view opposed polygamy absolutely and without exception: 15 years after the conversion of Sechele, Bishop Colenso was excommunicated, in part for expressing liberal views on the subject. Sechele had five wives. The principal (and in the eyes of the church the only) wife showed no interest in Christianity or in education: 'about the most unlikely subject in the tribe ever to become anything else than an out-and-out greasy disciple of the old school', as Livingstone described her. The other wives, and in particular two, Makhari and Mokokon, were probably the most intelligent, kind and most interested in Christianity of all the Bakwain: 'by far the best of our scholars' and 'decidedly the most amiable females in the town'. The parents of some of these women were leading members of the tribe and those who had given Sechele most help in his hour of need. The ramifications of the problem were endless. Small wonder then that Livingstone told Sechele that he had no desire that he should be in any hurry to make a full profession by baptism, and putting away all his wives but one.

Christian ideals were alienating the Bakwain. If Livingstone succeeded in converting Sechele, his prospects with the rest of the tribe remained negligible. For Sechele the risks were much greater: he not only lost the best and most devoted part of his family but could face deposition, possible exile or even death. As a young man he had suffered exile and ignominy after his father's murder. Now he was preparing to risk losing the achievements of a lifetime. If Livingstone made only one convert, that one possessed the courage and pertinacity of the great Christian martyrs. It is sometimes suggested that the chiefs only countenanced the missionaries at all because of the material benefits. In the case of Sechele, who had so much to lose and so little to gain, the message Livingstone brought must have been convincing indeed.

Sechele even suggested that he should go to England or elsewhere for a while to study, in the hope that his wives would forget him and remarry. Regretfully, Livingstone, conscious of the cost, advised that this was not practicable. When he applied for baptism:

> I simply asked him how he, having the Bible in his hand, and able to read it, thought he ought to act. He went home, gave each of his superfluous wives new clothing, and all his own goods,

which they had been accustomed to keep in their huts for him, and sent them to their parents with an intimation that he had no fault to find with them, but that in parting with them he wished to follow the will of God.

Livingstone in fact spoke to each of the four women immediately. 'Poor thing [Makhari], she was melted in tears, could not speak but with a choking voice. Offered me back her book "as she must now go where there is no word of God." Wished that they could have remained in the town that they too might be saved, but Makhari has no relations. She was much loved and worthy of it.'[17] She left that night, without her Bible. Mokokon was equally sad, and as she had a small child and no parents she was eventually allowed to remain in the town. The other two wives were enraged. These women were not only losing their husband, their homes and their way of life, they had also to leave their children behind. It is hardly surprising that the unbending Victorian version of Christianity did not find a universal welcome in Africa.

The first of October 1848, when he was baptized, was a sad day. On the previous night attempts had been made to intimidate the Chief. Indeed the pressure on him had been unremitting for months, with tribesmen making comments which in earlier days would have cost them their lives. He had once called a meeting and told those present that if they wished to kill him they should do so immediately. During the service of baptism Sechele, always a handsome man, was dressed in a long cloak sent specially from England. The mood changed to one of sorrow, with many openly weeping. There was also some surprise that, contrary to popular rumour, the converts (who included his children) were not made to drink an infusion of dead men's brains.

In the months afterwards opposition to the church increased. Attendance at services and school slumped. Sechele meanwhile delighted Livingstone by asking to learn English. He had read both the Bible and *Pilgrim's Progress* in translations made by Moffat. It was not until March that Livingstone realized that Mokokon was again pregnant. Livingstone was torn. He felt profound sympathy for Sechele and Mokokon, realizing that before he appeared they had seen nothing sinful in their relationship, and wrote to Tidman of his most becoming spirit and how he was always decidedly on the Lord's side. To Moffat he wrote of his own bitter grief and disappointment, though also of his hope that Sechele was now truly converted, unlike Isak, Paul's son, whose own lapse was discovered around the same time, thus increasing Livingstone's misery. It was agreed that the chief should be suspended from communion for some time.

This was a time of strong and mixed emotions for Livingstone. Mary produced their third baby Thomas Steele in March 1849. The dramas of the preceding months culminated in the missionary's decision to set out on a series of long journeys.

5
Lake Ngami, the River Zouga and Cape Town: the Traveller

The early months of 1849 were embittered for Livingstone not only by Sechele's lapse and the defection of Isak, but also by increasing friction between himself and the Boers. They demanded Livingstone's immediate recall, threatening otherwise to expel him themselves. Potgeiter, their Chief Commandant, even accused him at one point of fleeing, not daring to meet them. While the evidence is not clear, cowardice was not a charge frequently laid against the missionary.

His letters to his family in Scotland continued to be brusque, unsympathetic and unappreciative. This concerned Mary, who frequently took him to task for failing to thank his family for parcels sent or for sealing his own letters before she had included her own brief greetings to the parents-in-law whom she had never met. However, when she did add a postscript to one letter it did not demonstrate particular charm: 'My dear Mother, I have not much time to write to anyone. I intended to have written Janet, but a bonnet of her own size will do for me. I am going to beg for David too, he is very much in want of wo[o]llen stockings for winter. Missionaries' wives have not much time to knit stockings in this country, as they have to act as domestic drudge.'[1]

While life with three small children was permanently exhausting for her, the birth of Thomas had been easier than her two previous labours, despite Livingstone's inability to obtain the chloroform he so longed to be able to use to help her in childbirth, and Thomas was a relatively contented, healthy baby.

Livingstone devoted much thought to his younger brother Charles. The eight-year gap between them meant that David's memories of him were not of an equal but of a young boy in need of protection and guidance. This feeling of superiority always brought out the best in the older man and accounted for his kindness and consideration to Africans contrasted with his thoughtless cruelty to Europeans. He generally related well also to those for whom he acknowledged his admiration, such as his father-in-law or Risdon Bennett. The trouble came with those whom the world might consider his equals but who in his eyes failed to live up to his standards: other missionaries for example, or, later, European members of his expeditions.

Charles was considering leaving America to work as a missionary. He was also planning to marry an American girl who was reluctant to leave her home and family for the dubious pleasures of life as a missionary's wife. A few words with Mary might have increased her hesitation still further. But it was not Mary who wrote to her but her prospective brother-in-law. Charles might still accept his role as baby brother, grateful for advice and counselling. The American girl probably reacted somewhat differently to a letter[2] from a man she had never met, and who declared that they never would meet on earth. His letter started with an attack on Americans in general and went on to declare that her feelings about her parents (she was concerned about leaving them to go so far from home) were completely misguided. Yet David did not mean to be tactless: the letter ends 'though I feel inclined to say sharp things to some I have a warm corner in my heart for American Christians. You must excuse my want of politeness in this my first attempt at addressing you. I am so far out of the world and am among complete Barbarians. But I love Charles much and shall feel pleased if you can only gather from some parts of it that I love you for his sake.'

Disillusionment with the Bakwain, and Sechele in particular, made a letter from William Cotton Oswell inviting Livingstone to join him and Mungo Murray on an expedition to Lake Ngami particularly welcome. He was finding that converting the Africans to Christianity was more difficult than he had ever imagined. Dissatisfaction with his own lack of progress and a reluctance to follow Moffat's method of devoting a lifetime to a single village in the hope of saving a handful of souls revived his thoughts of working beyond other men's lines. He was temperamentally unsuited to staying in one place for long. He easily convinced himself, and did his best to convince the Directors in London, that brief visits to much larger numbers of Africans would be more productive since the alternatives were so unsuccessful. Conscious as ever of the need highlighted by Sir Thomas Fowell Buxton to bring commerce and civilization as well as Christianity to the heart of Africa, he dreamed of discovering a network of rivers beyond the Kalahari which would link the great unknown core of the continent with the open sea and thus the Western world.

This enabled him to undertake his first journey of exploration with a clear conscience. While Lake Ngami was well known to the Africans, previous European attempts had been defeated by the rigours of the Kalahari Desert. There were stretches of seventy miles or more, three days' travelling for the oxen, with the sand deep around the wheels of the wagons, without water at all. Once they were only saved when Oswell spotted a Bushman woman whom he induced to guide them to water. They had left Kolobeng on 1 June. On 4 July they reached the River Zouga. 'None save those who have suffered from the want, know the beauty of water. A magnificent sheet without bound that we could see, gladdened our eyes,' wrote Oswell later.[3]

The party consisted of Livingstone, Oswell, Murray and a reprobate European trader named J. H. Wilson, who was described by Livingstone at their first meeting as respectful and diffident, though Moffat more accurately wrote of him five years later as 'a man whose shameless character is a joke in the country'. The expedition with its twenty horses, eighty oxen, wagons, supplies and men, was financed by Oswell with some help from Murray. The men included Oswell's faithful servant John Thomas, a former slave, who later accompanied Oswell to England, spent some time as coachman to a country clergyman, was taught to write by the cook and to read by the lady's-maid, fought in the Crimean War, where he was reunited with Oswell, and finished his days as butler in an English country house. 'He was a perfect servant to a very imperfect master,' wrote Oswell, 'who, now that his friend is dead, feels that he did not value him half enough, though he never loved man better.'

Oswell and Livingstone made an excellent partnership. The sportsman was not only rich and generous but an exceptional man. He was highly esteemed by the great explorer Sir Samuel Baker.

> His character, which combined extreme gentleness with utter recklessness of danger in the moment of emergency, added to complete unselfishness, ensured him friends in every society; but it attracted the native mind to a degree of adoration . . . [His] only fault was the shadowing of his own light . . . although his retiring nature tended to self-effacement, all those who knew him, either by

name or personal acquaintance, regarded him as without a rival; and certainly without an enemy; the greatest hunter ever known in modern times, the truest friend, and the most thorough example of an English gentleman.[4]

The dour Scotsman was the perfect foil for this man and their skills too were complementary. Wrote Oswell in *Big Game Shooting*:

> We were the firmest of friends, both a trifle obstinate, but we generally agreed to differ, and in all matters concerning the natives, I, of course waived my crude opinions to his matured judgment. I had the management of trekking and the cattle, after he, with his great knowledge of the people and their language, had obtained all the information he could about the waters and the distances between them. This worked well.

Livingstone purported to despise the hunting of big game, though a number of his closest friends went to Africa for that purpose only. The sport certainly gave its devotees a knowledge and understanding of the territory through which they were journeying which enabled them to travel with impunity through areas hitherto considered impassable. The two men learnt much from each other. The shooting of game enabled them not only to feed their own party but to offer much-appreciated supplies of meat to the Africans they visited. Once, when travelling without Livingstone, Oswell was asked by a chief in time of famine to take large numbers of starving villagers on an expedition: he did so, and brought them back well nourished and healthy. When no other food at all was available, the two Britons were amazed at the amount of meat required. 'I certainly thought the dear old Doctor was very greedy, for he would eat 4 lb for his breakfast and the same or more for his dinner. On telling him my opinion of his performance, he retaliated, "Well, to tell you the truth, I've been thinking just the same of you!"'

Livingstone, on the other hand, with his command of the language and understanding of local customs and behaviour, made communication possible in a manner which was quite indispensable to the expedition. As Oswell expressed it, 'He could talk to the Kafirs ears and hearts, we only to their stomachs.'

The salient characteristic of Livingstone which impressed Oswell was what he described as his 'Scottishness', a species of obstinacy or patient, self-reliant, quiet determination. 'I have sat seven weeks with him on the bank of a swamp because he was unwilling to run counter to the wishes of the people. I pressed him to move on with the horses; no active opposition would have been offered but he would not wound the prejudices of the natives – and he was right.'

On their first expedition together they were hampered not only by the desert but by Sekhomi, chief of the Bamangwato, through whose territory they had to pass. The last thing Sekhomi wanted was for the white men to make a way through to the warlike Makololo tribe beyond, and perhaps supply that tribe with guns. He therefore, according to Livingstone, 'with true native humanity sent men in front of us to drive away all the Bushmen and Bakalihari from our route, in order that, being deprived of their assistance in the search for water, we might . . . be compelled to retire.' A similar problem arose at the end of their journey when, after reaching Lake Ngami, they wished to press on to the territory of the Makololo and their chief Sebitoane, but were prevented from doing so at that time by the refusal of the local chief to allow them the use of a boat. 'I could easily have swum accross [*sic*], and fain would have done it, but landing stark naked and bullying the Bakoba for the loan of a boat would scarcely be the thing for a messenger of peace, even though no alligator met me in the passage,' wrote Livingstone.[5]

One chief was keen that they should meet Sebitoane. Sechele regarded the chief of the Makololo as his friend and benefactor and longed for his white friends to meet him. In Sechele's boyhood, during tribal fighting when his father was killed, Sebitoane gave orders that Sechele and his brothers should be spared. Sechele was told that he could either remain with Sebitoane and be treated as his son or return to his own home with his mother. When he chose to return home, he was sent in safety with presents of cattle and beads. When, two years after their discovery of Lake Ngami, Livingstone and Oswell did eventually meet Sebitoane, they found him as remarkable as Sechele had told them. But for the present they were forced to return as they had come.

The expedition thus returned home somewhat disappointed, reaching Kolobeng on the 9 October. But the main objective had been achieved: they had become the first Europeans to reach Lake Ngami, then a large and impressive lake, which today has shrunk away. The way in which the news of this important discovery was received in Europe has been construed ever since as evidence of Livingstone's desire to claim all the glory which was in reality due to Oswell. This was not how either of the two men themselves saw it, at the time or subsequently.

Before they had ever started out, Livingstone had written somewhat gloomily of the need to wait for Oswell because of his generosity, commenting 'The honour of discovery will probably be given to him.' But fame did not interest Oswell: he made no attempt to report their discovery of the Lake, leaving this to Livingstone, who wrote immediately to his parents, father-in-law and the Directors of the London Missionary Society. While he did declare that 'they could never have reached this point without my assistance' and refers to Oswell and Murray as 'having come from England for the express purpose of being present at the discovery', he also goes out of his way in all his letters to emphasize the scale of their contribution: 'to their liberal and zealous co-operation we are especially indebted for the success.' Unless he was adopting the royal 'we' this sentence in itself indicates a team triumph. To his parents he avoids the use of any pronoun, referring to 'the discovery of a Lake & people hitherto unknown'.

If Oswell was given insufficient credit for his contribution, this was because he had no interest in the glory, though a cousin of his was the first to express her sense of injustice: ' . . . you, the prime mover in the great discovery, whereas . . . Mr Livingstone seems to have more than his due.' Livingstone, on the other hand, while he did not share Oswell's unusually complete disinterest in fame, was primarily motivated by a wish to justify his behaviour to the Directors. His conscience was not quite clear about the way he had abandoned his post and set forth as an explorer and not as missionary. However, the Directors too had their own motives. They appreciated, as Livingstone did not, that in their quest for financial support all publicity was good publicity. Thus it was Arthur Tidman who ensured that the missionary's report was widely read, which led in its turn to Livingstone being awarded a half-share in the Royal Geographical Society's Royal Premium, the sum of £25. That Society's new President, Sir Roderick Murchison, also sought publicity for his organization, so, having been presented with Livingstone's report, he made sure that it was widely circulated.

Yet the way in which other people reacted to the episode did cause a temporary deterioration in relations between the two men. When they resumed their explorations the following spring (1850), they set out separately. When Oswell arrived in May to find that Livingstone had left some weeks earlier, he remarked that Livingstone had been 'unable to resist the desire and opportunity of being the first to visit Sebituane'. Despite Livingstone's later claim that they had made no definite plan to join up, this allegation was almost certainly true. Later in the summer of 1850, he was still complaining, somewhat ungraciously considering all that Oswell had done for him, that Oswell was 'excessively anxious that I should promise to let him accompany me next year [1851], but I declined, yet I don't know how to get quit of him.'

The companions he took with him instead were less suited than the tough, experienced hunter to crossing the desert and reaching places from which no European, save himself in the preceding year (he had not even the excuse of ignorance), had ever returned. He took with him his wife Mary, once again heavily pregnant, and his three children, four-year-old Robert, Agnes, who was just three, and Thomas, who had had his first birthday. Perhaps Mary, lonely and miserable, preferred to go with him. Despite a lifetime in Africa, she had no experience of the type of country through which they were to travel, and little imagination. The first of the party to suffer were the oxen. This was Livingstone's first experience of the tsetse fly. Horses and cattle bitten by it rarely survived. His next experience was even more terrifying: malaria. Yet still the anxious father was pushed aside by the man of science: 'It is an interesting fever . . . Thomas had it in the remittent form, & Agnes in the intermittent.' Fortunately his medical skills proved equal to the occasion: he mixed some effective pills from quinine. Although he did not connect the disease with mosquitoes, he observed that 'I could not touch a square half-inch on the bodies of the children unbitten after a single night's exposure.' Mary's courage was recognized: he told her father that she took after him and behaved like a heroine, even when the wagon turned over with her inside it, but he acknowledged the physical toll the journey had taken on the family, with Thomas much reduced and Agnes not so robust as formerly. The whole family had enjoyed a visit to the shores of Lake Ngami the day before fever struck, and Livingstone's brain was already filled with the dream of finding 'a passage to the sea for supplies. A great and difficult undertaking, but my ambition mounts thus far, though I tell it to few,' he confided to Moffat. But after their illnesses the group was forced to abandon the plan to visit Sebitoane just when Livingstone had negotiated the exchange of a gun for help in crossing the Zouga.

Worse was to come. They met up with Oswell on the return journey, who was able to supply them with the water they so desperately needed and helped them back to Kolobeng before the birth of the new baby. But Mary's health had been seriously affected by the deprivations of the journey. Her baby, Elizabeth, was born on 1 August, a week after their return. A fortnight later one side of Mary's face became paralysed, she suffered considerable pain and her right side and leg were also affected: she was probably suffering from Bell's palsy. Fortunately the problem eventually resolved itself. On 18 September Livingstone wrote again to his father-in-law:

> Have just returned from burying our youngest child. Never concieved [*sic*] before how fast a little stranger can twine round the affections. She was just six weeks old when called away to see the King in his beauty. I have not the smallest doubt but that she is saved by one whom she could not know. She is home now, yet it was like tearing out one's bowels to see her in the embrace of the King of Terrors. She was a very active child, about same size as Robert was at her age. Had very fine blue eyes. Was smitten by the epidemic which is raging here, viz. inflammation of the lungs... I gave up hope four days ago, yet she held on and inspired some small expectation that she might be raised up from the gates of the grave as Robert was. I have not seen one recover in this country except him... Then at one o'clock she opened her beautiful eyes & screamed with a great effort to make her lungs work, and instantly expired. That scream went to our hearts, & will probably not be forgotten in Eternity. Wish we were all as safe as she is now.[6]

He wrote in his journal: 'It was the first death in our family, but just as likely to have happened had we remained at home, and we have now one of our number in heaven.' In an age when many, perhaps most, families did lose at least one child (Livingstone himself had two brothers who died in infancy and the Moffats had lost a six-year-old child), this statement had some validity, but the fact that he felt constrained to make it probably reflects a need to justify himself, to assuage his guilt.

If he persuaded himself of his innocence, he soon realized that not everyone shared his opinion. The family went to Kuruman for a period of rest and recuperation from November to February and relations between Livingstone and his parents-in-law were under severe strain. Robert Moffat and Livingstone normally enjoyed an excellent relationship based on mutual admiration, the best qualities of each being ones that the other could appreciate, and the older man, though a forceful character, had a sunny disposition. But at this time even he felt that Livingstone was not behaving responsibly towards his wife and children. Mrs Moffat, known as Ma-Mary in the same way that Mary herself was known to the Africans as Ma-Robert, was an altogether more abrasive character. When it became evident that the issue was not only one of past behaviour but of future conduct the atmosphere became oppressive. For Livingstone had determined to make a third journey to Lake Ngami and the country beyond, and he had resolved that his wife and children should accompany him. Further, though her parents did not know this at this stage, Mary was once again pregnant.

Mrs Moffat made her opinions abundantly plain. If Livingstone was determined to go, and if Mary could not remain alone at Kolobeng because of the risk presented by the Boers (a very real one, as was later proved) and because of the problems that would arise if the Bakwain moved their base and Mary was left without a house, she should stay at Kuruman. While Livingstone's objections (that this would give rise to gossip and that Mary needed to be with her doctor) were unconvincing, probably the real reason was that Mary did not wish to remain in her parents' home, subject with her children to the dictates of a domineering mother, preferring the company of her husband with all the attendant risks and discomfitures.

Mrs Moffat expressed her point of view in a letter which she wrote to her son-in-law as they prepared to leave Kolobeng.

My dear Livingstone

Before you left the Kuruman I did all I dared to do to broach the subject of your intended journey, and thus bring on a candid discussion, more especially with regard to Mary's accompanying you with those dear children. But seeing how averse both you and Father were to speak about it, and the hope that you would never be guilty of such temerity (after the dangers they escaped last year). I too timidly shrunk from what I ought to have had courage to do. Mary had told me all along that should she be pregnant you would not take her, but let her come out here after you were fairly off. Though I suspected at the end that she began to falter in this resolution, still I hoped it would never take place, i.e. *her going with you,* and looked and longed for things transpiring to prevent it. But to my dismay I now get a letter, in which she writes, 'I must again wend my way to the far Interior, perhaps to be confined in the field.' O Livingstone, what do you mean? Was it not enough that you lost one lovely babe, and scarcely saved the other, while the mother came home threatened with Paralysis? And will you again expose her & them in those sickly regions on an exploring expedition? All the world will condemn the *cruelty* of the thing to say nothing of the indecorousness of it. A pregnant woman with three little children trailing about with a company of the other sex, through the wilds of Africa, among savage men and beasts! Had you *found a place* to which you wished to go and commence missionary operations, the case would be altered. Not one word would I say, were it to the mountains of the moon. But to go with an exploring party, the thing is preposterous. I remain yours in great perturbation.

M. Moffat.[7]

Thus for Mrs Moffat, and for the society she represented, the Victorian missionary world, motivation was the crux of the matter. The wives and families of missionaries could be asked to endure all manner of dangers provided that the objective was the propagation of the Christian gospel in the accepted manner, that is by settling among the natives. Today few if any dangerous professions require or indeed permit a man to be accompanied by his wife and children. Livingstone could have insisted that Mary either remained at Kuruman or returned to Britain, as indeed a year later she did do. If she did in fact prefer to go with him, he would certainly have incurred censure one and a half centuries later had he refused to take her.

Probably she wanted them both to remain at Kolobeng or some similar base for the rest of their lives, like her parents. But Livingstone was not as other missionaries were. His drive and determination had set him apart from other men all his life. Men of destiny have rarely made good family men, nor even easy companions. He was sufficiently a man of his own time and culture to need to justify to himself any deviation from the traditional approach. Even at the end of his life, when the issues of wife and family had long ceased to apply, his conscience would not allow him to regard exploration for its own sake as a worthwhile pursuit. But at this time he had persuaded himself, and perhaps even persuaded Mary as well, that God was calling him to follow the path on which he had set his heart. 'It is a venture to take wife & children into a country where fever, African fever, prevails. But who that believes in Jesus would refuse to make a venture for such a Captain?' he declared. 'I am happy to say Mary reciprocates these sentiments.'

This year Mary and the children were fortunate in having Oswell to accompany them. He was not a man driven by destiny and ambition but a kind and thoughtful man, a devoted son who wisely delayed marriage and family commitments until he was ready to give up his nomadic way of life. He set off in front of Livingstone's group to open up the wells for them.

They spent the first night in a cave still known as 'Livingstone's cave' with a fearsome local reputation as the spot where witches were put to death. No one, the Bakwain were convinced, would ever emerge alive from it. While the missionary succeeded in breaking the superstition, it is to be hoped that his children were not aware of the gruesome record of the place.

More threatening in reality was the desert which lay before them. As they moved on Oswell's solicitude was of no avail: there were no wells to be opened up. At such moments Livingstone's facetious attempts to make light of suffering grate painfully when applied to his family. 'The less there was of water, the more thirsty the little rogues became,' he wrote in *Missionary Travels*, adding more soberly, 'The idea of their perishing before our eyes was terrible.' The mosquitoes too were as vicious as ever, though fortunately this time no one contracted malaria. At last they reached the River Chobe, a tributary of the Zambesi. Here the family remained with the wagons, while Livingstone and Oswell went on into the country of the Makololo to realize their ambition by meeting Sebitoane.

Of all the Africans with whom Livingstone came into contact, excepting only perhaps the two faithful friends of the end of his life, Susi and Chuma, this man was the most outstanding. A great warrior and tribal leader of vision and force of character, he had longed to meet the white men as much as they desired to meet him, probably in part because of the good relationship enjoyed by Livingstone's father-in-law with Mosilikatse, the only African feared by Sebitoane. No doubt too, like all the others, he hoped to obtain guns. He impressed Oswell immediately by the way he shook hands with them, though the custom was not one he could ever have seen or heard of. Yet he was nervous too. 'A sad, half-scared

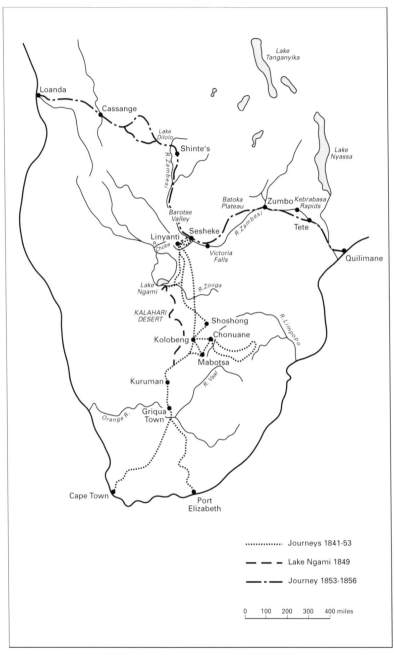

Livingstone's early travels, 1841–56

look never faded from his face,' Oswell recorded. 'He had wished us to visit him, but the reality of our coming with all its possibilities and advantages seemed to flit through the man's mind as a vision.'

That night he joined the two Europeans by their fire. They listened, enthralled, as he talked all through the night. 'By the fire's glow and flicker among the reeds, with that tall, dark, earnest speaker and his keenly attentive listeners, it has always appeared to me one of the most weird scenes I ever saw,' wrote Oswell. He told them of battles won and lost, of contests of speed and strength, of enemies destroyed by force of arms or subtle strategy, of bloodthirsty vengeance on his own deserters and extreme generosity to defeated enemies. He told them too of the visits of the Mambari, who came from West Africa laden with European goods, clothing and guns, which they would not exchange for the cattle in which Sebitoane's people measured their wealth, but only for people.

The horrified white men were soon to learn that the Makololo, unable to resist these allurements, would plunder subject tribes for slaves. Some indication of this had come before they met Sebitoane, when Oswell looked up and

> before me stood a tall stalwart Kafir, clothed in a lady's dressing-gown. It came scantily to his knee, and in other parts seemed hardly to have been made for him, and his appearance was so queer that I broke into a laugh. I saw the blood rise in his dusky face as he asked what I was laughing at. 'Why, you have got on a woman's dress from my country,' I told him. 'I don't know about that,' he said, 'but I gave a woman for it last year.'

Sebitoane told them other chilling tales. He sent an ox as a gift to a tribe, who returned it, saying they did not eat beef but only men. With some reluctance he sent them two captured slaves but they too were returned: their skin was too dark and only his own warriors would do. At this the chieftain drew the line. These were the first cannibals even he had encountered.

Each race held mystery for the other. Sebitoane asked the white men if it was true that they could make each other hear when miles apart and asked to be shown this magic. Livingstone took a tribesman out of earshot and asked him his name and his wife's name. Writing them down, he asked the tribesman to take the note to Oswell. 'Well, Ra'chobe, and how is Seboni your wife?' Oswell asked him, to the amazement and terror of the Makololo.

The new friendship between the chief and the two white men seemed to hold promise of many interesting developments, despite an unpleasant episode when the maid of a wife who had deserted Sebitoane and been executed was only saved from the same fate because of Livingstone's intercession for her. The chief asked to meet the missionary's family and invited them back to his village, and insisted on replacing all the cattle which had been bitten by the tsetse fly.

It was to be a tragically short interlude. Within a fortnight of their first meeting, Sebitoane was dead. An old spear wound in his chest led to an attack of pneumonia. The doctor dared not even attempt to treat him, fearing, rightly, that he would be held responsible for his death. Even an attempt to speak to the dying man of the afterlife led to suspicion and had to be abandoned. His last words were to ask a servant to take Robert for a drink of milk.

Although Sebitoane's daughter and successor was friendly to them, further extensive exploring was not practical. However, the two men did continue far enough to reach the mighty Zambesi River, wider and more impressive than anything either man had ever seen. So emotional was Livingstone when taken out onto the river by an old man in a canoe that only 'the fear that the old man who was conducting us across might ask, "What are you blubbering at? Ain't afraid of these alligators, are you?" made me hold my tears for some other occasion'.[8]

Livingstone, after long discussions with his friend, decided that he must now send his family back to Britain and continue his work alone. He wrote to Tidman proposing that the society should take over financial responsibility for them while he carried the Gospel into the new country. He concluded: 'I will go – no matter who opposes. But from you I expect nothing but encouragement . . .'

On the banks of the Zouga he insisted on a prolonged stop but would give no reason to Oswell. Eventually, after considerable pressure, he explained. Mary had had a son the night before. The baby was appropriately named William Oswell (rather than Charles, the original proposal) but was known throughout his life as Zouga. Livingstone was even more rude to his father-in-law, writing gloatingly to reiterate the theme of his boyhood: he could think for himself and anyone who tried to think for him must be 'a little soft headed'. This was provoked by the eventual arrival of Mrs Moffat's letter, written in April, which only now reached him. The reaction was particularly unnecessary: Mary's parents were right to be anxious. Although the baby thrived, she suffered a recurrence of the partial paralysis. Livingstone owed more to Moffat and to Oswell than anyone and liked both men. If he could behave so appallingly to them both and write so high-handedly to his employer, life for Mary cannot have been easy.

The party returned safely to Kolobeng where they enjoyed their last few days of family life in a home of their own. They had one visitor: William Frederick Webb, a big game hunter whom he had not previously met but who was to become a lifelong friend, a pallbearer at his funeral and his host for many months while he wrote his second book.

Oswell to their disappointment had refused to stay at Kolobeng but insisted on travelling on ahead alone. When they reached Cape Town in March 1852 they found that this was so that he could make financial arrangements for the near-destitute Livingstone family and equip them with a suitable wardrobe of clothes for their stay in the city, indicating that the money was their rightful share of the sale of the ivory. Even Livingstone was appreciative, writing frequently of 'the best friend we had in Africa' and 'he assisted me in every possible way. May God reward him.'

During the five weeks when the family stayed in Cape Town awaiting their passage to Britain, they had gradually to readjust to life in the civilized world. Despite Oswell's efforts, they must have seemed a strange group. Livingstone even had difficulty in coming down stairs, at first facing backwards as though on a ladder. When Mary and the children did eventually sail, there was still no confirmation from London that their stay in Britain would be paid for by the Society. Whether this worried Mary more than her husband it is impossible to tell. He assured her that they would only be separated for two years: in fact it was almost five before they met again. And, he told Tidman, when the children asked him 'When shall we return to Kolobeng? When to Kuruman?', the only homes they had ever known, he consoled them with the reply '*Never. The mark of Cain is on your foreheads. Your father is a missionary.*'

Tidman's response to the situation was sympathetic, and he tried to find a suitable travelling companion for Livingstone from among the missionaries. This provoked the inevitable torrent of invective against all of his profession with the solitary exception of Moffat. He was also involved in public controversy with the Boers.

On a more positive note, he was able at last to have an operation on his uvula, which he had long been desiring to improve his public speaking. Indeed, when they had been staying at Kuruman after the death of Elizabeth, he had tried unsuccessfully to persuade his father-in-law to perform the operation under his instructions with a specially prepared pair of scissors. He also spent considerable time studying under the guidance of the Astronomer Royal at the Cape, Sir Thomas Maclear. The two men became close friends and continued throughout Livingstone's life to correspond about his observations and calculations during his travels. Another new friend was William Thompson, a missionary who had previously worked in India. The two men first met at Mrs Sewell's house in London. After staying with him and his family in Cape Town, Livingstone carried on a friendly and light-hearted correspondence with him.

He left Cape Town early in June, but after problems with his wagon did not reach Kuruman until the end of August. There he learnt a few days later of the destruction of his family home and all his possessions, including his books, medicines and surgical instruments, at Kolobeng, the murder of more than sixty Bakwain and the imprisonment of some two hundred Bakwain women and children, including some of Sechele's own, as well as the capture of more than three thousand head of cattle. This was not the work of some other tribe but of the Boers. Had he not been delayed by the problems with his wagon, Livingstone himself would probably have been in the village at the time of the attack, as no doubt the Boers hoped that he would be. Kolobeng was importantly situated strategically, and Sechele, at the instigation of Livingstone, had shown himself reluctant to cooperate with the Boers. The Boers also at the time suspected Livingstone of supplying arms to the Bakwain. If he did so at all, this was on such a small scale as to be insignificant, as was indeed apparently admitted half a century later. One of the Boers involved was the young Paul Kruger. General Smuts told an audience in 1929 that he had once discussed the episode with Kruger, who said that it was a misunderstanding: a certain Gordon Cumming had supplied the arms and Livingstone was falsely blamed.[9]

Livingstone saw his escape as evidence that God had further need of him, and accordingly showed greater caution than was his wont in delaying his departure from Kuruman until his way ahead was clear of Boers. For the same reason he did not return to Kolobeng then or indeed ever again.

He did, however, have one further meeting with Sechele. He tried in vain, knowing that the attempt would be futile and frustrated long before it could be put into practice, to dissuade him from his plan of travelling to England to lay his grievances before Queen Victoria herself. Sechele refused to accept that, by signing the Sand River Convention that year, the Governor of the Cape had abandoned all claim to any authority in the territory north of the River Vaal.

It was to the north, much further north than Sechele's country, that Livingstone was now turning. Undeterred by events, the man whom Oswell described as a 'plucky little devil' was determined to open up the heart of Africa. This was the start of the greatest journey of his lifetime, a triumph unquestioned even by his detractors. He was to become the first white man to cross the continent of Africa from coast to coast.

6
To the West Coast of Africa: the Pioneer

Livingstone set out from Kuruman in contemplative mood. A long, mystical passage in his journal before departure starts in deepest gloom ('Am I on my way to die in Sebitoane's country? Have I seen the end of my wife and children?') then transforms into a paean of devotion to Christ. This was the first journey he had undertaken since his marriage without European company. His new companion, however, proved honest and helpful, while affording Livingstone an occasional quiet chuckle. George Fleming, a black merchant 'who is an American or perhaps was, for he calls himself a West Indian, for there freedom was proclaimed to the slave & I suspect he was once one', fancied himself as a cook and delighted in producing a plum pudding as they travelled through a remote part of the bush.

The men he and George had enlisted at Kuruman proved less satisfactory. They stole, told lies and revolted Livingstone by their behaviour. This group remained with him only until November 1853. They then returned to Kuruman with George while Livingstone himself set out from Linyanti, the Makololo capital, to Loanda on the West coast. From there he then completed his crossing of the continent.

He spent his first year after leaving Kuruman, until November 1853, in getting to know Sekeletu, Sebitoane's son, and the Makololo people, then in an exploratory journey 300 miles north-west up the Zambesi in the vain quest for a suitable site for a mission station.

Although Sebitoane had initially been succeeded by his daughter Mamochisane, she had found the pressures of sovereignty too great. Her father, fearful that, if she married, her husband would usurp power, decreed that she should sleep with any man she chose but marry none of them. After his death, Mamochisane, finding that this brought her no happiness but only the resentment of the other women, resolved to abdicate in favour of her brother Sekeletu. He was at first reluctant, but eventually became chief with his sister as his most trusted adviser. An attractive young man, though lacking his father's outstanding ability, it was clear from the way his eyes lit up when Livingstone spoke of Sebitoane that he had idolized his father.

Inevitably there was a wicked uncle, or, in this case, cousin. Sebitoane had a nephew named Mpepe. Mpepe had hoped to succeed his uncle and, during Mamochisane's brief reign, had done his best to persuade her to have her brother put to death and to marry him. Her wise old father had pointed years before to Mpepe's house, where he was alleged to indulge in vile sorcery, and remarked to Sekeletu 'if that house does not eat me it will eat you'.

Worse still, Mpepe was in league with the slave traders, negotiating directly with the famous Portuguese slave trader and explorer, Silva Porto. Ivory, cattle and slaves were handed over to the Portuguese. 'A man who did not like his wife sold her for a few pieces of cloth.'[1] There was little doubt that he was doing this in return for a promise of help in overthrowing Sekeletu.

The country into which Livingstone wished to travel was the area where Mpepe had most power. Sekeletu, eager to befriend the missionary for the same reasons as his father – that is a belief in the benefits that European civilization could confer and a particular wish to be associated with a close relation of Moffat's because of the older missionary's influence on the dreaded Mosilikatse – accompanied him.

As they approached Mpepe's stronghold, the man himself came running out towards them. He had an axe hidden on his person, but Sekeletu, rightly suspicious, avoided him. Their meeting was delayed until they sat down together in a hut that evening. Livingstone, unconscious of the plotting, sat between the two men and was the first to get up to go to bed. Sekeletu rose too, to show him to his tent, and thus was saved by Livingstone standing between them from the second attempt on his life that day. Livingstone was still unaware of the part that he had played, though he realized later that he had been lucky not to have been killed himself by the murderous Mpepe. That night, so quietly that Livingstone knew nothing until the following morning, Mpepe was put to death.

Later in their travels they reached the village where Mpepe's father was headman. Sekeletu told him that it seemed strange that he had not reproved his son Mpepe. He and the other headman were told to stand. Sekeletu's men appeared from nowhere to ensure that there was no trouble. The two men were marched to the river, hewn down with axes and their bodies taken out to the centre of the river by canoe to be fed to the crocodiles. Within two hours of 'our stopping we were again on our way', Livingstone recorded in his journal. Taken completely by surprise and deeply shocked, he remonstrated with Sekeletu's counsellors. 'We are Boers, we are not yet taught,' they replied. On reflection, Livingstone accepted the inevitability and perhaps the justice of the sentence. He also found that in minor disputes the tribe had some sense of justice: when matters were brought before the chief for arbitration, each man was allowed to put his side of the case without interruption from his opponent. Later, when they were in the country controlled by the Portuguese, two of the Makololo asked him to arbitrate on a minor dispute. The Portuguese were amazed and impressed with the way in which he dispensed justice. He took no credit, since he was merely operating the system of the tribesmen themselves.

Livingstone's approach to his missionary duties was becoming more realistic. Perhaps drawing a different conclusion from the case of Sechele from that which other missionaries of the time, including Moffat, would have drawn, he no longer saw success in terms of conversions of a handful of souls, each individual's spiritual development being the subject of detailed analysis over a period of years. He wrote to his father: 'The conversion of a few, however valuable their souls may be, cannot be put into the scale against the knowledge of the truth spread over the whole country,' and in his journal he made a similar comment, drew an analogy with missionary successes in India and concluded: 'The general knowledge is the criterion . . . Where missionaries in the midst of masses of heathenism seem like voices crying in the wilderness . . . future missionaries will see conversions following every sermon. We prepare the way for them.' Perhaps his preaching was more successful than even he believed: a missionary visiting that country nearly thirty years later found old men there who could still remember Livingstone's sermons in detail.

No other missionary of the time would have reacted as Livingstone did to Sekeletu. When the young chief declined to learn to read 'lest it should change his heart and make him content with one wife' Livingstone merely commented 'I like a frank objection. One cannot get hold on a "Ya, Mynheer". They are too oily.'[2] As a compromise, Sekeletu delegated learning to read to two members of his family as guinea pigs so that he could see the effect on them. Both showed such enthusiasm that they had mastered the alphabet perfectly in a single day.

Livingstone's first meeting with the Portuguese slave trader and great explorer Silva Porto was not propitious. The trader was travelling in magnificent style with a retinue of 200 and was conspiring with Mpepe to extend the slave trade and destroy Sekeletu. A visit to his stockade revealed gangs of miserable chained men, women and children whom he had enslaved. Livingstone showed more tolerance than might have been expected in persuading the Makololo not to expel him or withhold food. He hoped this would prevent increased suffering by the slaves and forestall any repercussions against himself from the Portuguese when he later reached their territory. He went further and had dinner with the man, who had first-hand knowledge of the country he was about to cross. This willingness to associate socially with men who represented all that he most deplored was a remarkable characteristic of Livingstone's, which was repeated time and again in the last years of his life when he became increasingly dependent for survival on the Arab slave dealers he was aiming to destroy. That it was evident at this time when his sole motive was convenience or perhaps curiosity is interesting. It shows practicality taking precedence over principles. Livingstone did, however, draw the line by rejecting the suggestion that they should travel on together, and altered his route to ensure that he was passing through different country. Silva Porto celebrated his own departure 'by seizing and chaining 2 men & a woman as tribute'. The Makololo proved a match for him on this occasion, however, and refused to allow him to cross the river until he had released his captives.

If he did arouse Livingstone's curiosity it is not surprising. It has been alleged since that much of the glory attached to Livingstone's name should rightfully belong to the slave trader. Certainly he was a European who had been travelling extensively in the Zambesi region for many years before the arrival of Livingstone. He did not, however, cross the continent. It is an interesting suggestion that much of Livingstone's reputation, many years before he met Stanley, was undeserved. It seems improbable that the lone missionary, without money or influential friends to support him, was a more effective self-publicist than the rich and ostentatious merchant.

Strangely for a doctor, Livingstone was unsympathetic to physical suffering. Although, in a moment of self-mockery, he once suggested that he could sympathize only with broken bones and toothache, at that time the only problems from which he had himself suffered, he was in fact so stoical himself that he would never admit that pain or illness was anything but a weakness to be overcome by determination. For years he mocked all those with malaria, which he described as bilious attacks rather than fever, and laughed openly at George's anxiety that they would all die. In May 1853 he succumbed himself for the first time and in the next seven months had eight attacks. While he now had a greater understanding of the disease, he kept himself going by sheer willpower, as he was to do for the rest of his life, and even persuaded himself that reduced activity made one more susceptible. Further, 'there is a good deal in not "giving in" to this disease. He who is low-spirited, and apt to despond at every attack, will die sooner than the man who is not of such a melancholic nature.' No wonder colleagues found him a hard taskmaster. But he had eventually to accept that the twin evils of malaria and the tsetse fly made the country virtually uninhabitable for Europeans and their livestock.

Early in November 1853 Livingstone prepared to set out from Linyanti for the west coast of Africa. Despite all the hazards, he was intent on finding an accessible route from the sea to the heart of Africa. The decision to head west rather than east was a somewhat arbitrary one: he claimed that the choice was made because it was nearer.

In spite of his relief at the departure of the Kuruman men, he was well aware of the limitations of the Makololo men with whom he would have to replace them. He had spent the summer travelling with those accompanying Sekeletu and wrote to William Thompson:

Hope the gospel will yet be established in these savage lands. I travelled in a company of 160 in 33 canoes. From the chief downwards all strove to shew kindness. Nine weeks' intimate intercourse, hearing their conversation, anecdotes, quarrelling, roaring, dancing, singing, and murdering, have imparted a greater disgust at heathenism than I ever had before, and on comparison with Southern tribes, a firm belief that missionaries effect a great deal more than they are aware of, even when there are no conversions.[3]

All arguments, he noted, tended to degenerate into 'How many men have you killed, you are a coward, you never killed anyone &c. &c.,' and stories were enlivened with imitations of the death cries of their victims. He found this a remarkably poor substitute for the conversations he used to enjoy with Oswell in the evenings. Sekeletu offered to lend him 27 men as well as his own canoe, and gave him food, oxen and ivory. Generous though this was, it constituted a tiny retinue: most travellers took around 200 men with the additional goods they could carry. His own possessions, firearms and ammunition, tea, sugar and coffee, a few beads for trading, clothes, books, medicines (though many of these including most of the quinine were stolen before he left Linyanti), a small tent, sheepskin and a rug, all fitted into four tin chests. He had also a sextant, artificial horizon, chronometer, pair of compasses and magic lantern carried separately. Some of these were presents from his friend Captain Steele and from Mr Freeman of the London Missionary Society, and some bought with the money awarded to him by the Royal Geographical Society. He was quietly proud of travelling so light, convinced that he would suffer less from want of 'knicknacks advertised as indispensable for travellers' than from want of pluck. And pluck, as Oswell had pointed out, was never in short supply with Livingstone.

For some time now he had kept a journal, despite a scornful response when Tidman first proposed that he should. His wide range of scientific and geographical interests coupled with his acute powers of observation made it one of the most fascinating and detailed accounts of a country ever written. People, plants, birds, animals, insects, fish, the constellations and the country through which he was passing as well as the adventures which took place: all are recorded in minute detail, in beautiful handwriting, often with neat, accurate little illustrations. He was the natural forerunner of modern makers of wildlife documentary films. He would write it up in the evening after the daily building of the camp and eating such supper as was available, when the men were asleep – probably the most pleasant part of his exhausting day.

For he was constantly ill, sick, sweating and suffering from diarrhoea and exhausted by the raucous chatter of his men. When travelling by canoe there were regular rapids to be negotiated, in water seething with crocodiles and hippopotami. On land they were trespassing in the country of the rhinoceros, buffalo and lion. Vegetation was often so tall and dense as to be virtually impenetrable.

And all the time it rained. Livingstone rode much of the journey on an ox. He fell off constantly and the surly beast, known as Sinbad, rarely missed an opportunity of dragging him under a low branch or kicking him on the ground. All the shooting of game for food had to be done by Livingstone. He neither enjoyed doing this nor was particularly good at it but the Makololo were such bad shots that he could not afford to allow them to waste the precious ammunition.

Early in 1854 they passed from Sekeletu's territory into that of the Balonda tribe. The local ruler was a woman named Nyamoana, who had a 20-year-old daughter Manenko. Livingstone would never pass through an area without paying his respects to the chief and explaining his intentions, even when this could cause considerable delay on a mere whim: he deemed it neither politic nor courteous. He would lay down his arms some distance away and offer greetings according to the local tradition by clapping his hands. Once good relations were established he had many tricks for capturing the confidence and curiosity of his hosts. They enjoyed comparing the different texture of his hair with their own, and the different colour of his skin. They were particularly intrigued with the whiteness of his chest contrasted with the dark tan of his hands and face. His watch and compass always aroused much interest, but the chance to look at themselves in a mirror caused endless merriment, except for one sad man who, thinking himself unobserved, murmured 'People say I am ugly, and how very ugly I am indeed!'

Nyamoana was determined that her visitors should not continue their journey by river, but travel overland to meet her brother and overlord, Shinte. This was in fact a smaller diversion than Livingstone feared, but it was rare for him to change his plans in response to local pressure. Her threat of violence from the next tribe upstream brought the reaction that 'I had been so often threatened with death if I visited a new tribe, that I was now more afraid of killing any one than of being killed.' She changed tack and indicated that the threat was not to Livingstone himself but to his men. With the Makololo thus terrified, further resistance was rendered pointless by the appearance of Manenko, virtually her only covering a mixture of fat and red ochre, and otherwise 'in a state of frightful nudity'. As Livingstone reluctantly yielded, Manenko patted his shoulder with 'a motherly look, saying, "Now, my little man, just do as the rest have done." My feelings of annoyance of course vanished.'[4] Manenko further decreed that the improved relations between her

tribe and the Makololo should be sealed by Livingstone's spokes-
man, who had the greatest understanding of the local dialect, taking
a local wife, an idea which so appealed to him that it led to his
eventual desertion of Livingstone.

Eventually they set out for Shinte's town with the formidable
Manenko outwalking them all through the dark jungle in the pouring
rain and dictating throughout how the expedition should be managed. Shinte gave them a memorable reception. He himself was
seated on a throne draped with leopardskin, dressed in a checked
jacket and scarlet and green kilt with beads around his neck, his
limbs bedecked with bangles and a plumed helmet on his head.
Livingstone and his men stood watching from the shade of a tree
40 yards away. An entourage of around 100 women in scarlet robes,
musicians, speakers and many others, around 1000 people in all,
stood behind the chief. Then there was a sudden roar and a host
of 300 warriors, armed and in battle regalia, swords drawn, screaming battle cries, their faces contorted with savage violence, charged
the visitors. Livingstone nonchalantly continued to prop up his
tree. Disappointed, the warriors turned to salute their chief. Nine
separate speakers then made orations, musicians played and guns
were fired. Throughout the whole performance, Shinte never took
his eyes off the white man.

In the middle of the night a messenger came to summon Livingstone to the ruler's presence. His Makololo adviser, much concerned,
was eager to appease the autocrat. Livingstone, feverish with malaria,
opposed to 'deeds of darkness' and prepared to take orders from
no one, refused to go. Their meeting next day was marked by mutual
respect. The traveller presented his host with an ox, which was
graciously received, though Shinte took it in good part when his
niece insisted that it should have been given to her, had her men
remove it and gave her uncle only a leg.

One evening Livingstone gave the people a show of Biblical pic-
tures with his magic lantern. He admitted later that it was the only
mode of instruction he was ever pressed to repeat. On this occasion the effect was even more dramatic than usual: the first picture,
of Abraham with his knife raised as he prepares to kill his son
Isaac, seemed so realistic that when he moved the slide the women
thought that the knife was about to strike them. '"Mother! Mother!"
all shouted at once, and off they rushed helter-skelter, tumbling
pell-mell over each other, and over the little idol-huts and tobacco-
bushes: we could not get one of them back again.'

At each successive settlement the evidence of slave trading became worse. Gangs of chained women held by Portuguese slave traders shocked the Makololo at Shinte's town, and children were kidnapped for sale during their visit. One evening Shinte summoned Livingstone and offered him a little girl as a present. Livingstone's attempts to explain his objections were misunderstood and he was offered a bigger girl instead. He toyed with the idea of taking her to grant her her freedom but realized that this would be misinterpreted as well as presenting practical difficulties. But Shinte was not to be thwarted in his generosity: he came secretly to Livingstone's tent one evening and presented him with a large shell of great value.

The nearer they approached to Portuguese civilization at the coast, the worse was the evidence of slavery. After Shinte's town the people he met on the way became less and less friendly. Demands for hongo, or payment for the right to pass through their territory, were frequent. Sometimes he could bluff his way through: an ancient shirt might be accepted and guides and food offered in return. But when he reached the Chiboque, most unpleasant of all the tribes he met, his customary offer of meat was ignored. A moment later, his camp was surrounded by armed men, their guns and swords all pointed at him. He calmly sat down, his gun across his knees, and bade the chief sit with him. The chief alleged that one of the Makololo had spat on one of his men and, although it was accidental, a fine of a man, an ox or a gun must be paid. In the ensuing discussion, the young tribesmen became increasingly aggressive until one made a charge at his head from behind. The young ruffian found the barrel of Livingstone's gun against his teeth, which he had filed to sharp points, and hastily took a step back. Meanwhile the Makololo, trained by Sebitoane, had quietly surrounded the group. Livingstone told the Chiboque that, if they wanted to fight, they must strike the first blow. A long silence followed. 'It was rather trying for me, because I knew that the Chiboque would aim at the white man first; but I was careful not to appear flurried, and having four barrels ready for instant action, looked quietly at the savage scene around.'⁵ Eventually a compromise over presents of food was reached.

This combination of cool courage, refusal to yield to blackmail and what Stanley later described as 'mildness of speech' proved amazingly effective. Livingstone hardly ever fired at a man, except with intentional inaccuracy as a threat, and was welcomed on friendly terms by the vast majority of Africans. There were, though, many showdowns similar to his first with the Chiboque, from all of which both sides emerged unscathed. When this is contrasted with the record of most of the other explorers it is remarkable. Two decades later Stanley, for example, who had already massacred some 30 or 40 tribesmen and wounded a further 100 in one town, fought 32 battles in his journey down the Congo as well as looting and plundering many villages.

Livingstone's own men on this journey were generally remarkably loyal to him. Once when crossing a flooded river, he let go of the tail of his ox. His men, convinced that no white man would be able to swim, plunged in immediately to save him, and were amazed to find him swimming strongly. But a week after the episode with the Chiboque he had a mutiny on his hands. Weak with fever, he found the men complaining and his orders ignored with mocking laughter. They had lost confidence in him, and were even convinced that the sea to which he had promised to lead them was a figment of his imagination. Seizing a pistol and pointing it at them in such a fierce way that they fled, he soon restored discipline. Next day, when Livingstone was ill, the leading mutineer showed himself ready to give his own life to save his master from an aggressive group of tribesmen.

His health was deteriorating fast and he was finding the Chiboque's incessant demands ever more wearing, though occasionally he struck on an effective ploy. Finding that one of his oxen was rejected by the tribesmen because it had lost part of its tail and was thought to be bewitched, he speedily 'bewitched' the rest of the oxen to render them less attractive to strangers.

On 4 April 1854 they reached the first outpost of civilization. The Portuguese with whom he stayed in a succession of houses amazed Livingstone by their generous hospitality. This was particularly remarkable since they must have known of his opposition to the slave trade on which their prosperity depended. While he later heard that some of them had not always led the blameless lives he at first attributed to them (one particularly welcoming host had not only been guilty of fraud in the past but also of killing his own father) their treatment of him and his men was superb. Although Cassange was still hundreds of miles from Loanda, and he was a sick man, he was no longer facing a constant struggle to feed and protect his men.

On 31 May he entered Loanda. Told that there was but one genuine

English gentleman in the city, 'I naturally felt anxious to know whether he were possessed of good nature, or was one of those crusty mortals, one would rather not meet at all.'[6] Few men could have been possessed of more good nature than Edmund Gabriel, Her Majesty's Commissioner for the Suppression of the Slave Trade in Loanda. He took one look at his visitor, put him to bed and nursed him devotedly for many weeks. He became a great admirer of Livingstone's. As late as July, he wrote on the missionary's behalf to the Directors as Livingstone himself was still too ill to be able to do so. The latter was well aware of all that he owed to Gabriel. 'The unwearied attentions of this good Englishman from his first welcome to me when, a weary, dejected and worn-down stranger, I arrived at his residence, and his whole subsequent conduct, will be held in lively remembrance by me to my dying day,' he wrote. He realized too how close he had seemed to death that day. 'I nearly marched off from the land of the living,'[7] he told Thompson.

It has been suggested that he subsequently played down the extent of his sufferings in an attempt to persuade the Directors that conditions between the coast and Linyanti were better than was in fact the case so that his schemes for the area could go ahead.[8] While his stubborn and persistent nature is not in question, he was less devious than the suggestion implies. He was an incurable optimist for whom the glass was always half full, never half empty, and he would always minimize or attempt to laugh off any physical suffering. His description of the attack by the lion might have been written by an impassive observer devoid of feeling, the tale of his dental problems is made almost comic, the discomforts and deprivations of travelling through desert or jungle are brushed aside. To have made what he would have considered a fuss about his own illness would have been anathema to him.

He was fortunate that the ships in harbour in Loanda at this time included HMS *Polyphemus*. The naval surgeon on board, a Mr Cockin, did much to speed his recovery. However, to his bitter disappointment, there was no mail awaiting him in Loanda and none arrived for him in the months he stayed there. Probably Mary had not known in time of his destination.

His men were finding their visit to Loanda a thrilling experience. The respect shown to their leader and the attention offered to themselves surprised and delighted them. They had been frightened by tales of white men who would fatten them up for dinner. Instead they were welcomed on board British ships by men who told them that they had been sent out to prevent Africans being enslaved. Hitherto they had not known that ships bigger than their own canoes existed: 'It is not a canoe at all, it is a town, and what sort of town is it that you must climb up into with a rope?' They were taken to High Mass in the Cathedral where, they said, 'they had seen the white men charming their demons', a remark which did not entirely displease the Scotsman, and the Bishop gave them all new blue and red outfits and other presents, including a horse and a Portuguese uniform for Sekeletu. They found employment in loading 'stones that burn' (coal) onto the ships.

Livingstone too was most generously treated by the Portuguese: he remarked that this was because he had approached from behind. An English missionary going inland from the coast would have been less popular. The Bishop embraced him, but 'I would have preferred a kiss from my wife to a hug from this benevolent and kind-hearted celibate in crimson silk gown & golden cross hung round his neck.' He also enjoyed the company of the officers and men from the British ships, and in particular a certain Lieutenant Norman Bedingfeld. Perhaps all that he had gone through clouded his judgement: certainly he was later to regret bitterly the enthusiasm which led him to invite Bedingfeld to join his expedition to the Zambesi.

That decision lay in the future. He had another, even more important, one to take immediately. He was offered a free passage home on the mail-packet *Forerunner*. He could go back to Scotland, have a real rest and recuperate, see the elderly parents he had not seen for so many years, be with Mary and the children and discuss his future plans with the Directors in London. Indeed his old father, when he later heard, sighed 'Man David, I wish you [would] come now – for I don't think I'll live to see you.'[9] Nor did he. Life was not proving easy either for Mary and the children, and all these things he must have guessed or suspected.

But there was never any possibility that he would accept the offer. He later said that this was because he had promised to take the Makololo home, but when he eventually reached the East coast two years later he left them there without compunction until after his visit to England. The answer lay rather in what he had once told Moffat: 'I shall open a path into the Interior or perish.' Although he himself had made his way through, he had not found the highway he sought. God was still calling him, indeed he had declared long ago in February 1853 that he was thankful to Him: God had allowed no European yet to reach the Falls Livingstone was later to name for his Queen but 'bestows tokens of the appreciation of my fellow men by throwing discoveries in my way'.[10] He was convinced that he bore a charmed life until he had completed the work God wanted him to do, and 'if I live I must succeed in what I have undertaken. Death alone will put a stop to my efforts.'

So he completed all his letters, reports and maps, packed them up and delivered them to Bedingfeld to be carried to England on the *Forerunner*, and allowed the ship to sail without him. In October the ship went down. All Livingstone's papers were lost, as were all hands on board with the sole exception of Bedingfeld. God did indeed appear to be watching over David Livingstone.

7
Across Africa from West to East: Great Leader of Africans

Livingstone declined the company of an Austrian botanist keen to go with him on the journey back to Linyanti, fearful lest the man should take the credit for discoveries already made by Livingstone. He started slowly, taking the opportunity to look at Portuguese agriculture and industry in the region, visiting coffee plantations and a sugar factory, as well as a number of deserted monasteries, while he waited for his Makololo to recover from various ailments. His Portuguese hosts were hospitable and charming as ever though they found him difficult to fathom. If he was a missionary, how could he also be expert in the study of latitudes and longitudes and a doctor of medicine too? If he was a priest, how could he also have a wife and children? To that he would reply 'Is it not better to have children with a wife than children without a wife?'

One friend who had been particularly kind to Livingstone on his way to Loanda fell ill during his visit on the way back. He was forced to stay longer to look after him and found the experience a revelation since it was the first time that he had stayed for long in a household of slaves. 'Pity the poor mortal who falls sick among his slaves,' he wrote to his brother Charles. 'This is a most kind and considerate master, yet he says to me, "If you had not been here, I think they would have knocked me on the head." They run riot among the eatables. . . . Let who will vote for slavery. I vote for the freeman.'[1]

The news that all his papers had been lost decided him to stay until New Year's Day 1855 with Colonel Pires, a rich and charming merchant prince, and rewrite all his dispatches, letters, journal and maps, a mammoth task. His fame was growing in Britain now, as well as in Africa. Gabriel forwarded a cutting from *The Times* to him describing his work as 'one of the greatest geographical exploits of the age'. Glasgow University gave him an honorary degree and the Royal Geographical Society awarded him the Patron's Gold Medal, its highest honour. He was reluctantly persuaded by Gabriel to write of his journey to both the Foreign Secretary Lord Clarendon and to Sir Roderick Murchison. The correspondence with Murchison, conducted at first through Maclear, led to a lifelong friendship and unfailing support from the most influential man in Britain on exploration. Murchison, so far from crying out 'My dear fellow, no more of your nonsense,' as Livingstone had feared, was soon writing '*I thank you most heartily* for having made me your correspondent.'

For as long as Gabriel was able to forward periodicals to him, he was able to keep in touch with world affairs, learning of the Charge of the Light Brigade and of how his old friend Thomas Steele was mentioned in dispatches in the Crimean War. He particularly enjoyed reading *Punch,* though Sinbad would not allow him to peruse it as he rode through the jungle any more than the ox would tolerate him holding up an umbrella. Instead Livingstone thought of his future as he rode. The children worried him: 'the country explored is unfit for a European family,' he wrote to a friend. The possibility of a government post passed through his mind. The Makololo, impressed by all that they had seen in Loanda and with the respect accorded to their leader, were giving little trouble: 'When I can get the natives to agree in the propriety of any step, they go to the end of the affair without a murmur,' he wrote. 'I speak to them and treat them as rational beings and generally get on well with them in consequence.'[2]

But once again as they passed into the country controlled by Africans close to the Europeans, trouble erupted. His thoughts on Africans and the effect of Europeans on them were constantly fluctuating. Sometimes, dependent on geographical conditions as well as his own state of mind, he saw them as enjoying an idyllically easy life, while on other occasions he compared the lot of their grandest chiefs unfavourably with that of the poorest factory worker in Britain. He usually adhered to his belief that the Africans were sorely in need of the Christianity, Commerce and Civilization which he struggled to bring to them. It was simple enough to contrast this with the horrors of slavery, but at times like the present he was painfully aware that contact with many aspects of European life and the consequent breaking down of tribal society had a deleterious effect on the Africans.

While Livingstone was lying ill in one village, one of the Makololo hit the headman. The villagers used this excuse to escalate demands and were soon firing shots. A sudden attack forced the missionary himself to threaten their chief with his gun and the chief gave way immediately but said that he dared not turn his back to leave in case he was then shot in the back. Livingstone replied that he could shoot him in the face just as easily, and the Makololo warned him that it was a trick to make him turn his own back. But Livingstone ignored them and, by turning his own back to mount his ox, defused the situation.

The next chief to cause trouble provoked some of the Makololo to try to stay and fight, and Livingstone was forced to threaten his own men with his gun and give one a 'punch on the head with a pistol' to ensure they followed him. The tribesmen hid their canoes and demanded more goods before they would allow them to cross the river. One of the Makololo outwitted them, however, finding a hidden canoe and using it by night to enable the whole group to cross.

When he reached the little Lake Dilolo, Livingstone observed that water flowed out of it in two different directions and worked out that water from the Lake was flowing into both the Atlantic and Indian Oceans: 'I was not then aware that anyone else had discovered the elevated trough form of the centre of Africa.' He was subsequently more amused than irritated to find that Murchison, from his desk in England, had come to the same conclusion and written a paper to that effect some months earlier.[3]

Then he was back among the chiefs who had befriended him earlier, exchanging gifts with some and arbitrating in a complex dispute for Shinte, who had held the matter up to await Livingstone's return. His sister Nyamoana lent them five canoes in return for their help with a buffalo problem. In other villages they received a rapturous reception because they 'had not only opened up a path for them to the other white men, but conciliated all the chiefs along the route.'

There was just one small tragedy: Sinbad the ox died, or rather he became seriously ill having been bitten by tsetse flies. The unsentimental Livingstone was for killing and eating him immediately but 'my men having some compunction, we carried him to end his days at Nariele.'[4] As they left there the canoe was almost overturned in a most unusual attack by a hippopotamus whose young had been speared the day before. At last they were back in the land of the Makololo. The men who had travelled with him took pleasure in showing off their new clothes and telling tales of all their adventures, seemingly unconcerned by the discovery that many of their wives had remarried during their absence. They talked excitedly of ships which ate black stones, of reaching the end of the world, and their chief delighted in wearing his new colonel's uniform. He had also to accept a severe rebuke from Livingstone for marauding the neighbouring tribes during their absence. The European wisely followed the advice of Sekeletu's father-in-law: 'Scold him much, but don't let others hear you.'[5]

Awaiting him was a package delivered by Moffat a whole year earlier to Moffat's friend Mosilikatse and eventually brought back, after a full year lying on an island near the Victoria Falls – the subject of endless suspicion of witchcraft or treachery between the two tribes, by the Makololo. The foodstuffs were mostly fit only to be thrown away, but the letters and papers were all the food and drink he craved, especially as they included one of the few letters ever to reach him from Mary. She must have reproached him for the time he spent in Cape Town as well as later, for he wrote:

> Don't know what apology to make you for a delay I could not shorten. But as you are a merciful kind-hearted dame, I expect you will write out an apology in proper form, and I shall read it before you with as long a face as I can exhibit. Disease was the chief obstacle. The repair of the waggon was the 'source of attraction' in Cape Town, and the settlement of a case of libel another 'source of attraction.'[6]

The two Moffats also gave him family news, and told him too of their irritation at the criticism levelled against him for refusing to accept the traditional missionary's role by travelling instead into unknown territory, or, as he phrased it in his reply, 'they seem to believe their do-nothingism is better than my blundering do-somethingism!'[7] He probably delighted more in the professional praise of the leading men of science. Maclear remarked on how much his observations, which he had sent to the Cape, had improved as he became more experienced, concluding 'But upon the whole I do not hesitate to assert that no explorer on record has determined his path with the precision you have accomplished.' Four months later he wrote to tell Livingstone that the President of the Society had 'said there was more sound geography in the last sheet of foolscap which contained the result of your observations than in many imposing volumes of high pretensions . . . O may life be continued to you, my dear friend! You have accomplished more for the happiness of mankind than has been done by all the African travellers hitherto put together.'[8]

The parcel contained also two unrecognizable portraits of his parents and the news that his son Tom had been allowed on account of illness to stop studying, a decision of which his father predictably strongly disapproved: 'he has nothing else but his abilities and learning on which to depend.'[9]

In his letter to Tidman he assessed the health hazards of the country, pointing out that in the twenty years that the Makololo had been living in that area the mortality rate had been so high and the birth rate so low that the tribe was approaching extinction, a gloomy prediction which in fact came to pass after the death of Sebitoane in 1863. He soon returned characteristically to a more optimistic approach: while malaria was a problem there were very few other diseases, and by improving the diet and getting soaked less often even attacks of fever might be less frequent. After all, he concluded, none of his men had died: the real danger came because 'neither doctors nor patients hurry themselves'. Despite reservations, he saw it as a field for missionary expansion. 'I can speak only for my wife and myself. *We will go, whoever remains behind.*'[10] At this time, he seems to have had every intention of settling with Mary in the Makololo country in traditional missionary style.

It was at this time that he started to spell his name with a final 'e', as it is now always spelt, although he himself occasionally forgot at first and reverted to the spelling he had used hitherto. The 'e' had originally been included, but his father elected to drop it because, according to his daughter, 'he thought his name long enough without it'. Why the old man later changed his mind remains a mystery, but he wrote to all his children asking them to use the final letter.

For the continuation of his journey he had the chance to accompany Rya Syde, an Arab, to Zanzibar 'with the opportunity to discover Tanganyika or Lake Nyassa' on the way (the Arab's discoveries did not count: only Europeans were seen as eligible to compete). However, he neither liked nor trusted the man and felt in any case that this was diverging from his true aim of following the Zambesi to assess its possibilities as a highway to the heart of Africa. Sekeletu offered to accompany him as far as the great falls of Mosioatunya, Smoke does Sound There. On the first night of their journey there was the worst thunderstorm Livingstone had ever known. The young chief chivalrously insisted on covering Livingstone with his own blanket, lying uncovered himself. Had he known then that the missionary would never return, with his wife, Moffat's daughter, as their insurance against Mosilikatse, to live with them as both men then envisaged, perhaps he would have regarded the white man somewhat differently. They took as their most capable guide Sekwebu, an exceptional man who was to dedicate the remainder of his tragically short life to Livingstone.

For many years now, Livingstone had heard the Africans talk of the great falls. Now he was to see and hear them for himself. Only one canoe had been brought instead of two so that Sekeletu was unable to accompany him, for they approached by water, the most impressive, if dangerous, route. He was still five or six miles away when he first saw the spray, rising like smoke in great white columns. As he came near with the roaring sound ringing in his ears the beauty of the whole scene overwhelmed him. Many of the place descriptions in his book contain comparisons for the benefit of his untravelled readers to scenes in England or Scotland. Here no comparisons were possible. 'No-one can imagine the beauty of the view from anything witnessed in England,' he wrote later. 'It had never been seen before by European eyes; but scenes so lovely must have been gazed upon by angels in their flight.'

Half a mile from the falls he moved to a smaller canoe and was expertly navigated through the rapids to the island in the middle of the river which now bears his name and reaches right to the top of the Falls themselves. He crept forward to peer over the edge into the seething mass of water plunging down, down into the narrow canyon far beneath. The water was low at that time, enabling him to get so close, though this meant that he did not see the Falls at their most spectacular, when, as the Africans told him, they can be seen and heard from much further off even than on that day. The weather must also have been dull since he barely mentions the rainbow effect so conspicuous on sunny days. The description written for *Missionary Travels* is more arresting than his original version, though the image of angels seeing much that he saw in Africa before him had already surfaced more than once in his writing.

His first account, written without the encouragement of his

publisher John Murray, was characteristically less evocative, more scientific, more detailed and so understated that the measurements he gives as estimates are frequently only half what are now known to be the correct figures. He was irritated by his failure to produce accurate measurements, for the only line he had to use broke and he could not remember how to use the sextant for the purpose. 'That I once knew it, and that it was easy, were all the lost ideas I could recall, and they only increased my vexation.'

Next day he returned with Sekeletu, for whom the sight was also a new experience, and planted a little garden on the island with peaches, apricots and coffee seeds, but sadly it did not survive: he was fearful at the time that the hippopotami would trample it.

Livingstone had long dreamed of naming something for his Queen, though up to now he had used only African names for the places he had visited. He toyed with 'the smoke-sounding Falls of Victoria' but eventually chose the simpler Victoria Falls. He broke another of his own rules too, though not quite, as he claimed, for the first time, by carving his initials and the year, 1855, on a tree.

Sekeletu then returned home leaving 114 of his men with Livingstone as well as much ivory. East of the Falls and north of the Zambesi, lay the Batoka Plateau, a much healthier, more fertile region than any Livingstone had encountered. He was convinced that this area showed potential for the future and longed to pass on news of his discovery to the rest of Christendom. It was, however, more than 800 miles from the coast for any potential European settlers and the Batoka people he found exceptionally repellent. Their way of greeting strangers was to roll on their backs on the ground, stark naked, slapping the outside of their thighs and saying 'Kina Bomba'.

Early in 1856 he reached the point where the River Loango flows into the Zambesi from the north, near the deserted Portuguese city of Zumbo. As always when approaching the outposts of Portuguese settlement, relations with the tribesmen deteriorated. Nor was anyone prepared to tell him why the Portuguese had left Zumbo 20 years before. To cross the Loango he was dependent on local help and the use of their canoes.

Men gathered in increasing numbers, armed, standing back, silently watching. They would provide only two canoes, they said, and later this was reduced to one, though they had others within sight. Tension mounted throughout the day. With so few men able to cross together, inevitably for long periods small groups would be left unprotected and vulnerable. While Livingstone's subsequent account in his book is relatively laconic, he seems almost to have visualized what he wrote that night in his journal being found weeks afterwards, sole evidence of the end of his expedition and of himself.

> Thank God for His mercies thus far. How soon may I be called upon to stand before him, my righteous Judge, I know not. O Jesus, grant me resignation to Thy will and reliance on Thy powerful hand. But wilt Thou permit me to plead for Africa? My family is Thine. They are in Thy hands.
> It seems a pity that the important facts about two healthy ridges should not be known to Christendom. Thy will be done.

By evening he had reached a decision. He remembered the words of Jesus:

> 'Lo, I am with you always, even unto the end of the world.' It is the word of a gentleman of the most sacred and strictest honour, and there's an end on't. I will not cross furtively by night, as I had intended. It would appear as flight and [quoting the Old Testament] should such a man as I flee? Nay verily. I shall take observations for latitude and longitude to-night, though it be my last. I feel calm now, thank God.[11]

Next day as the canoe slowly plied its way back and forth between the bank and an island in the middle, ferrying across his goods, cattle and men, Livingstone stood at his post of honour showing the armed tribesmen around him his watch, lens 'and other things to keep them amused'. As he finally climbed into the canoe, the last of his party, he thanked the tribesmen for their kindness, and wished them peace. 'After all, they may have been influenced only by the intention to be ready in case I should play them some false trick, for they have reason to be distrustful of the whites.'

This episode increased Livingstone's faith in God, but also his conviction that God had a plan for him and would protect him for as long as he was fulfilling that plan. 'If I am cut off . . . I am no longer needed by Him who knows what is best,' he wrote to his parents.

For his next decision, God was not guiding him, though it was to be some years before he realized what a disastrous mistake he had made. He resolved to cut across a corner to the town of Tete, omitting a loop of the Zambesi, to save a few miles and some rough walking. He thought that by regular calculations based on the boiling point of water, which is in direct ratio to the altitude, he would know if the river passed over any major rapids, cataracts or falls. Unfortunately he got his sums wrong. Until his return years later he remained unaware that the Zambesi dropped 600 feet between Tete and the point where he had left it. The Kebrabasa Rapids, lying as they did between steep, sheer high rocks, ensured that the Zambesi would never form a navigable highway to the Plateau of Batoka. It was not, as he convinced himself, mere indolence that prevented the Portuguese from making full use of the natural highway. He dreamed of returning to set up a missionary base with Sekeletu, assuring Tidman that 'there would be no difficulty in coming down to Quilimane, for there is no impediment to canoe navigation except a small cataract about 20 miles above Tete'.

Tete was a somewhat derelict place. But the Portuguese Commandant, Major Sicard, proved as hospitable as Gabriel had been in Loanda. The party stood as much in need of help as they had on the previous occasion. Food supplies were exhausted, and in the last stages two men were lost, one to disease, the other probably to a lion, the first casualties of the whole journey. He stayed there for some six weeks, having planned to leave earlier before the whole household was stricken with malaria. Livingstone recovered sooner than Sicard and his son which enabled him to repay part of his debt by treating them. When he went, he left most of his Makololo in the care of the major, who ensured that they were able to keep themselves until Livingstone should return, far distant though that time was in fact to be, and refused even to accept a share of the ivory. Just a small group of men, led by the guide Sekwebu, came on to the coast with Livingstone.

On 20 May he finally reached Quilimane, almost four years after he left the Cape. His joy in arriving was dissipated by the discovery that British ships had regularly been sending boats over the bar at the mouth of the river to ask for news of him and a recent one had sunk with all those on board drowned.

He had six weeks to wait, catching up on mail and reflecting on what he had achieved and what he had yet to do before HMS *Frolic* docked in Quilimane and offered him a free passage. With her came his old travelling companion George Fleming, sent from Cape Town by Thompson to bring him supplies and welcome him. Many of the Africans begged to accompany him to England but he agreed to take just one, his guide, interpreter and friend Sekwebu. The poor man, so sensible, tactful and resourceful as they crossed Africa, found the sea terrifying. He seemed briefly to be coming to terms with life on board ship and starting to learn English (even his master was finding his own native tongue something of a mystery after so many years away from any English speakers). However, the strain continued to build up in his mind and eventually he became insane. Livingstone would not allow the officers to put him in chains, terrified lest the poor man should think he had been entrapped into slavery. But his freedom was of little benefit to him for eventually he flung himself overboard and drowned himself.

Livingstone's reflections even before this tragedy were of a somewhat depressing nature. The post he received at Quilimane included a letter from Arthur Tidman. While the Directors were keen to congratulate him on his achievements and show appreciation of all he had endured, he was probably relieved as he started to read that there had been no possibility of listening to their opinions before he set out: 'As anything in the way of friendly counsel or discussion would now be fruitless, we can only... hope...' Even his return to England meant that 'immediate interests will be injured by your absence'. However, they were glad that he would now be able to discuss future plans with them directly. Livingstone did not share their enthusiasm.

While Tidman wrote with pleasure of the accolades heaped on Livingstone in England, he struck a note of caution. 'The Directors... are nevertheless restricted in their power of aiding plans connected only remotely with the spread of the Gospel.' Livingstone's letters had failed to convince them that the way forward lay in a wider dissemination of the word of God rather than in the conversion of a few souls in a small community. Further, his description of the country convinced them that it would be prohibitively expensive at a time when the Society was already overdrawn, as well as dangerous, to attempt to send out other missionaries.[12]

Livingstone responded with a relatively mild synopsis and justification of his movements in Africa, though he could not resist an acerbic conclusion.

Which of the plans is it that the Directors particularize when they say they are restricted in their power of aiding plans only remotely connected with the spread of the gospel? It cannot be the last surely, for I had their express approval before leaving Cape Town, and they yield to none in admiration of the zeal with which it has been executed. Then which is it?[13]

But he adds a few words of mollification, conscious that it is too soon to provoke an open rift with the Directors, although he told several of his friends that if necessary he would leave the Society. He wrote to William Thompson (8 August 1856): 'I shall not boast of what I have done, but the wonderful mercies I have received will constrain me to follow out the work in spite of the veto of the Board. If it is according to the Will of God means will be provided from other quarters.' A month later (17 September 1856) he wrote to Thompson of 'my certain severance from the L.M.S.'

In March (2 March 1856), before he received the Directors' bomb-shell, in another letter to Tidman, he had summarized his own view of his position. 'I am not so elated in having performed what has not to my knowledge been done before in traversing the continent, because the end of the geographical feat is but the beginning of the missionary enterprise. May God grant me life to do some more good to this poor Africa.'

All this gave him plentiful food for thought during the weeks he spent in Quilimane and the month he stayed in Mauritius after the death of Sekwebu. When he continued his voyage home, the vessel was shipwrecked close to Malta. As passengers and crew prepared to climb into the lifeboats, a wind got up and carried them to safety. He apologized to Mary for the consequent delay, but inevitably made so light of the whole episode that she must have wondered if the other passengers took the matter as calmly as did her husband.

But at Cairo news awaited him which did shatter his tranquillity. His father was dead. Much of the pleasurable anticipation of returning home after so long was destroyed. The joyous welcome awaiting him would now be muted, the father who would have listened with so much pride to all he had to tell would never now hear his tales, at least in this world. While for years he had assumed that he would never see any of his family again, to have come so close to doing so and then be thus disappointed gave him pain.

8
Britain: National Hero

A hundred thousand welcomes, and it's time for you to come
From the far land of the foreigner, to your country and your home
Oh, as long as we were parted, ever since you went away,
I never passed an easy night, or knew an easy day.

Do you think I would reproach you with the sorrows that I bore?
Since the sorrow is all over now I have you here once more,
And there's nothing but the gladness and the love within
my heart
And the hope so sweet and certain that again we'll never part.

A hundred thousand welcomes! How my heart is gushing o'er
With the love and joy and wonder thus to see your face once
more.
How did I live without you these long long years of woe?
It seems as if 'twould kill me to be parted from you now.

You'll never part me darling, there's a promise in your eye;
I may tend you while I'm living, you will watch me when I die;
And if death but kindly lead me to the blessed home on high,
What a hundred thousand welcomes will await you in the sky.

Mary went to Southampton to meet her husband although, because
of the shipwreck, he in fact landed at Dover. He hurried to
Southampton to join her early in December 1856 where she greeted
him with this poem. He had heard so little from or even of her
and the children during the four and a half years of their separation that he must have wondered how she was feeling and what
she was thinking. In Africa he had longed for letters but dreaded

opening them in case of bad news, though once he was reassured of his family's physical well-being there is little evidence of speculation about their way of life or relations with his parents and sisters. He was not an imaginative man and the assumption that he could categorically assure Tidman that Mary would wish to do whatever he did in the missionary field was taking much for granted after such a long time apart.

As the poem indicated, the time Mary spent in Britain without her husband was not happy. She took the children first to stay with her parents-in-law in the little house where they now lived in Scotland. Neil Livingstone was in his mid-sixties by then and his health was failing. He had always been a somewhat pedantic, strict, narrow-minded man who had expected his own children to accept his opinions without question. His wife had been a good mother to children who had been born into a confined world in which five or more people ate, slept and lived in a single room, where the working day lasted 14 hours and the hours and space available were not negotiable. It had never been easy, but at least the children had been used to the restrictions. At their age too, the grandparents were inevitably set in their ways.

For Mary, on the other hand, and especially for her children, life had often been hard, so hard indeed that survival itself was frequently in question. But they had always enjoyed the freedom of space. Whatever the hardships and dangers, there was room to be alone or with the companions of your choice. In Scotland, even in summer, the weather must have seemed freezing to children used only to the heat of Africa, forcing them to stay indoors more than other children. Even the language was a struggle for the children: Livingstone told his brother while the children were still with him that Robert spoke the native language well but felt much at a loss in English, despite his parents' efforts and Agnes (nicknamed Nannee) 'is all fun & frolic, perpetually inventing new modes of merriment. She gabbles what she can in pure Sitcuana.' This must have made the transition to broad Scots somewhat confusing. As for Robert, his father had commented even then 'He is excessively obstinate at times. Never saw one so very determined at his age. It often causes us sorrow.'[1] The paternal resemblance does not appear to have occurred to his father.

In such circumstances, to confine four children, the oldest barely six, and their mother to a tiny cottage already the home of the children's grandparents and their two maiden aunts was inevitably a recipe for disaster. And so it proved. Before six months were up, Mary had scooped up her brood and fled, bidding her parents-in-law to make no attempt to keep in touch with any of them. Within a year of their arrival in Britain, Neil Livingstone was writing to the LMS to say that on account of Mary's 'remarkably strange conduct' he 'had resolved to have no more intercourse with her until there is evidence that she is a changed person'. 'Mrs. L. does not write to us, nor are we anxious that she should, neither do we wish her to know that we are enquiring about them. Yet we do love the children much,'[2] he wrote, adding that they were sorry for the boys and were willing to take Robert and Thomas and educate them. Perhaps it was not thought necessary to educate Agnes.

Mary meanwhile was learning that life in Britain without a roof over your head with four small children presented many difficulties unimaginable in Africa. After she left Hamilton she stayed in turns in Hackney, Manchester, Kendal and Epsom, sometimes in lodgings, sometimes with friends of her father's. She struggled to live on the money sent her by the LMS, and the problems became more acute when she sought their remedy, or at least oblivion, in alcohol. Although her health had originally improved on the long sea voyage, she had bouts of serious illness when she was dependent for care on the kindness of others.

She had been confident at first that David would be back with her in two years, but as the two stretched into four and a half she became increasingly depressed. Nor did his letters retain the charm of the first devoted love letter he sent her from Cape Town. The messages to her increasingly took on the tone of a sermon. Much shorter than those he wrote to her father, they included such admonitions as: 'I am thankful that you are where you are, and if you improve your opportunities you may have cause for gratitude through life. Hope you give much of your time to the children. You will be sorry for it if you don't.'[3] This tone was even more marked in his letters to the children. None of the light-hearted banter and friendly teasing which he delighted in in letters to friends was ever sent to them. They are bidden to work, learn, be brave, fear to sin and remember they are now the children of Jesus.

Rebuilding relationships with the different members of the family must inevitably have been difficult, particularly for such a direct, tactless, insensitive man as David Livingstone. His mother was newly widowed – she had recently lost a grandson too when John's son, David's namesake, was drowned aged 11 in Canada – and she and his sisters had had much to bear through the way in which he had handed on his own family responsibilities. His only reaction to news of ill health among them had been to write from Quilimane to tell them they should emigrate to Australia as they had not gone to America. His children hardly knew him, his wife was drinking heavily. But, if there were problems on the home front, the British nation certainly gave him 'a hundred thousand welcomes'.

Every generation looks for different qualities in its heroes. Excessive adulation in the modern world is reserved for pop singers and film stars. In the 1850s courage, determination and piety were fashionable virtues. Livingstone had them all. In an age of science, Livingstone enjoyed the admiration and in some cases friendship of many of the leading men of science, the astronomer Maclear, the geographer Sir Roderick Murchison, the inventor of paraffin James Young. His former teacher the eminent zoologist Sir Richard Owen spoke fulsomely in his praise. He stayed in London with the renowned surgeon Sir Risdon Bennett.

In an age of exploration 'Darkest Africa' was what the Moon was to become just over a century later. Livingstone was the first European to cross it from coast to coast. In an age of philanthropy Lord Shaftesbury, the greatest philanthropist of all, took the chair at a dinner in his honour given by the LMS. Angela Burdett-Coutts went out of her way to befriend him. In an age of commerce Livingstone painted a rosy picture of the prospects for businessmen in the continent he had done so much to open up to the world.

Yet for all the grand names, Livingstone was no establishment figure. That again was in his favour at a time when the horrors of the Crimean War had left the public disenchanted with establishment generals whose incompetence could lead to the slaughter of the Charge of the Light Brigade, establishment administrators whose arrangements for the care of the wounded ensured even greater slaughter until the arrival of Florence Nightingale. Livingstone had gone into a factory at the age of ten. For those destined to a similar fate that gave hope. For those who owned or profited from factories, it was proof that working in them could be a beginning and not an end, which was soothing for their consciences. The ethic of hard work was important to Victorians. None exemplified it better than Livingstone. The image of the family man was important too. Livingstone appeared with his devoted wife and small children and had a much loved elderly mother at home in Scotland.

Heroes should also be romantic figures, with something strange and unusual about them. His dark hair and flashing eyes, deeply tanned, furrowed face and stern, almost dictatorial expression gave him an imposing, somewhat foreign appearance. His manner of speaking increased the impression with an accent unlike anyone else's and a lack of fluency which he explained (with some exaggeration) as the consequence of speaking no English for nearly 16 years. Then he would tell an amusing story in broad Scots, reminding his listeners that he was after all just a homespun Northerner. As the events of his life became better known, and especially after the publication of his book, he became even more of a storybook figure. All the best heroes have been attacked by a lion, or survived a shipwreck or seen some natural phenomenon unequalled anywhere in the world. Livingstone had done all these things.

As soon as he returned to London from Southampton with Mary in December, a flurry of honours landed gently all about him, outlasting the first few flakes of winter snow, although their brilliant dazzling white quality too was soon a memory. First came the presentation of the Royal Geographical Society's Gold Medal, a memorable evening with speeches by Murchison and Owen. Of all those there, he was probably most pleased to see his old friend William Cotton Oswell. Next night the reception was given by the London Missionary Society, another impressive ceremony, though his deteriorating relationship with his employers meant that the sparkle of this occasion already showed signs of melting away. After this a new experience awaited him, his first journey to Scotland by train, to visit his mother. Here the sight of his father's empty chair reduced even the hard-bitten traveller to tears.

There followed the presentation of a testimonial by the Lord Mayor of London at the Mansion House, the granting of the Freedom of the City of London, and later of Edinburgh and Glasgow too, together with another testimonial and honorary degrees including a DCL at Oxford. Prince Albert received him, and later the Queen herself. He spent an hour and a half with her, even succeeding in making her laugh heartily when he told her that up to now African chiefs had been astonished when he admitted to them that he had never seen his chief. They would then ask if she was wealthy and when he said that she was very wealthy they would ask how many cows she had got. Finally in 1858 he received the highest honour of all when he was elected a Fellow of the Royal Society.

Like most of those who suddenly find themselves famous, his reactions were mixed. He could sometimes be uncommunicative to those who plagued him with questions. When mobbed in the middle of Regent Street, he fled to the sanctuary of a cab. Even going to church could be an ordeal: once he succeeded in slipping in quietly and anonymously, but the preacher, recognizing him, foolishly mentioned him in a prayer. The congregation swarmed round, even climbing over the pews, desperate to see and shake hands with the great man.[4] He maintained that he hated to be lionized, but, being human, there were occasions when he revelled in the attention and later missed it when it faded.

From the moment when he agreed with John Murray that he would write a book, any possibility of keeping to his original intention of returning to Africa within two or three months disappeared. John Murray's offer had been most generous: not only was Livingstone to receive two-thirds of the profits but he was also to have an advance of two thousand guineas on publication. *Missionary Travels in South Africa* is dedicated to Sir Roderick Murchison. It was completed in just six months and is almost 800 pages and some 250 000 words long. Livingstone was writing in his London lodgings with the children living with him, proving that the ability to concentrate whatever the distractions around him had not left him since his days in the mill at Blantyre. He had some secretarial help from his brother Charles, who was now in London, but wrote the whole book himself by hand.

The book is rambling and somewhat disjointed, but gives a vivid picture of people and events and a fascinatingly detailed observation of all that he had seen: animals, birds, insects, trees, plants, rocks, stars, the geographical nature of the country, rivers, forests, the soil, diseases suffered by men and beasts, tribal customs. His catholic interest in everything around him enabled him to write sufficiently detailed descriptions to satisfy the scientist while simultaneously painting a vivid enough picture to enthral the lay reader. Five years before he had thought of writing a book similar to White's *Natural History of Selborne*.

He does not include, intentionally and contrary to advice from his publishers, any of the religious reflections which frequently occur in his journal, an omission which led to complaints from some of the more pious of his readers. More controversial is the way in which, as always, he paints a rosier picture than the facts justified of conditions in the interior of Africa. Although this is in part temperamental, reflecting the reluctance he always felt to dwell at length on difficulties surmounted or dangers survived, it is also symptomatic of his determination to promote future expeditions to the same area. In this respect the book was disingenuous and dangerous.

The element of danger to others will be considered later when the extent of Livingstone's responsibility for the disastrous Makololo mission is considered. However, it is worth noting here that although Livingstone has attracted more opprobrium for the way in which he single-mindedly pursued his objective of sending as many Europeans as possible into the central plateau of Africa than for almost anything else he did, his motives for this were not selfish. Had he been primarily concerned with any glory he hoped would ensue, he would have been keen to take as large a part personally as possible. On the contrary, as will be seen later, he avoided all personal involvement. He had a vision for Africa as a whole and this part of it in particular. He was absolutely convinced that Africans would benefit from sharing in European culture, from legitimate trade which would take the place of the slave trade, and from the spread of Christianity, its broad principles rather than its dogma. Europeans too, he felt, had much to gain as well as a duty to fulfil. Since the infiltration of Africa by Europe in the longer term was inevitable, Livingstone's desire to have this movement led by the sort of Europeans he hoped to encourage was not something to be deplored.

This aspect of his book prompted little comment at the time. Indeed, 13 800 copies at a guinea apiece had been ordered before the first 12 000 copies were available. Seven editions were published in quick succession. Nor was his readership composed only of the unthinking. 'I have been following a narrative of great dangers and trials, encountered in a good cause, by as honest and courageous a man as ever lived,' wrote Charles Dickens, never usually a fan of missions to Africa, in *Household Words* in January 1858. He went on to applaud Livingstone's independence of 'mischievous sectarian influences' and appreciation of the need to link 'every legitimate aid' with the preaching of the Gospel.

The impoverished missionary who had returned from Africa no richer than when he set out 16 years before suddenly found himself an extremely rich bestselling author. He did not enjoy the work: 'I think I would rather cross the African continent again than undertake to write another book,' he declared in the Introduction, but it enabled him to make adequate provision for his family as well as for a Moffat missionary brother-in-law whom he was keen to help.

After the completion of the book, he started a lecture tour through-out Britain, speaking in Dublin, Manchester, Glasgow, Oxford, Leeds, Liverpool, Dundee, Halifax and Birmingham as well as Blantyre and the church in Hamilton. His speeches in the industrial cities em-phasized the commercial possibilities of central Africa. In particular, cotton could be grown there under English control across the world from the slave-based cotton plantations of America. When he went to speak at Cambridge he had no plans to make the evening special. But something in the fervour of his audience inspired him. He told them first that they were the sort of men who were needed. In his final sentences his voice rose to a shout:

> I beg to direct your attention to Africa. I know that in a few years I shall be cut off in that country, which is now open. Do not let it be shut again! I go back to Africa to try to make an open path for commerce and Christianity. *Do you carry on the work which I have begun. I Leave It With You!*

No one there ever forgot the impression his speech created. His privileged, cultured, academic audience was enthralled by the vision he showed them. The little man with a throat problematic enough to prevent him preaching confidently to a congregation of Africans, who had almost forgotten his own language, was heard to the end in absolute silence. Then came the applause, deafening, unending. Money was immediately collected to replace the books he had lost at Kolobeng. More importantly, as a direct consequence the Oxford and Cambridge Mission (which also included the Universities of Durham and Dublin) was established. It was later known as the Universities' Mission to Central Africa, or UMCA.

Livingstone had never doubted that he would return to Africa as soon as possible. The question which confronted him was to de-cide in what capacity. He had been brought up to believe that the only way in which he could serve God overseas was as a mission-ary. Even then he had had reservations about committing himself to any particular sect, hence his choice of the LMS. Sixteen years in Africa had convinced him that the traditional life for missionar-ies, tied to a single village or small community, was not for him. He found it too restricting and he no longer believed in what it set out to achieve. He attached less importance to the conversion of an individual soul and more to the propagation of Christian ideals throughout a wider community. His increasing doubts were reinforced by the receipt of Tidman's letter in Quilimane. He had mentioned the possibility of a government job in Loanda. When he received Tidman's letter he wrote at once to Murchison, dropping hints that provided he could ensure financial security for his family he would 'prefer dissolving my connection with the Society and follow out my own plans as a private Christian'.[5]

Tim Jeal maintains that the way in which Livingstone handled his employment negotiations at this time are revealing about his character: 'Duplicity and ruthlessness are by no means uncommon in exceptional men, but when they occur in the personality of a man usually considered to have been honest to a fault and gentle in his dealings, it does call for remark.' He suggests that the previous assumption that Livingstone parted cordially with the Society was not supported by the facts. The chronology and statement of facts given below adheres precisely to those given by Jeal: only the interpretations and conclusions are different.

Even before Livingstone received Tidman's letter, he wrote to Edmund Gabriel from Tete saying that the Directors would want him to go on a lecture tour on his return as a means of raising money. However, they had already begrudged Mary the sum of £30 when asked: 'Expect me to go begging after that.'

The positions of both Livingstone and Tidman had been dramatically altered by the realization that Livingstone was now a famous man. Tidman saw this as excellent for the all-important matter of fund raising, since the Society had an overdraft of £13 000, making it vital to retain Livingstone. On the other hand he was concerned that it would enable Livingstone to pressurize the Society into opening up new missions it could ill afford in the area which interested Livingstone. This was why Tidman wrote the cautionary letter to Quilimane, failing to anticipate the fury it would arouse in the other man's breast.

Livingstone on the other hand saw his fame as a source of power for achieving the three objectives which most concerned him. He sought financial security for his wife and family, a suitable opening for himself, and the chance to promote the opening up of the central Batoka Plateau area. The first, although it can be presented as mercenary, seems eminently reasonable, especially in the face of the criticism he had incurred for his treatment of Mary and the children. No one made less use of what he termed 'filthy lucre' for their own ends than did Livingstone. The second too seems unobjectionable. The third he probably sought for altruistic motives, though it is possible that he was intentionally turning a blind eye to the inherent problems. The questions which arose were how if at all the second two objectives should be combined, and what measure of responsibility and personal involvement he should have been prepared to take for the opening up of the country.

On 5 January 1857 Murchison organized the Mansion House meeting which set up the testimonial fund and on the same evening wrote to Lord Clarendon, the Foreign Secretary, to suggest that he might be able to make use of Livingstone's talents for speaking African languages and communicating with the natives. Murchison followed this up with a second letter just six days later proposing a meeting between Clarendon and Livingstone.

While they knew nothing of either letter, the Directors of the LMS were displeased about the testimonial fund, feeling that the money should be coming to the Society and not to Livingstone. The dangerous financial independence this gave him determined them to discuss future plans with him just a week later. At the meeting Livingstone told them that two new missions should be set up, one to the Makololo and one, to reassure the Makololo, to the Matabele. That to the Matabele should be set up by Moffat and (according to the Minutes) 'in his [Livingstone's] judgment the result would be promoted by the residence of himself and Mrs. Livingstone amongst the Makololo.' This was confirmed by an LMS Committee on 22 January, conditional on a Moffat heading the Matabele mission. Further, 'a missionary [was to] be appointed to assist Dr. Livingstone in the organisation of the intended mission among the Makololo.' As Jeal points out, this does not indicate that Livingstone himself would no longer take a direct part. This was confirmed at a meeting on 14 May without complaint from Livingstone.

By this time Livingstone knew that there was a good chance that he would be offered a suitable government post. He told Murchison in April that he had suggested and Clarendon had approved 'a consulship to the Makololo and other central African tribes.' Details were not finalized and few people choose to give up an existing job before they have finalized the arrangements for a new position: Livingstone wrote to Maclear in May saying 'I am not yet fairly on with the Government but am nearly quite off with the Society.' But he went further. He told Murchison in April that he did not wish to finalize the deal at this moment because this would enable the LMS to present the matter in such a way that it would harm his reputation.

Ever the optimist, he may have hoped at this stage that he could give adequate cover to the Makololo Mission while fulfilling his government undertaking. Certainly his arrangements with Clarendon were progressing fast.

Meanwhile Tidman was in no hurry. He did not even write to Moffat until April, when he told him 'No step to be actually taken.' He had no enthusiasm for the proposed new missions and no doubt hoped, as Jeal suggests, that Livingstone would become impatient and go on his own. Meanwhile the public appeal launched in March on Livingstone's reputation continued to bring in money.

Thus it was in the interests of both men not to make public Livingstone's imminent departure from the Society. Jeal rejects the notion of collusion between them because of the risks of discovery. But no collusion was necessary. Whether Tidman in fact suspected or discovered Livingstone's plans is irrelevant: so long as the public had no suspicion, the money would continue to pour in. If eventually Livingstone had other plans, so much the better. The proposed new missions could be forgotten and the money used to clear the Society's overdraft.

This was where Tidman made a serious error of judgement. Livingstone was happy until October, when he eventually informed the Society of his changed plans, to allow the appeal to benefit from his name and reputation. But he considered that the money had been collected for a specific purpose, and one particularly close to his heart: the establishment of a mission to the Makololo. He was not prepared to allow this plan to be dropped and in February he told Tidman so. Tidman was forced to go along with this.

Both men had been playing the game to achieve their own ends. Those ends were not selfish ones. They were what each considered to be in the best interests of the Society and of Africa. For a long time their interests had followed the same track. But when the divergence came, Livingstone held the winning hand.

It was unfortunate that Livingstone's judgements were based on the assumption that nothing was impossible. He refused to accept that, without more help than he was prepared to offer, the mission might be doomed to failure. He was no more guilty of duplicity and ruthlessness in his dealings with Tidman than was Tidman with Livingstone. He was guilty of a gross error of judgement in a field where he was to make the same type of mistake time and time again. He knew that when he looked at a sheet of water he found it difficult to assess distances with any degree of accuracy. He never understood that when he aimed to assess the capabilities of other men, he overestimated them to an alarming degree. This was his greatest weakness, and never did it have more tragic consequences than on this occasion.

Livingstone's declared objectives for his government-sponsored expedition were to open up the Zambesi for trade, build up commerce with the Portuguese so as to drive out the slave trade and start growing cotton. He hoped that the Prince Consort would initiate negotiations with Portugal, for the king was his cousin, but Albert declined to do so. Relations between Portugal and Britain were not good at this time and Portugal refused to include Sena or Tete in his consulship. Livingstone was appointed Consul in the District of Quilimane on the Eastern coast of Africa with a salary of £500 and given official letters in the Queen's name for presentation to tribal chiefs. There was no official uniform, but for some years he had worn, in England as well as Africa, a navy blue peaked cap. He now added a gold band to this. He was authorized to appoint his own expedition members.

The three oldest children were to remain in Scotland with their grandmother and only Zouga was to accompany his parents. After a sad farewell, they embarked on the steamer *Pearl* at Birkenhead on 6 March 1858.

9
The Zambesi and Shire Rivers: Flawed Leader of Europeans

Livingstone had proved that he could succeed against apparently impossible odds, winning through by determination, hard work and persistence, with virtually no help from anyone. Conversely, at the start of his Zambesi expedition, he seemed to have everything he could ask for. He was being paid by the government to do what he most wanted to do, virtually on his own terms. He could choose his own team, his budget was larger than he required at this stage and his terms of reference were elastic. Yet the expedition ended in complete disaster. His good qualities remained intact. But he lacked judgement and the ability to lead a team.

His lack of judgement became apparent as soon as he started to pick his team. In part, this was inevitable. He knew nobody well and had no experience of working closely with others. Conscious of the first of these difficulties, he decided to select at least one person on whom he could rely. This led to his first and greatest mistake. He asked his brother Charles to join the expedition as general assistant and 'moral agent'. Charles was also supposed, erroneously, to have some skill as a photographer ('So far,' remarked his colleague Kirk, himself an excellent photographer, 'he has only made a mess of it'[1]) and knowledge of the cotton industry, this being based purely on the fact that he had spent most of his adult life in America. Livingstone mistakenly perceived the little brother of whom he had been so fond in their boyhood in Scotland as a younger version of himself. Two years passed before his eyes were opened, two years during which Livingstone's blind faith in all that his brother said and did caused incalculable harm to the expedition.

The most unbiased account of the different characters involved and all that happened is generally accepted to be that given by John Kirk, Livingstone's one truly inspired choice of team member, in his diary. Kirk was unimpressed by the younger brother from the start. 'He has never had anyone under him and is awkward and ungracious in his dealings,' indicates that Charles shared David's faults. He did not share his good qualities. David could never have been accused of 'lounging indoors and never exposing himself without an umbrella and felt hat', nor of becoming 'so tired with the walk as to be fit for little more than sleep'. While the older brother was devout but very private in his devotions, the younger's approach to religion was so narrow-minded as to verge on bigotry. David could be critical of those who failed to meet his own high standards: Charles set no standard of his own but rarely had a good word for anyone with whom he came into contact.

If Charles was ultimately the most disastrous choice of all, the second worst selection and the first of the group to cause trouble was the only other one whom Livingstone knew personally beforehand. He selected as his second-in-command Commander Norman Bedingfeld, the naval officer whom he had liked and admired most of all those whom he had met in Loanda. He admitted later that Captain Washington of the Admiralty, who tried to help him with selecting his team and equipping the expedition, had warned him against Bedingfeld, who had twice been reprimanded for insubordination, once being dismissed from his ship, for 'contempt and quarrelsome conduct towards his superior officer'.[2] Bedingfeld, whose pay far exceeded that of any of his colleagues since he continued to receive half his naval salary in addition to his expedition money, was used to commanding several hundred men. An arrogant man, and officially second-in-command to Livingstone, he may have been sufficiently misguided to consider the other a mere figurehead and himself leader in all but name. Certainly he never doubted that in any matters connected with navigation his word would be law. In Kirk's words, 'he comes out as perhaps the great man and forgets that he is but the equal of others when the Doctor is present.'

It soon became apparent that even in matters of navigation, Bedingfeld's knowledge was inferior to that of the dour Scots navigator George Rae. Born at Blantyre, his morose nature did nothing to lessen his leader's appreciation of his competence. He, in company with Kirk and Charles, completed his two-year contract, unlike the other three members of the expedition.

Richard Thornton at 20 was the youngest of the group. He came

I The room at Blantyre where Livingstone lived with all his family.

2 Shuttle Row, Blantyre, *c.* 1870.

3 Robert Moffat, Livingstone's father-in-law.

4 Mary, Livingstone's wife.

5 William Cotton Oswell, who discovered Lake Ngami and met Sebitoane with Livingstone.

6 David Livingstone. This picture was taken in Cape Town in 1852.

7 Livingstone and his family, 1857.

8 Bishop MacKenzie, leader of the Universities Mission, who tragically died in 1862.

9 Livingstone and his daughter Anna Mary, 1864.

10 Henry Morton Stanley and his African protégé Kalulu.

11 Susi, Horace Waller, Chuma, Agnes Livingstone, Mrs Webb, William F. Webb and Tom Livingstone at Newstead Abbey, 1874.

1 The room at Blantyre where Livingstone lived with all his family.

2 Shuttle Row, Blantyre, *c.* 1870.

3 Robert Moffat, Livingstone's father-in-law.

4 Mary, Livingstone's wife.

5 William Cotton Oswell, who discovered Lake Ngami and met Sebitoane with Livingstone.

6 David Livingstone. This picture was taken in Cape Town in 1852.

7 Livingstone and his family, 1857.

8 Bishop MacKenzie, leader of the Universities Mission, who tragically died in 1862.

9 Livingstone and his daughter Anna Mary, 1864.

10 Henry Morton Stanley and his African protégé Kalulu.

11 Susi, Horace Waller, Chuma, Agnes Livingstone, Mrs Webb, William F. Webb and Tom Livingstone at Newstead Abbey, 1874.

as a practical mining geologist from the Government School of Mines, on the recommendation of Sir Roderick Murchison. He failed, however, to find favour with his leader, who was soon writing to warn Murchison that he suspected Murchison's protégé was an idle young man. The Doctor was not alone in this opinion: Kirk recorded that Baines, the final member of the expedition, had commented: 'Young Livingstone and Thornton are not of much use... when it comes to a day's work.'

Thomas Baines himself was perhaps the most enigmatic of the group. He was enlisted as artist and storekeeper, an interesting combination. He was recommended by the Royal Geographic Society. Initially Kirk too was impressed. Before they reached Africa he wrote 'Mr. Baines is a trump and does more than anyone else. If anything is required from any case in the hold he is down working and sweating.' In the battle between him and Livingstone many factors besides the personalities of the two men were to come into play, with Baines increasingly affected by ill health and Livingstone being influenced more and more by his mischief-making brother. Reports on Baines in his later life were also contradictory.

The last and best member of the expedition was John Kirk himself. A qualified doctor aged 25 when he joined, he was listed as an economic botanist. The combination of the medical and botanical roles was one of the attractions to him: he showed considerable talent in both fields though botany was his first love. He was also an excellent amateur photographer, at that time a hobby which demanded considerable scientific expertise, and was capable of expressing himself clearly and effectively in debate. He was one of 50 applicants accepted from some 700 volunteers for service in the hospitals of the Crimea, where they had more free time than anticipated, enabling Kirk to learn the Turkish language as well as develop an understanding of the Moslem faith and customs, which were all to stand him in good stead in later years. He became a good shot though a bad horseman and proved himself, in the many adventures in which he was involved, enterprising, courageous and diplomatic. The decision to join Livingstone meant that in the course of his long life he would make full use of all these qualities. In his future career in the diplomatic service, when he served 21 years on the island of Zanzibar, Sir John Kirk played a decisive role in the final destruction of the slave trade.

On the voyage out to Africa in the *Pearl*, the steamship which had been sent out by the government to take the expedition to the mouth of the Zambesi and as much further as should prove practicable, Livingstone presented every man with a letter of instructions drafted by himself. These stated that the objects were to increase knowledge of the natural resources and encourage the natives to develop these so as to trade them with England. It was hoped that this could be made more profitable for the Africans than the slave trade. Each member had specific instructions for his department: Kirk, for example, was to investigate the tsetse fly and ivory, among other things. A number of detailed admonitions were included concerning behaviour and the principles to be followed in relations with the Africans. They were expected to learn Sechuana as spoken by the Makololo. The contract was for two years, although Livingstone had extensive powers to dismiss them earlier.

These formalities could not be completed until the initial attack of seasickness had been overcome. One member of the party did not recover as fast as the others. Livingstone realized with a shock that Mary was once again pregnant. (She had suffered a miscarriage during their time in England together.) She was probably more upset than her husband by the inevitable decision that she and six-year-old Oswell should not accompany the expedition but travel instead to Kuruman. When the *Pearl* docked in Cape Town, they found that Mary's parents were already there, having heard that she was on board the *Pearl*. They were also waiting to greet the ill-fated missionary party despatched at Livingstone's instigation and bound for the country of the Makololo.

Livingstone's reception in Cape Town was very different from that on his previous visit there. He was feted by the Governor, wined and dined by every branch of the establishment in the city and presented with a silver casket containing 800 guineas which had been collected for him.

His father-in-law was less enthusiastic. Moffat found the news of Livingstone's split with the LMS 'perfectly confounding and very painful'[3] and was equally shocked to learn that his own son John had also severed his connection, which he had been enabled to do by the generous annual sum paid to him by Livingstone. He was deeply concerned too by anxieties over the missionaries destined for the Makololo mission, pondering with prescient gloom on their probable fate if they reached the Makololo before Livingstone had arrived to persuade that tribe that they could move to safer country away from the risk of malaria without fear of attack by their old enemy Mosilikatse and his Matabele.

115

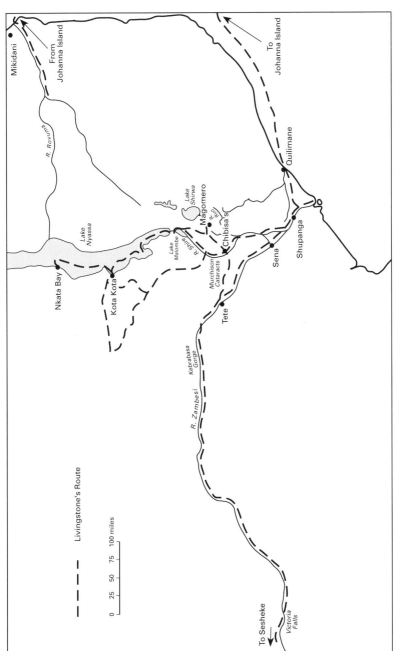

The Zambesi expedition, 1858–63

Mikidani

From Johanna Island

R. Rovuma

To Johanna Island

Quilimane

Lake Shirwa

Magomero

Rio S.

Chibisa's

Lake Nyassa

Lake Malombe

R. Shire

Murchison Cataracts

Shupanga

Sena

Nkata Bay

Kota Kota

Tete

Kebrabasa Gorge

R. Zambesi

Livingstone's Route

0   25   50   75   100 miles

To Sesheke

Victoria Falls

After ten days in Cape Town, Livingstone bade his wife and son and her parents farewell. He did not see Mary again for four years or Zouga for six, and he never met either of his parents-in-law again. Yet the heartfelt tribute paid him by old Robert Moffat after his death was deeply moving in its sincerity. Moffat appreciated his faith, his courage, his self-sacrifice and, more controversially, his humility, recalling it particularly on this visit to Cape Town. He spoke of him as one whose 'ruling passion was to live for suffering humanity' and 'whose loving spirit could not but endear him to all'.[4]

The *Pearl* reached the mouth of the Zambesi on 14 May 1858. The original plan had been to travel in her as far as Tete but the river proved too shallow. They were forced to assemble the steamboat specially made in England for use on the Zambesi. She was called the *Ma-Robert* after Mary's African name (mother of Robert) and had been built under the supervision of Commander Bedingfeld. She was to prove a major factor in the failure of the expedition. Soon nicknamed *The Asthmatic*, her engine, Livingstone wrote, was 'evidently made to grind coffee in a shop window'.[5] The wood she consumed in one day in action required one and a half days to chop, partly because of the quantity consumed and partly because only very hard woods were suitable. The steel plates wore away at an alarming rate, becoming paper-thin and rusting into holes. Her performance was so disappointing that Livingstone was convinced that Bedingfeld had been tricked when he watched the trials, and cursed himself for accepting 'the opinion of a naval donkey'.[6]

Although the *Ma-Robert's* problems continued to dog them throughout her life, irritation over the part played by Bedingfeld fuelled the fires of discontent which soon flared up against him. 'There is an evil spirit between the Captain and the Doctor, and I rather think the Captain does not try to make matters go smoothly,' wrote Kirk. 'In fact also I rather think Bed. is tired of the service; he seems to have expected to live the life of a man-of-war commander and has no idea of being a subordinate.'

The trouble started between Bedingfeld and Captain Duncan of the *Pearl*, a man whom Bedingfeld saw as his professional and social inferior, but who won the support of the rest of the expedition, including its leader. Livingstone handled the matter with a conspicuous lack of tact, culminating in a letter telling Bedingfeld that suitable medicine for his bowels might improve his outlook. After considerable altercation over the manner of his dismissal, Bedingfeld eventually left for England.

It took six months from the arrival of the *Pearl* at the mouth of the Zambesi for the *Ma-Robert* to ferry everything from their provisional base on an island there to Tete. Livingstone was not a natural skipper but took on this role after Bedingfeld's departure, even though, as he himself admitted, he frequently confused port and starboard. In November too Mary gave birth to a daughter, Anna Mary, though it was a full year before the news reached Livingstone, by which time mother and daughter were back in England.

Before this, in August, Livingstone found his old Portuguese friend Major Sicard who allowed them to use part of his house at Shupanga. It was here that he first met two young Africans, Amoda and Susi. Both were with him when he died 15 years later, and it was Susi who led the expedition which culminated in Livingstone's burial in Westminster Abbey. Here too at Shupanga Livingstone was to know the greatest grief he ever suffered, for it was here that Mary died and is buried.

More moving at the time than these shades of the future was Livingstone's return to Tete, where even the unemotional Scotsman was reduced to tears by the rapturous way he was greeted by his Makololo. They were overjoyed to see their 'father', having been taunted by the locals that he would never return. He told them sadly of the death of Sekwebu and they told him how thirty of their number had died of fever and six been murdered by a local chief. There were problems at Shupanga too, for the Portuguese were engaged in fighting with tribesmen. In some of the bloodthirsty battles expedition members played a walk-on part, doctoring the wounded or witnessing scenes of horrendous massacres.

The next challenge was to investigate the loop of the Zambesi which he had omitted on his original journey alone. He knew that within this loop lay the Kebrabasa Rapids. He had made light of this hazard during his time in England, but if it was not possible either to navigate the river through the rapids or, at worst, to carry vessels round a short impassable stretch of the river with reasonable ease, then the whole concept of God's Highway to the heart of Africa and the imagined paradise of the Batoka Plateau was destroyed.

Livingstone's airy confidence was fast vanishing as rumours of the true nature of the rapids reached him. He began to talk of using gunpowder to blast a way through. Kirk was appalled. It was decided that Baines and Thornton, who were both suffering badly from malaria, should remain at Tete with Charles while the other three and one of a pair of Englishmen, temporarily seconded when their ship had docked at Quilimane, should survey the rapids accompanied by some volunteer Makololo. As they entered the gorge the river narrowed and the *Ma-Robert* was in danger of being smashed on the rocks. They tied up the boat and started to walk across the smooth rocks in heat so intense that Kirk thought his load of just one revolver and a compass excessive. As the cliffs on either side soared higher the gorge became increasingly narrow, the water restricted to a fierce current. What they saw was not encouraging: by the time they returned to Tete Kirk at least was convinced that it was impossible to get the launch up. This time the whole group returned and struggled on for four days, the Makololo, their feet burnt by the rocks, declaring Livingstone mad. 'The Doctor changed his appearance completely from the first time he saw the rocks . . . and in the shaking of his head we could see that things were not working well,' Kirk reported.

Livingstone then proposed that he should continue alone. Kirk, offended, offered to join him and the two men climbed over rocks almost too hot to touch, the banks soaring 2600 feet above the narrow, gushing river, where they saw a fearsome waterfall 30 feet high. On their return to base, incredibly, Livingstone wrote to England reporting that the river would be navigable without difficulty at high water. 'The Doctor gives a very favourable account of the rapids, much more so than I could do,' commented Kirk.

Livingstone knew really. He had already written in his diary 'Things look dark for our enterprise. This Kebrabasa is what I never expected. No hint of its nature ever reached my ears.'[7] Two weeks after their return to Tete, leaving the other three there, Livingstone, Kirk and Rae left the Zambesi and set off north up the Shire River. It was a remarkable change of plan, abandoning the Batoka Plateau, the Makololo and his design of using the Zambesi as God's Highway to the heart of Africa.

During 1859 Livingstone turned his attention to this new country. There were many problems: the tribesmen were exceptionally hostile, firing poisoned arrows as they passed, and the villagers fled screaming in terror: it soon became apparent that the slave trade was affecting the whole country on a massive scale. Only one of the chiefs, a jovial man fond of laughing named Chibisa, was friendly. Much of the country was unhealthy and, apart from the physical problems, Kirk at least was very conscious of the bad effect malaria had on sufferers' tempers. 'If the Doctor keeps good health one can manage [the Manganja tribe] . . . but, if his digestive system don't go alright, he loses his diplomatic power wonderfully.'

The Shire too was interrupted by cataracts, which Livingstone named after Murchison. However these were a less insuperable barrier: it might be possible, if difficult, for porters to carry everything around them, including a boat which could be dismantled. For regular use, however, a gang of sappers would be needed to build a road. Kirk and Livingstone continued on foot. Kirk believed them to be the first white men to reach Lake Shirwa, and later the enormous expanse of Lake Nyassa too, though Livingstone should have realized that the trader Candido Cardosa, whom he had met, had almost certainly reached both places before.

There were political problems also. It soon became clear that the most vicious of the local people, the Ajawa, were running a large-scale slave-trading operation, passing on the slaves to the Arabs. There was some Portuguese involvement too, particular after Livingstone's expedition itself opened up the route from Quilimane to Lake Nyassa. While Livingstone got on well with a number of Portuguese personally, he developed an ever greater loathing for the race as a whole and its government, which he was not at great pains to conceal. The sentiment was reciprocated: his motives were mistrusted, in one respect with more justice than possibly even his associates in the British government realized.

Long before he left England, he told a few close friends of his secret dream: colonization. At the time, amazing as it may seem in the light of late Victorian imperialism, this was a dirty word. Livingstone's own ideas fluctuated, but his ideal was to allow each country to benefit from what the other had to offer. Africa had space, raw materials, untouched country. Britain could offer technical and commercial expertise, democratic institutions, education, leadership and, above all, Christianity. He longed to give each the best of both worlds, and, with his curious ability for turning a blind eye to aspects he did not wish to see, conveniently ignored the inevitable conclusion that the worst of each culture would be quite as certain to surface.

The British government resisted these suggestions as they filtered through on pragmatic grounds. 'I am very unwilling to embark on new schemes of British possessions,' Palmerston wrote. 'Dr. L. . . . must not be allowed to tempt us to form colonies only to be reached by forcing steamers [up] cataracts.'[8] The Portuguese, deeply suspicious, could not believe in such philanthropy and saw only a British plot to take their rightful possessions. Livingstone sometimes forgot that as they controlled the mouth of the Zambesi and its junction with the Shire they held all the cards.

These journeys of exploration were interspersed with returns south, and on one visit to Tete Livingstone became convinced that neither Baines nor Thornton should remain with the expedition any longer. Both men had been seriously ill, and therefore, as Kirk pointed out, irritable, and probably less capable of doing their work satisfactorily, but the real trouble-maker was Charles, who no sooner rejoined his brother than he succeeded in poisoning his mind against them. Thornton was portrayed as incurably idle, but Baines was considered to be dishonest in his handling of the stores for which he was responsible. The unfortunate Kirk was made to return to Tete down the Shire, only just surviving a serious attack of fever on the way. He had to investigate the charges and dismiss both men. He found no conclusive proof of dishonesty; probably there had been some genuine confusion attributable in part to the inefficiency of the system and in part to Baines' confused state of mind, though it is interesting that a later employer commented on the excessive amount of food consumed by Baines: perhaps he ate the stores rather than selling or giving them, as alleged, to the Portuguese.

Both men were forced to leave the expedition under a cloud, feeling, with reason, that they had been badly treated. Baines was not even allowed to eat with the rest of the party before his departure, and neither he nor Bedingfeld are mentioned by name in Livingstone's book, written in collaboration with Charles, *Narrative of an Expedition to the Zambesi and its Tributaries*.

At the end of January 1860 the two-year contracts expired. Rae was keen to return to England where Livingstone asked him to supervise the building of a steamer to patrol Lake Nyassa in the hope that it would be possible thus to control the slave trade. Livingstone was willing, if the government was not prepared to pay for this, to spend his own money on the project. Kirk and Charles agreed, without enthusiasm, to stay with him and devote the next six months to taking the Makololo back home. The Makololo themselves were reluctant. Many had settled where they were and preferred life under the Portuguese to returning to Sekeletu. Some made this clear immediately, others waited till they had started then slipped away.

Despite the unpromising start, Livingstone was closer to recapturing his old delight in travelling through Africa on this journey than at any other time on the Zambesi expedition. Kirk was seriously ill at one point, but he was impressed with the Batoka Plateau and had the delight of seeing the Victoria Falls. Here they unexpectedly rescued an Englishman who, inspired by Livingstone's account, had found his own way there but been arrested by the local chief for bathing in the river and risking being eaten by crocodiles. The chief feared the English might hold him responsible. The arrival of Livingstone himself amazed and delighted everyone. The only jarring note was struck by Charles, who became increasingly difficult throughout the journey until even his adoring brother lost patience.

When they reached Sesheke they found Sekeletu ill with a form of leprosy. The two doctors, after diplomatic discussions with the tribal doctor, were able to give him some relief, but he had not many years to live. Worse news than this awaited them, however. Livingstone at last heard the consequences of his insistence that the LMS should use the money raised through his name to send a mission to the Makololo even though he himself was not prepared to lead it.

The missionaries had reached Cape Town just after Livingstone left: Moffat had been there to meet them. The group sent out had not impressed Maclear. 'I must say, the strangest lot I ever met with . . . Mr. Moffat said nothing about them, but Mrs. Livingstone was astounded at the *tout ensemble* of the party, and to me expressed a hope that they might not be so located as to hamper you,' he wrote to Livingstone.[9]

The group was led by Holloway Helmore accompanied by his wife and four of their children. The other missionary was Roger Price, with his wife and a baby born in Africa. None had medical training. All, and Moffat as well, were apparently convinced that Livingstone would meet them there although he had made it quite clear to Tidman that he had no intention of doing so unless he happened by chance to be close by. For Sekeletu, as Livingstone, Moffat and Tidman well knew, the sole attraction of a mission was for it to include one of the Moffat family as a guarantee against attack by Mosilikatse, particularly if he was to be asked to move his tribe to the healthier ground closer to the Matabele. As a result, he was bitter and angry when they arrived, and was not prepared to move.

The group, in their haste as they thought to arrive at the same time as Livingstone, travelled at the worst time of year for fever.

Consequently, all became ill: Price's suspicions of poisoning were unfounded. Relations between Europeans and Africans deteriorated fast. Sekeletu claimed that he had established a good relationship with Helmore but that Price had behaved badly, kicking one of the Makololo, tying another to his wagon wheel and threatening to shoot people. Price not only denied this but claimed that Sekeletu had stolen most of their possessions including Helmore's wagon, refused to allow them to leave when they became ill and given them no help at all. Eventually all except Price himself and two of the Helmore children died an extremely unpleasant death, albeit of natural causes. Even after she was buried Mrs Price could not rest in peace. Her body was dug up and decapitated so that her head could be used for magic purposes.

Livingstone has been accused, at the time and since, of moral responsibility for the whole tragedy. Once he decided not to take part in the mission himself he had no right to insist that it should be sent. He failed to brief anyone concerned adequately beforehand on the many aspects of the situation which he alone was in a position to understand. The LMS elected to send out a group with no medical skills (Kirk too criticized the LMS bitterly for this decision) but Livingstone made no attempt to pass on to them the knowledge he had acquired relating to the treatment of malaria. He claimed that his treatment was not scientifically proven and it would have been unethical to publish it, but made no attempt to pass this information on to the group in an informal way. No one had asked for his help or advice, he said. While they were all aware of the importance of involving the Moffat family, the missionaries, fresh from England, had no guidance on the right way to establish good relations with tribal chiefs.

All this is true, and by insisting that the expedition should be sent Livingstone did incur some responsibility. On the other hand all his knowledge and experience were acquired by his own initiative. He also went out originally untrained in all these respects with far less information than even the Helmore group possessed. None of this excuses his deplorable behaviour after the tragedy. He accepted everything that the Makololo told him and refused to believe the account given by Price, but then Sekeletu had always been a good friend to Livingstone, whose own wagon and supplies were still safe and untouched where he had left them in Sekeletu's care at Linyanti, whereas he had no personal knowledge of Price or Helmore. He showed a total lack of sympathy and understanding, perhaps in reaction to his own feelings of guilt, and belittled the scale of the tragedy which had occurred.

Roger Price went on to become a successful missionary earning the nickname of 'the great Lion of Bechuanaland'. He married Mary Livingstone's sister and, even more remarkably, walked behind Livingstone's coffin up the aisle in Westminster Abbey.

10
The Shire and Rovuma Rivers: the Husband

They left Linyanti in September 1860 and Livingstone never saw Sekeletu or the rest of the Makololo again. After Sekeletu's death three years later the tribe, already drastically reduced in numbers and ravaged by disease, was totally destroyed by its enemies.

Livingstone had lost too the only close confidant other than Mary he ever had. Charles remained with his brother for a further three years but the expedition of 1860 had finally opened David's eyes and from then on they merely tolerated each other's presence. Before they even left Tete, Charles criticized his brother's leadership style so cuttingly that the older man realized he had been bottling up endless grievances. This spurred him to look at Charles with a more critical eye and finally acknowledge that his brother had made no worthwhile contribution to the expedition whatever. He belatedly realized too how credulously he had accepted his brother's criticisms of others. Violent arguments broke out between them with increasing frequency, with such language that Kirk was appalled. Just after they left Sekeletu on the way home, Charles, with remarkable stupidity as well as brutality, lost his temper with the Makololo headman lent them by the chief and kicked him viciously. Kirk was amazed at the restraint shown by the Makololo. 'Nothing but [their] high personal regard for Dr. L. avoided bloodshed in that case. The spear was poised and needed only a stroke of the arm to send it to the heart . . . For Dr. L.'s sake he held back.' 'The Commander should keep him by himself, for he is utterly unsafe,' was Kirk's conclusion.

The worst threat to Kirk's life, however, was occasioned by the Doctor and not by Charles. When they reached Kebrabasa, Livingstone decided that they should attempt to shoot the first set of rapids.

To the end of his long life 62 years later, Kirk recalled this as the most terrifying moment he ever lived through: 'There have not been many escapes more miraculous.' Although all three men survived, Kirk lost all his possessions, revolver, surgical and dental equipment, clothes, bedding and, worst of all, eight precious irreplaceable volumes of botanical notes, the fruit of all his work on the expedition.

They were cheered on their return to Tete by letters from home. A new steamship, the *Pioneer*, was on its way out to replace the *Ma-Robert*, though the second ship Livingstone wanted for Lake Nyassa would have to be paid for out of his own pocket. His exploration of the country towards Lake Nyassa was appreciated, but his colonial plans were rejected. Most important of all, he learnt that the Universities Mission, set up as a result of his Cambridge speech, would be sending out its first members early in 1861. He had hoped that the new missionaries would have the support of his planned colony. Since the colony was not to be, even Livingstone was somewhat concerned for their welfare in the Shire Highlands.

The mission leader was a bishop, Charles Mackenzie, an intelligent, energetic, friendly, enthusiastic and practical man who had already spent five years working in Natal. The two doctors and the bishop took to one another immediately, although the younger Livingstone resented his High Church Anglicanism. There were five more Englishmen, three of them clergymen or prospective clergymen, with two others, a clergyman and a doctor, expected shortly. Horace Waller, who had yet to be ordained, was to become one of Livingstone's closest friends, a member of that select group of eight who were the pall bearers at his funeral. It was Waller too who was responsible for the editing and publication of his last diaries.

Mackenzie had been hoping to make a start on the new mission straight away, but Livingstone had other plans. The Portuguese were threatening to block access to the Shire river and he was keen to take the *Pioneer*, his new steamship which had arrived with the missionaries, 600 miles north along the coast to explore the Rovuma river as an alternative way of reaching the Lake Nyassa area. So most of the missionaries were taken to Johanna, an island opposite the mouth of the Rovuma, Mackenzie reluctantly agreed to join Livingstone in the *Pioneer* on the Rovuma, in return for a promise that this diversion would last no more than three months. Perhaps this time limit was fortunate: the river proved disappointingly shallow and the *Pioneer's* draught, which was deep enough to enable her to withstand the journey out to Africa, meant that had they persisted for more than five days from the river mouth they might have run aground and been unable to return.

The journey up the Shire was dogged by similar problems, with the steamer spending as much time aground as afloat. But the Bishop retained his cheerful good humour, writing light-heartedly of their 'picturesque appearance', the Livingstone brothers in blue serge, David with his distinctive cap, he himself wearing a 'broad-brimmed wide-awake with white cover, which Livingstone laughs at, but which, all the same, keeps the sun off'.[1] He made light, too, of his first attack of fever, declaring Livingstone's cure to be worse than the disease.

Then word reached them of slave raiding, near Lake Shirwa, further upstream from Quilimane than ever before (slavers round Lake Nyassa were selling to the Arabs in the north, not the Portuguese to the south) proving, in Kirk's words, that 'we had been the means of opening a slave hunting country.' The knowledge hardened Livingstone's attitude. The Bishop was away from his friends, washing, one morning when six armed men marched into the village blowing horns with a train of 84 slaves, many of them secured by long, forked, heavy poles fastened round their necks. They told piteous tales: 'one woman, . . . unable to carry both her load and young child, had the child taken from her and saw its brains dashed out on a stone,' while others had been shot, Kirk recorded. The Englishmen, encouraged by the villagers, set about releasing them, sawing through the heavy sticks and cutting the ropes. It was the first time that Livingstone had taken positive action of this sort, even though the slavers, one of whom they recognized as himself a former slave of Major Sicard's, had fled without firing a shot. Among those freed were two boys, Chuma and Wikatani, the first of whom was with Livingstone 12 years later when he died, partnering Susi in the leadership of the expedition to take his body back to England. The whole group chose to stay and form the basis of the new mission centre. A site was chosen with the help of a Manganja chief at Magomero.

After rescuing other, smaller groups, inevitably the Englishmen found that they themselves were in danger from the Ajawa, the most aggressive raiders. While Kirk was pursuing another group, Livingstone went out unarmed to talk to them. Soon poisoned arrows were flying at him, one landing between him and the Bishop as they stood together. They returned the fire with their guns, the

Bishop handing his to Livingstone, who was unarmed, then they set fire to the Ajawa town.

It was the first time that Livingstone had ever attacked Africans, although three years previously he had replied to a letter from a pacifist, 'I love peace as much as any mortal man. In fact I go quite beyond you for I would fight for it.'[2] He had enlarged on this theme, indicating that, while he hoped never to have to do so, there would be circumstances in which he would be prepared to kill. On the other hand, up to this moment he had always avoided taking sides or intervening physically in tribal warfare. The Manganja could behave quite as cruelly as the Ajawa, and the latter had no monopoly of the slave trade in the area. The inevitable consequence was to alienate permanently those attacked without creating any lasting peace with those supported by the Englishmen. Hitherto the fact that he travelled alone save for his Africans meant that this dilemma had not confronted him. Now the English group was of sufficient size and possessed of sufficient firepower to be a force to be reckoned with in local politics.

It was a perplexing situation for both men. Before Livingstone left Magomero three days later, he attempted to impress on the Bishop the inadvisability of becoming entangled in such affairs, except in self-defence. But the episodes which had already occurred created an impossible situation for the Bishop. He could hardly preach against the slave trade yet refuse practical aid as cases arose. He had not the strength, whatever his convictions, to police the whole area impartially. Thus haphazard intervention was bound to appear one-sided. He became increasingly enmeshed in a moral maze in which he would befriend groups of Africans provided they took oaths concerning their future behaviour. Livingstone would have avoided such semantics. Some weeks later, as the Bishop learned more of Ajawa atrocities, 'his blood rose and theories vanished', as Kirk later wrote. Crozier in one hand and loaded gun in the other, he waged war on the slavers aggressively, not just in self-defence. Livingstone, when he first heard, shared the disquiet felt in England and was anxious to disown the Bishop. Later, he came to sympathize with his action.

Livingstone and Kirk meanwhile were exploring Lake Nyassa. They had a large party of Africans with them who had been needed to help carry everything past the Murchison Cataracts and could not now be left alone in alien territory, so in addition to the sailing boat a large group had to walk along the edge of the lake and the sailing boat slow to walking speed. It was not a happy voyage. The natives were unattractive, curious and intrusive, constantly staring at them, occasionally stealing or wantonly destroying their possessions. Horrifying evidence of the slave trade was all around them. The Irish fisherman with them, used to rough conditions at sea, had never seen such waves before and frequently insisted on staying on land for days at a time for the storm to calm. Livingstone no doubt learned much seamanship from this man, which was to stand him in good stead when next he left Africa. They were ravaged too by further attacks of fever, which, as always, deepened their gloom.

Sometimes the walking party, led by Livingstone where the Africans were endangered by slavers, was out of touch with the boat for days at a time, each group battling with myriad problems. A fierce group of armed savages confronted Livingstone, ordering him to sit in the sun while they sat in the shade. He refused, ignored their terrifying rattle of weapons and spoke quietly but fearlessly till eventually they slunk away. As another chief remarked in similar circumstances, 'How could I give the signal to kill a man who smiled?'[3] When finally reunited, Livingstone, Kirk recorded, greeted them laconically with, 'What on earth made you run away and leave us?'

The mountains closed in ever closer on either side of the lake, convincing them that they were close to the northern extremity. They were running short of food, having used most of the cloth they brought to barter with, nor, as the country became increasingly barren, was there anyone with whom to barter. They turned for home, having surveyed the west side of the Lake with great accuracy and precision to that point but unaware that it extended for many miles further. Kirk remarkably also observed a resemblance between the flora and fauna of Lake Nyassa and those of the Sea of Galilee, thousands of miles away. Both are now known to form part of the Great Rift Valley.

On returning to the *Pioneer* at Chibisa's, they had a brief meeting with the Bishop and a new member of the mission named Henry Burrup, who had just arrived from England. They liked him and learned that another ship was on its way to Quilimane bringing his own young wife, the Bishop's sister and Mary. Delighted though Livingstone was at the prospect of seeing Mary, he was beginning to realize that the site of the mission at Magomero was not a healthy one, and he began to doubt his own wisdom in sanctioning the arrival of the women. The Bishop's news was even more worrying: Livingstone and Kirk were deeply concerned by the aggressive stance he had been adopting, although they understood only too clearly how the situation had developed.

When they parted for Mackenzie and Burrup to go briefly to Magomero, it was agreed that the two missionaries would come down to the point where the River Ruo flowed into the Shire on 1 January to meet the women and escort them up to Magomero. Livingstone meanwhile was to go to the mouth of the Zambesi to collect the women in the *Pioneer* and bring them back to the agreed meeting place, the furthest point which the *Pioneer* could reach by that time of year.

Unfortunately both parties met with serious delays. The natives around Magomero were so aggressive that Mackenzie and Burrup did not reach the meeting point until 11 January. Shattered by the fighting in which they had been involved and desperate not to miss the meeting, they suffered appalling conditions on the journey, when the canoe capsized and they were repeatedly soaked to the skin and lost all their medicines. Soon both men were desperately ill. They arrived to find that Livingstone had indeed been there a few days earlier, not with the women but still on his way downstream to the coast to meet them. He also had had problems: they had had to drag the *Pioneer* all the way down over sandbanks. As he missed his rendezvous with the ship on which the women were travelling, the *Hetty Ellen* escorted by HMS *Gorgon*, they were forced to put to sea once more and it was not until 31 January that they reappeared. Joyful signals were exchanged: 'Wife aboard.' 'Accept my best thanks.'

The celebrations were premature. On that very same day, on an island where the rivers joined, Bishop Mackenzie died. Burrup struggled to bury him then somehow dragged himself back to Magomero. Three weeks later he too was dead.

Livingstone meanwhile, reunited with Mary, and unaware of the tragedy, was intent on assembling the steamer which he had paid for himself, the *Lady Nyassa*, which had arrived, contrary to his instructions, in pieces. Captain Wilson of the *Gorgon* therefore offered to take Miss Mackenzie and Mrs Burrup on ahead to the planned meeting with their menfolk. Kirk and Dr Ramsay from the *Gorgon* joined them. Miss Mackenzie was an elderly, querulous, infirm spinster. Mrs Burrup on the other hand was a bright, active, positive young woman who had been married for less than a year. Both women showed equal courage in their reception of the tragic news which awaited them. They remained with Dr Ramsay while Kirk and Wilson paid a brief visit to Magomero during which Wilson was desperately ill. The two men then returned to escort the grieving women on the first stage of their journey back to England.

When Livingstone eventually learnt what had happened, his grief and shock were weakened by a selfish reaction in which he blamed the men for their own fate, just as he had done with the Makololo mission. This time, however, he was more directly involved in the decisions taken and the two men who had died had become personal friends. He was keen to repudiate personal responsibility as well as being concerned over the effect the tragedy would have on missionary work in the area. He wrote to James Young immediately: 'It may be well to publish a connected account of the Ajawa affair and that I disapprove entirely of the bishop taking the offensive as it is possible his party may put all the blame on me.'[4] His own determination, inevitably, was unaffected: 'I shall not swerve a hairbreadth from my work while life is spared,' he wrote in his journal. The manner in which the Bishop had taken sides with the Manganja against the Ajawa raised many complex issues, both practical and moral. The Doctor's initial tendency to distance himself from the course pursued by Mackenzie was eventually reversed when he learnt that Dr Pusey had criticized the missionaries for failing to die as martyrs. So farcical did this argument appear to Livingstone that from that moment his conversion to the Bishop's point of view was absolute.

For Mary, unaware for some weeks of the tragedy, this was the first time that she had been working with her husband in Africa since their last journey with Oswell ten years before. The intervening decade had not been kind to Mary. Never renowned for her looks, she had become grossly overweight, coarse and vulgar. The qualities which had made her 'the best spoke in the wheel' in a family as impressive as the Moffats had been eroded by despondency, loneliness and alcohol.

Perhaps in the circumstances James Stewart, the handsome young missionary who had travelled out with her, had more cause for complaint than she had when rumour mongers started to link their names. The scandal predictably originated with an old maid and a man who judged others by his own behaviour. Miss Mackenzie, of whom Stewart wrote 'age has chilled her sympathies and what are not already frozen are tied up in denominational bands',[5] was a prim old spinster, prying and disapproving by nature. George Rae, dour Scotsman that he was, had himself been suspected by Kirk of attempting to seduce one of the Portuguese wives. Livingstone, rightly, did not believe a word. More upsetting than the rumours themselves was the basis of fact which had sparked them. Stewart had indeed frequently visited Mary's cabin late at night, in an attempt to help her maid contend with the problems caused by her drinking. Stewart had come out filled with hero worship for Livingstone. Even the reality of his morose, unattractive, alcoholic wife did nothing to alter the image Stewart had built up for himself of a saintly missionary. The disillusionment of reality gradually transformed Stewart from the Doctor's most ardent fan into his most severe critic. Stewart's journal shows how easily he was shocked. 'I could hardly have credited that Dr. L would have said "Go forward, you useless trash!"' he wrote, then 'I do not feel satisfied with the Sabbaths on board the Pioneer. Dr. L. is more faulty on this matter than I supposed. At noon, when we should have had service, he was writing.' His criticisms became increasingly bitter: 'Talk at night . . . Strong feeling against Livingstone for his mis-statements. His accursed lies have caused much toil, trouble, anxiety and loss of life, as well as money and reputation, and I have been led a dance over half the world to accomplish nothing.' Eventually, just before they parted, a year after their first meeting, he wrote: 'I part with Dr. L and have no wish whatever to meet him again. Bad [?faith] and insincerity will always come out.' Yet Stewart later overcame his disappointment with Africa, which he blamed on the false image he believed he had imbued from reading *Missionary Travels* (in a fit of histrionics, he threw his copy in the Zambesi before his departure), and with Livingstone himself. Years later, after Livingstone's death, he returned to Lake Nyassa to establish a successful missionary station. He named it Livingstonia.

During February, March and early April, as she struggled to help her husband to assemble his ship, the *Lady Nyassa*, in the unhealthy country around Shupanga, Mary was not well. Overweight and alcoholic, occasional surges of playfulness and fun were counterbalanced by much depression. Particularly worrying to her husband was her seeming loss of faith. Eventually she became feverish. A week later, despite all that Livingstone and Kirk could do, she died on 27 April. Livingstone was devastated. His journal and letters to all his friends pour out his grief and devotion to the wife whom he had lost. He worried too about the state of her soul at the time of her death, though perhaps summarized it best himself in one of his letters: 'she was a sincere if somewhat dejected Christian.'[6]

He derived much comfort at this time, surprisingly, from James Stewart, rather than from Kirk. Stewart had the advantage of having known Mary well and his own disillusionment with her bereaved husband was not nearly as marked then as it was to become. Stewart conducted the funeral service for Mary and afterwards frequently talked long into the night with Livingstone.

Two years were to pass before Livingstone sailed from Africa, two years of disappointment and blighted hopes. Although he became somewhat more sympathetic after Mary's death, he was also increasingly driven to push himself beyond the limits of human endurance in fatalistic mood. His efficiency and organizational skills had been heavily criticized by an officer on the *Gorgon*. Yet many of the seamen had a profound admiration and affection for him and were deeply impressed by his humanity, his kindness, his humour, his modesty and above all his courage.

He started with an abortive trip up the Rovuma. Nothing was achieved and relations between Livingstone, his brother, Kirk and Rae deteriorated to the point where Livingstone was enduring abusive language from Rae which he would have found intolerable from anyone earlier in the expedition because he could not risk losing the engineer's skills. Kirk in his journal becomes increasingly bitter about Livingstone, whom he eventually describes as 'a most unsafe leader'. The most noteworthy event was an attack by natives which Kirk repelled by shooting two men dead. This outcome of the episode is never referred to by Livingstone. Another drama had also to be resolved by Kirk's gun, when a hippopotamus overturned a boat carrying ten men.

Next they attempted to take the *Lady Nyassa* up the Shire. Relations between the four Europeans did not improve and now morale was further lowered by the sight of the appalling suffering inflicted on the area by the slavers. There were so many corpses floating in the river that they had literally to be regularly disentangled from the boat's paddles. Even the crocodiles who had earlier fought over them were now sated. Everywhere men were starving.

The expedition members' spirits were temporarily boosted early in 1863 when Richard Thornton rejoined them. After some discussion with Livingstone of the basis on which he did so, the original charges against him were withdrawn. Then a desperate appeal came from the missionaries who had replaced Mackenzie. More of their number were dying. Thornton responded by travelling to Tete to bring back a herd of sheep and goats. The journey finally exhausted him and on the 21 April he too died. In the same week Charles and Kirk both obtained permission to return home, though when Livingstone himself suffered an exceptionally bad attack of dysentery Kirk remained to nurse him. When the two men did eventually part, Kirk was the more embittered of the two, and wrote most venomously about him after he reached England. Livingstone on the other hand wrote to Kirk: 'You were always a right hand to me and I never trusted you in vain. God bless and prosper you.'[7] He named a mountain range 'Kirk's Range' and did all that he could to advance Kirk's future career. Waller, who was still with the Mission, was one of the few Englishmen closely associated with him at this time whose admiration continued unabated, and the more so when Livingstone took the trouble to make a handsome apology for a remark to Waller which he later accepted was unjustified.

The Mission was now headed by the coldly logical Bishop Tozer, who shared none of Livingstone's passionate feelings on slavery and was predominantly interested, to Livingstone's disdainful fury, in removing the mission from its perilous position in the front line first to the relative safety of Morumbala and eventually to Zanzibar. When he decided to leave behind most of the Africans dependent on the Mission for protection from slavery, Waller revolted and, with the backing of Livingstone but independently of the UMCA, led them to the Cape.

It was unfortunate that Tozer was responsible for the transmission of the terse official despatch which finally brought the expedition to a close. He allowed its contents to be read and discussed openly before sending it on to Livingstone in the hands of a man who, as soon as he was within hailing distance, bellowed 'No more pay for you Pioneer chaps. I brings the letter as says it.'[8] Livingstone was justified in lodging an official complaint, though he was well aware that the recall was inevitable. An attack in *The Times* in February 1863, vicious but accurate, pointed out that there was no trade, no converts and the bill was excessive. Further, the members of the expedition had almost all departed.

And yet the expedition had achieved much. Its original object had been to increase knowledge of the area and its natural resources. This had been done. If it appeared at the time that Livingstone was unduly optimistic about the potential for growing cotton, half a century later the cotton industry was the largest in the country then known as Malawi. The missionaries too were to return with greater success, acknowledging the source of their inspiration in the names of Livingstonia and Blantyre. Many of the most effective blows at the slave trade were struck, as Livingstone had known they could be, from Lake Nyassa.

Livingstone accepted the recall of the expedition and his duty to hand over the *Pioneer* at the coast according to instructions, but while awaiting the next rainy season he characteristically put the intervening weeks to good account. He set off on foot to explore the western side of Lake Nyassa, turning inland and almost reaching the country to which he was eventually to return to die a decade later. In all he covered some 750 miles. By his return he had not only seen a new part of Africa, he had also recovered much of his old spirit of delight in exploration, undertaken independently.

11
The Indian Ocean: Ship's Captain

Everyone who knew Livingstone considered his outstanding characteristic to be his courage. Never was this more clearly demonstrated than in May and June 1864 when he sailed the *Lady Nyassa* from Zanzibar to Bombay, 2500 miles away in a different continent. He was a landsman with no experience of the ocean. His crew was little better, including as it did three Europeans, two of whom were seasick, the third mutinous, and nine Africans, two of whom were mere boys (though one of those was Chuma) and none of whom had ever seen the sea before. The *Lady Nyassa* had been designed for shallow rivers and Lake Nyassa. He set out with only 14 tons of coal and, when dependent on fuel if the wind failed for sailing, she consumed about four tons of fuel every 24 hours. He was informed, on what he believed to be good authority, that the voyage would take around 18 days. In fact it lasted 45 days. He left Zanzibar on the 30 April knowing that the monsoon would break sometime between the end of May and the 12 June and that the Consul thought it very doubtful that he could reach Bombay before that happened.

In these circumstances, courageous would not be the unanimous choice of adjective for describing his state of mind. Yet he himself saw the decision as the inevitable culmination of the sequence of events. He does not even, on this occasion, appear to have been courting danger for the satisfaction of feeling that his escape was an indication of God's favour. There were moments on the voyage when he was convinced that he faced imminent death. He accepted this with resignation, grieving only that he would not after all be able to do all that he hoped to do for Africa.

Before he ever reached Zanzibar, he had experience of his little craft in a hurricane. He refused to sell the *Lady Nyassa* in Quilimane, knowing that the Portuguese who were keen to buy her would use her for slaving. The *Lady Nyassa* and the *Pioneer* were towed by two British cruisers, the *Ariel* and the *Orestes* respectively, from Quilimane to Mozambique. Livingstone refused an invitation to go on board the larger ship, preferring to stay on his own ship in company with a number of African passengers, left at the mission by Bishop Tozer. Instead, he sent Waller, who was suffering from seasickness, in his place.

On the 16 February a hurricane struck with such force that the engine of the *Ariel* was put out of action and the two vessels only just avoided colliding. Three times the hawser linking the two had to be replaced, a remarkable feat of seamanship watched with admiration by Livingstone, and the waves were such that he and his companions could see first the bottom and then the deck of the larger ship as it tossed forward and back, rearing up and plunging almost vertically in each direction. To those on the *Ariel*, the plight of those on the smaller vessel appeared considerably worse even than their own, an opinion which Livingstone was reluctantly forced to endorse when, after the storm abated, he finally agreed to accept a rest on the cruiser.

After a stop at Mozambique for a few necessary repairs, Livingstone spent a week taking his boat on to Zanzibar, where he was still hopeful that he would be able to sell her, realize his capital and book a passage home. He was still accompanied by Rae, but Rae had received an offer of employment elsewhere which he now decided to take up, influenced in part by his not unnatural terror of journeying further in the little vessel. He was particularly nervous since he had been involved in a frightening shipwreck four years previously. This decision was devastating news for Livingstone, for Rae, a skilled, professional engineer, was irreplaceable, however much Livingstone might mock him for his cowardice. But when it once more became clear that the *Lady Nyassa* was unsaleable except as a slave ship, Livingstone was convinced that he had no option. He must sail her across the Indian Ocean away from the coast of Africa with its hideous trade.

They left Zanzibar on 30 April. Progress was depressingly slow. Lack of wind frequently compelled them to steam. Two of his three European colleagues were successively useless with sickness. The dolphins following them were joined by sharks, 'All ill-natured,' he recorded, 'and in this I am sorry to feel compelled to join.'[1]

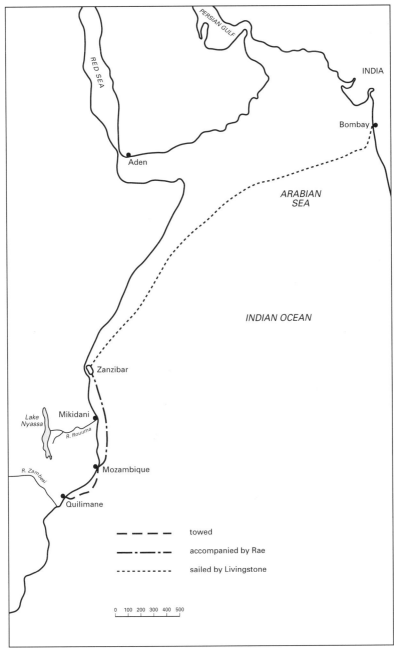

Taking the *Lady Nyassa* from Quilimane to Bombay, 1864

Soon his journal became as fascinating as it was when he travelled by land, filled with detailed observations of all that he saw, fish, birds, mammals and even water snakes, how they looked and how they behaved, of weather, sky and ocean. All this is interspersed with the random reflections of a highly intelligent man. Sometimes he is recollecting the pleasures of travel on foot in Africa, sometimes he considers the ways in which the African continent might develop, carefully assessing the nature of colonization, and the part which Britain ought to play, or contemplates the nature of the country itself. Next he may reflect on the way in which he feels the mission societies have treated him badly. Latin quotations and their translations are laced with disparaging comments on scholars whose time would have been better spent translating the Bible into a spoken language.

As May turned to June, weather and tempers alike showed signs of deterioration. One of the Englishmen was so surly as to be close to mutiny, and Livingstone exerted his authority without hesitation. The Africans on the other hand worked hard and courageously: their Captain must have been most relieved at seeing their reactions when he reflected on the fatal panic which had overtaken poor Sekwebu when he went to sea.

With increasingly stormy conditions and the calendar conspiring to warn him of the imminent approach of the monsoon, he considered other stopping places closer than Bombay, but the wind was in the wrong direction for him to approach Aden, and as he crept nearer to Bombay he resolved to press on despite everything, rejecting other alternatives including the first land sighted 115 miles short of Bombay. The squalls became increasingly severe, and the more responsible crew members spent long hours without sleep. Late in the afternoon of the 13 June, when the port was shrouded in mist, they sailed into Bombay. 'The vessel was so small, that no one noticed our arrival,' he noted and accordingly completed the customs papers with the words 'I am consigned to Nobody and I do not know a single soul in the place.'[2] Necessary formalities were soon completed and when word of his arrival reached the Governor, Sir Bartle Frere, he was invited to stay with him. The two men got on well and had long and productive discussions on the problems of slavery. Livingstone enjoyed the ten days he spent in India, finding it strange to adapt to a land where buffaloes were kept for their milk and elephants used like horses in Britain. As he wrote to Sir Thomas Maclear, they 'invariably made the question glance across the mind, "Where's your rifle?"'[3]

He had two important transactions to complete. The *Lady Nyassa* was made safe, eventually to be sold for just £2300, the sum being invested in a bank which collapsed before Livingstone could withdraw it. In material terms he had risked his life for, literally, nothing, though the men were generously paid off. Chuma and Wikatani he left with the head of the Free Church Missions Schools, Dr Wilson, who proved himself worthy of the trust. Livingstone also found employment for Susi and Amoda, the two older men who, with the boys, were to rejoin him when he came back 18 months afterwards.

After ten days, Livingstone embarked for England. He visited a number of interesting places on his way, including the Suez Canal, then half built. In the course of the journey he considered what project to undertake at the end of his holiday. At this stage his mind was filled with the atrocities of Portuguese slave trading. He longed to reveal this to the world, and to establish a settlement beyond the reach of that nation close to the source of the Rovuma. His time in England was to turn his thoughts in an entirely fresh direction.

12
Britain: Author and Father

When Livingstone arrived in England on 23 July 1864, while he was no longer the popular icon of the masses as on his previous visit, during his first week in England he accepted invitations from the Prime Minister, the Duchess of Wellington, Mr Gladstone and the Lord Mayor of London, to name but a few of the eminent people keen to associate with him. Lord Palmerston, the Prime Minister, was now 80, but Sir Roderick Murchison assured Livingstone that the slave trade was at the top of his list of priorities.

Lord John Russell, however, the Foreign Secretary, Livingstone found 'very cold in his manner'. For him the whole Zambesi expedition had been a sore trial. For the government to be spending money on something which made good relations with Portugal almost impossible to maintain, involved interference in local tribal warfare and resulted in the deaths of some of the finest group of missionaries to have been sent out from England for many years, without producing any tangible or immediate benefits, was painful to the statesman.

After a week of frenzied social and political activity in London, Livingstone travelled to Scotland by train and spent two days with his old friend 'Paraffin' Young before continuing to Hamilton. The two men remained close throughout their lives and Livingstone relied heavily upon Young for help in handling financial and family matters of all sorts. Young combined considerable business acumen with sound judgement in his dealings with people and these, with his close proximity to the family home at Hamilton, made him an invaluable support. Their correspondence is full of friendly banter. On the one occasion when some friction arose, after Young had entered into a business deal with Livingstone's brother John in

America (probably in a benevolent attempt to help John) and the arrangement turned sour, Livingstone was very quick to conclude a letter to Young discussing the question with the words: 'If you take a totally different view of the case from what I do pray do not trouble yourself to reply on the subject but let us continue our correspondence as heretofore.'[1] He had an easy friendship too with Mrs Young, whom he always called Majames in the African fashion. He wrote to her just after his visit apologizing for removing her 'worse half' for 24 hours: 'I am trying to get him to the jeweller's but he won't promise to buy, the ne'er do well that he is.'[2] Young was in fact a generous man: four weeks later Livingstone was thanking him for the beautiful watch he had given to his daughter Agnes.

For Agnes was no longer a child. She was an affectionate, friendly young woman of 17, well used by now to taking responsibility for the whole family, and the only one of his children with whom Livingstone formed a close relationship. She arrived at Hamilton the day after her father, bringing her two younger brothers with her. Neither of the boys was physically strong, and the 15-year-old Thomas was suffering from a serious kidney disease. He died at the age of 26, only two years after his father, having worked for some time in Egypt. Oswell, who was just approaching his thirteenth birthday, was probably the most intelligent of the boys (though Tom was handicapped by constantly finding his education disrupted by ill health) and eventually became a doctor.

Livingstone had not seen any of his children for six and a half years, but the youngest, Anna Mary, was now five and this was their first meeting. He found her 'a nice sprightly child'. As an old woman of 80, a year before her death, Anna Mary recollected how she did not like being kissed by him because of his moustache and would have preferred a white doll to the black one he gave her. Although he took her for walks, 'I was very shy of him and did not speak much, and perhaps he was a little shy of me!' She had more fun with her Uncle Charles and could only remember her father as 'always writing letters'.[3] Yet Anna Mary inherited much from her father. With her husband Frank Wilson, nephew of an old friend of her father's, she devoted much of her life to working with the Mission to Deep Sea Fishermen and later to voluntary evangelical work in Sierra Leone.

The last member of the family, Robert, was the real victim of their fractured family life. His independent, stubborn nature he inherited from his father but, where David had aimed for a life beyond the narrow confines of the mill and the single room in which he had been reared, perhaps because Robert had started with the freedom of Africa and gone to the restrictions of Hamilton life, he was merely rebelling against his surroundings. The tiny house, the strict, narrow-minded aunts and old-fashioned grandparents, then the squalid penury of the years with his mother before his father's first return to England, and later the restraints of unimaginative trustees and inappropriate schools with no home, no parents and no family basis of love and support (his father had had all these last three needs fulfilled) to give cohesion and structure to his life: all these contributed to undermine the self-confidence which had stood his father in such good stead. As a child he had declared that he was going to be a traveller like his father, but his father's letters were not designed to inspire and encourage: they were negative, critical, destructive.

Yet his father told James Young[4] he supported Robert when a schoolmaster overstepped the mark with a threat to thrash the boy. The master's wife 'advised me to reprove him for running away. I could not conceive what I should say, so said nothing. It was well he had spirit not to submit to what you never authorised Mr. Hall to do,' but perhaps Robert never knew of this support, only that his father deplored his decision to turn to bad company and drink rather than his father's friends. Later Robert thought of joining the navy, where the combination of discipline, responsibility and the opportunity to travel could have been just what he needed, but the Trustees (with the exception of Young) 'would not hear of it, on the plea that I would disapprove, and never said a word about it to me till all was over . . . But I would not have objected,' wrote his father.[5]

Eventually, just after his mother's death, it was agreed that he should travel to Natal. He hoped first to stay with his uncle, Robert Moffat, but the latter sadly died before the young man arrived. His widowed aunt showed him kindness, however. Robert wrote, 'besides £1, I owe [her] a great deal, perhaps more than I shall ever be able to repay.' She must also have sent word to his maternal grandmother, who sent him a delightfully loving, supportive letter, though it is uncertain whether this ever reached him. Thomas Maclear also tried to help him, though other connections of his father's were less cooperative. Various plans to enable Robert to join his father on the Zambesi proved abortive, and, after a series of unfortunate events and misunderstandings, he found himself enlisted in the US army, kidnapped, so he said, on board a ship, though he may have had more choice in the matter than he suggested.

Livingstone, before he learned what had actually happened, was worried. He wrote to James Young 'I cannot free myself from blame in his having so little of fatherly care. I am very heartsore about him.'[6] It was almost a year before he learned more. In July 1864 he wrote to Kirk with chillingly brutal prescience: 'My heart is rather sore – that bad boy has got into the American Army and will be made manure of, for those bloody fields.'[7]

In October he received a final, heart-breaking letter from the boy himself. Robert explained how he came to be taking part in the American Civil War, telling of his part in one battle and two skirmishes, of how he fired high to avoid killing anyone and controlled his passion sufficiently to take his opponent prisoner despite the 'furious madness' of a bayonet charge. He spoke of his craving for travel, of throwing away his chance of an education and of his use of the pseudonym Rupert Vincent to avoid bringing further dishonour on his father's name, he of whom his father had recently written that his sole interest was to make capital out of having a famous father.[8] He started this letter 'My dear Sir, Hearing that you have returned to England I undertake to address a few lines to you, not with any hope that you will be interested in me but simply to explain the position,' and concluded it, 'Your quondam son, Robert.'[9]

His father strove to pull strings to have him sent home but to no avail. Robert was captured soon after in another skirmish and died in a Confederate prisoner of war camp on 5 December 1864 aged 18.

While his father had no official confirmation of this until Stanley reached him in Africa in 1871, he was under no illusions. He commented many times that they would never hear of him again in this world, saying, 'I am proud of the boy. If I had been there I should have gone to fight for the North myself.'

For Robert had died in his father's cause, fighting against slavery. Livingstone's shock and grief at the assassination of Abraham Lincoln the following April must have been exacerbated by recollections of Robert.

The long months of uncertainty probably affected Agnes more than her father. Brother and sister had been very close, and with the optimism of youth she continued to hope long after her father had accepted the inevitability of Robert's fate.

Livingstone's mother never realized what had happened to her adored grandson but continued to ask the rest of her family where the 'puir laddie' was. She did not at first recognize David and throughout the few months of life which remained to her constantly confused the generations, thinking him a brother to his own children, asking about Robert as if he were David's brother and lamenting that David had not more time to play with his 'little sister' Anna Mary.

While in Scotland at this time, Livingstone made a number of visits of very different types. As well as seeing friends and family, he called to discuss politics with the Duke of Argyll at Inveraray, spent a day on Ulva, looking for the remains of the croft where his grandfather had lived and went with Agnes to the launching of a Turkish frigate on the Clyde. The Turkish ambassador told him that it was him the crowd was cheering, and, when Livingstone denied this, said, 'I am only what my master made me; you are what you made yourself.' A moment later one of the crowd proved the point by insisting on shaking Livingstone's hand.

His own health was a cause of some concern so he went to Glasgow to consult Professor Syme about his piles. However, when the specialist recommended an operation, he decided not to go ahead with this as the bleeding had stopped and the operation would incapacitate him for some time and inevitably be reported in the press, which he would find embarrassing. It was a decision which was eventually to cost him his life.

Having reached an agreement with John Murray for a second book, it was now time for him to start writing. The question was where he should base himself. His mother's house at Hamilton was clearly not suitable. He considered renting a cottage in or close to London with Agnes to keep house for him.

Before he even left Bombay he had received a letter from William Frederick Webb, the big game hunter whom he had first met more than twelve years earlier at the end of the journey with Mary, the older children and William Cotton Oswell, just after the birth of his son Oswell. Webb considered that he owed his life to the Doctor, for Livingstone had learnt that there was a white man lying sick somewhere in the vicinity of Kolobeng, set out to find and treat him and brought him back to stay with him and Mary until he had fully recovered.

Webb was some 16 years younger than Livingstone, an intelligent, thoughtful man who was now happily married to an exceptionally capable and charming woman, who was probably a stronger personality than her husband. They had bought Newstead Abbey in

Nottinghamshire as a family home in which to bring up their young daughters and nothing gave them greater pleasure than to fill the house with like-minded friends who might stay for ten days or a fortnight and share their pleasant way of life.

Newstead was originally built as a Priory in the twelfth century. After the dissolution of the monasteries it was bought by the Byron family. Every corner of house and estate thus had its associations either with monastic times, with the poet or with his great uncle the 'wicked' Lord Byron. There had been one other owner, a Colonel Wildman, from whom the Webb family bought Newstead, and he was responsible for the somewhat incongruous addition of the so-called 'Sussex Tower'.

Mr and Mrs Webb, with characteristic hospitality, proposed that Livingstone should come and stay at Newstead for the whole of his time in England to write his book. He hesitated. He did not know William Webb well and had never even met his wife. They might not get on. It was also a tremendous imposition. Besides, he wanted to see as much of his children as possible, and gave this as his reason for refusing. Mrs Webb brushed this aside: Agnes should stay with him throughout and the boys would be most welcome for part at least of their Christmas holidays. Still he demurred. He was keen for Agnes to have good music lessons while she was with him. Once again his hostess had an answer. She promptly decided that her eldest daughter now needed a governess and ensured that the governess selected was an outstanding musician and piano player.

A friend later described Livingstone's visit to Newstead as 'perhaps all things considered, the eight happiest months of his life'. Mr and Mrs Webb lived up to their reputation as the perfect host and hostess. More remarkably, Livingstone proved himself equally successful as a guest. To remain on such good terms with a family when living with them for such a long period demands qualities on both sides which the members of the Zambesi expedition would have been amazed to discover Livingstone possessed. At Newstead he was without responsibility, except for the writing of his book, and able to relax. He took an interest in all his host's activities, learning about the running of a large estate, participating with enthusiasm in experiments in trout breeding then being pursued by Webb and taking part in field sports. One evening the two men watched duck coming into a pond too late in the evening for a shot. Next morning Webb decided to get up early and return to the pond. Although he was early he was not the first: he met a wet, muddy but delighted Livingstone returning along the same path with a gun under his arm and a brace of wild duck in the other hand. Despite his failure with Anna Mary, he proved himself a tremendous success with the Webb children. Little Ethel, with her dark hair and rosy cheeks, was his particular favourite, and he would concoct exotic treats of scones with clotted cream and jam for her to the horror of the nanny, justifying them by claiming superior knowledge as a doctor. But 'NaNa', like everyone else in the house – hosts, children, other guests or staff – was captivated by the charm and kindliness of the man so often described as dour and impossibly difficult. When one of the children was miserably cold, and her parents were unsympathetic, Livingstone would speak kindly to her and lend her his own gloves. At Christmas time, when the boys came to stay, sleeping in a room adjoining his with the big four-poster in the Sussex tower which had been made over to him, he joined in singing, dancing, word games and even blind man's buff, despite cutting his head open on the stone fireplace when blindfolded.

Agnes too, gentle, quiet and shy, intelligent and kind, was much loved by all, and her father delighted in watching her set out for dances, looking a credit to her hostess, who had taught her how to make the most of her natural good looks. Father and daughter were proud of each other and delighted in each other's company. She helped him with his writing, which he worked at every morning before enjoying the rest of the day, and as time became more pressing, forcing him sometimes to work late into the night, all the Webb family started to help with making fair copies. The book appeared under the name of Charles as well as himself to enable Charles to receive royalties in America, though the incorporation of his brother's notes proved a hindrance rather than a help. He also helped and encouraged Charles to obtain the position of Consul at Fernando Po.

In an age of intolerant religious bigotry, the relaxed way in which Livingstone accepted and welcomed all forms of Christianity caused astonishment. When he wrote that he would much prefer to see the Africans good Roman Catholics than idolatrous heathens, men marvelled. In the same way, he encouraged Agnes to be confirmed during her time at Newstead and thus become a member of the Church of England, whereas he arranged for Anna Mary to be educated at a Quaker school. But Livingstone was no ordinary Presbyterian minister: even his dress appeared shocking to some.

His scientific interest in geology was deemed by the more old-fashioned to be incompatible with religious faith. But this was one of the many interests he shared with his host and more especially with Sir Roderick Murchison, when he and his wife came to stay at Newstead. Lady Murchison caused much amusement. With her quick brain, ready wit, copious fund of anecdotes and total lack of discretion she could keep any dinner party enthralled all evening.

Sir Roderick was an old friend of both Mr and Mrs Webb and Livingstone, but the hosts were equally keen to entertain any friends of Livingstone whom they did not themselves know. Endless attempts were made to bring William Cotton Oswell and his wife to Newstead but her health prevented this, although, as Mrs Webb was herself pregnant, she would have welcomed a companion to sit quietly with. Oswell was one of the proofreaders for Livingstone's book and the two men were in constant communication throughout Livingstone's time in England.

Conversely, some of the regular visitors to Newstead were particularly keen to come while Livingstone was there and Mr and Mrs Webb took trouble to avoid embarrassing him. Once, however, when those there were all close friends and his escape from the lion came up in conversation, he reluctantly and uncharacteristically allowed them all to feel his damaged arm with its so-called 'false joint'.

One visitor who was not universally popular at Newstead but kindly treated by Mrs Webb was the strange but brilliant Lionel Hayward. On this occasion he was acting unofficially for the Prime Minister when he approached Livingstone and asked what the government could do for him. Livingstone, who had not found Hayward a sympathetic character, was taken off guard. As he wrote many years later in Africa, 'It never occurred to me, that he meant anything for me or my children, till I was out here. I thought only of my work in Africa, and answered accordingly.'[10] He requested that the British and Portuguese governments should have a formal treaty granting free access to the African highlands through the Zambesi and Shire rivers. This took place, but thus he missed an opportunity to help his children for the future.

Negotiations with the government concerning his future plans did not go well. Ministers applauded his stance on the slave trade but, with a certain lack of logic, desired to disassociate themselves from his attacks on the Portuguese. While he was apparently not discontented with an informal offer of £500 and the rank of Consul, a subsequent letter declaring in stark and insulting terms that, apart from this, no salary would be paid nor pension considered caused him grave offence and led to his declaration that he did not like to be treated like a charwoman. The tone precluded further discussions if circumstances changed and Russell, prompted by Murchison, was apparently ready to retract it but in fact never did.

Livingstone was in discussion with the RGS too, though the precise object of his projected journey was not yet agreed. An expedition would cost around £2000. His intense interest in geographical issues was first aroused in September 1864 when he was asked to speak on the African slave trade before two and a half thousand people at Bath. His speech proved controversial, partly because of Portuguese reaction and partly because he was thanked by Bishop Colenso, whose heretical religious views were then quite unjustly thought to be held by Livingstone also.

The most important part of the evening, however, was a debate between the two great explorers, Burton and Speke. These two men had jointly discovered Lake Tanganyika. Speke had then, without Burton, discovered Lake Victoria Nyanza (Lake Victoria) and declared it, accurately as is now known, to be the source of the Nile. Meanwhile another explorer, Samuel Baker, discovered Lake Albert and suggested this as a possible source of the Nile.

Burton and Speke were now deadly enemies and rivals. Since the country had not yet been sufficiently explored, Burton would be able to argue that there was no proof that Lake Victoria was the source. Further, even if both Lake Victoria and Lake Albert did flow into the Nile, it was possible that Lake Tanganyika also had a river flowing from it into the Nile. It is now known that this is not the case, but had it been so this much more southerly Lake would have been the true source.

Livingstone in anticipation of the debate, became increasingly interested in the issue. He too believed that Lake Tanganyika was indeed the true source. He was scornfully dismissive of Speke's theories though looking forward to meeting the man, while he intensely disliked Burton. Burton's amoral outlook and racist attitude to Africans appalled Livingstone. The atmosphere at the debate would be charged with electrifying clashes of personality.

But it never took place. Speke was out shooting alone the day before when his gun went off as he climbed a wall. His death was almost certainly accidental, though it was widely suggested that the prospect of disputing publicly with Burton had driven him to suicide.

From then on, the possibility of Livingstone going out on behalf of the RGS to resolve the mystery of the source of the Nile was increasingly discussed. Finally he was offered £500 on certain stringent conditions to do so. Combined with the offer from the government, he was now halfway to being able to afford to mount an expedition. He was fortunate in his friends. Young came to his aid by providing the missing £1000.

Precisely what Livingstone himself wished to do probably even he did not know. He asked Kirk to accompany him, but the doctor wisely but tactfully declined, and Livingstone helped him to obtain a post at Zanzibar from which Kirk progressed to become Consul in the year of Livingstone's death. Livingstone declared in several letters that he was not interested in purely geographical issues. Murchison on the other hand regarded the missionary motive as an unhelpful diversion. Livingstone was interested in the question of the source of the Nile and he had backing from the RGS. He was very interested in stopping the slave trade and he had governmental support. He was sponsored too by Young, to whom he had repeatedly reiterated his missionary inclinations, and summarized in his preface to *The Zambesi and its Tributaries* as 'another attempt to open Africa to civilising influences'.

He left Newstead at the end of April, soon after finishing his book, and sailed in August. In between he returned to Scotland, where his mother's health was deteriorating fast. He left her briefly for a visit to Oxford, and it was there that a telegram reached him telling him of her death. She had told him the last time he left England that she would have liked 'one of her laddies to lay her head in the grave'[11] and he was able to render her this last service.

A short time before he had taken part in a happier family occasion. He was persuaded, with reluctance for he knew that he would not avoid making a speech, to attend Oswell's school prize giving. Oswell had been confident of winning first prize in three different subjects: in fact he won the prize in six. Tom, too, got a prize for drawing, and, his father acknowledged, the drawing was very good. Livingstone concluded his speech to the boys with the words 'Fear God and Work Hard.'

Livingstone had resolved that, when he left the country, Agnes should continue her education in France, an unusual idea for the time. He had selected a suitable lady to take charge of her, a relation of the Protestant French missionaries he had known near Kuruman, who had previously been governess to Queen Victoria's daughters, but had lost her post through an unintentional indiscretion. Agnes had three very good friends in England: the family at Newstead, James Young and Cotton Oswell. Oswell, whose memories of her went back to when she was a toddler in Africa, once wrote to her: 'If you are within a hundred miles of me, let me know, and I will come and shake you by the hand. I will always come even to the end of the earth, if I can be of any use to you, or you want me.' He in fact went to Paris to bring her home when the time came.

Livingstone's farewells to all his friends were sad. Perhaps they had a premonition that they would never meet again in this world. On 8 August Webb and Kirk went with him to the London Zoo, where their combined knowledge of many of the species probably exceeded that of the keepers. Next day he said goodbye to Mr and Mrs Webb, with Mrs Webb in tears, and later to Oswell and his wife. Kirk and Waller escorted him and Agnes to Folkestone.

13
Lakes Nyassa, Tanganyika and Moero: the Explorer

After he had parted from Agnes in France, Livingstone travelled on to Bombay, where he spent most of the next four months with the Governor, Sir Bartle Frere, who became a close friend. However, Frere did not advise him well in the selection of men for his expedition. The first and most serious mistake was to enlist 12 sepoys in the charge of a havildar. African porters Livingstone understood. Indian soldiers baffled him, and the particular ones selected proved cruel, idle and selfish. Livingstone did not appreciate that as soldiers they considered carrying goods demeaning, nor did he understand their customs and outlook. Africa was as strange to them as to any Englishman. When they eventually killed and ate the expedition's buffalo calf, they insisted that it had been taken by a tiger, naively assuring Livingstone that they had seen its stripes.

Next he visited the mission school at Nassick, set up to help young African boys rescued from slavery, and took nine boys. He later wrote to Kirk 'To send such Africans forth as having been taught trades and being Christians is little less than a public fraud.'[1] They lacked even basic training in their professed trades and had had no discipline, since the school authorities 'dreaded their desertion ... bringing an ill report on the Institution'. While some eventually turned out well, others later even took to slaving on their own account.

Livingstone returned too to Dr Wilson, who had taken charge of Chuma and Wikatani, the two boys rescued from slavery whom he had brought over to India in the *Lady Nyassa*. Both were decent, quick-witted lads and Chuma was eventually to prove himself, with Susi, the most loyal and capable of all Livingstone's Africans, but they were at this time also giggly, irresponsible teenagers. They constantly lost his knives and forks and forgot to do any routine work without repeated reminders. They smoked hemp, got involved with women and Wikatani drove Livingstone mad by 'singing Dididy dididy or weeweewee.'[2] When the expedition passed through Wikatani's home country, he met a brother and decided to return home. Livingstone was sorry, appreciating that, like Chuma, he showed potential despite the irritations. Some years later Wikatani acted as interpreter for E. D. Young, the naval lieutenant who had served for some time with Livingstone on the Zambesi expedition. Although he had by then forgotten most of his English, he could still sing a hymn Livingstone had taught him, no doubt hoping at least to vary his musical repertoire, and had evidently derived nothing but good from his experiences with the explorer.

Susi too, who with Amoda rejoined Livingstone in Zanzibar when he arrived there and found them working together, although an older man, was far from the mature, responsible, loyal follower he eventually became. He also caused problems with his womanizing, was once described by Livingstone as 'a habitual thief'[3] and at one stage led a revolt against his leader.

Frere's help was more effective for the manner in which he introduced Livingstone to the powerful Sultan of Zanzibar. The Bombay government was about to present the Sultan with a ship, the *Thule*, and Frere arranged for Livingstone to travel in her to Zanzibar and make the presentation to the Sultan, thus establishing his credentials as a man of importance in Britain. The Sultan, suitably impressed, had his band play 'God save the Queen' and 'The British Grenadiers' at his reception, 'as if', Livingstone wrote to Agnes, 'the fact of my being only five feet eight . . . ought not to have suggested "Wee Willie Winkie" as more appropriate. I was ready to explode, but got out of sight before giving way.'[4] There were more tangible results, however; he was given an official document entitling him to help and support from all the Sultan's subjects with whom he came in contact. As the part of Africa to which he was now preparing to travel was that where the Arabs, rather than the Portuguese, held sway, his relationships with them were vitally important. Although he found in practice that most of the Arabs whom he met were unable to read this document, its purport and word of the Sultan's attitude probably contributed much to the reception he met with from the Arabs he encountered.

His position was an extraordinary one. The Sultan accepted, indeed possibly overestimated, the esteem in which he was held by the

British government. He also valued highly his own excellent relations with Britain. On the other hand, Livingstone's avowed purpose in life was well known to be the abolition of the slave trade. Everyone in Zanzibar, every Arab travelling on the African mainland, from the Sultan down, depended on the slave trade for a high proportion of his wealth. The situation in many ways mirrored that with the Portuguese during Livingstone's earlier expeditions, yet it became increasingly intense as Livingstone during his travels became more and more dependent personally on the goodwill and kindness of individual Arabs but more and more vehement in his horror of slavery. Probably the Arabs, including the Sultan, deemed it best to humour him outwardly and privately mock his lack of power. After all, they had seen that the Portuguese, despite much official indignation, had had nothing to fear from him. The British government in the end rated good relations with Portugal more important than listening in detail to the rantings of a lone eccentric. It is remarkable that ultimately that lone eccentric, now old, exhausted and isolated, caused the treaty suppressing the slave trade in Zanzibar to be signed within a month of his death.

The way in which Arabs, including the Sultan, humoured Livingstone can be attributed to politics, to a desire by the Sultan to ingratiate himself with the British and by the other Arabs to ingratiate themselves with the Sultan, combined with an underestimation of Livingstone's effectiveness. They also seem to have liked him as a man and enjoyed his company. More puzzlement has been caused by the way in which Livingstone himself was prepared to accept more and more help from the Arabs. Yet the terrible suffering of his last journeys left him little choice in the matter. To continue his mission, indeed to continue his life at all, he had to accept help from the only people able to offer it to him. Always a pragmatist, he justified his behaviour in various ways, but he had never seen martyrdom as preferable to continuing God's work for as long as possible. He had made this clear when he heard Pusey's comments on Bishop Mackenzie. He soon learnt too that the individual leading slave merchants frequently had many qualities which made him prepared to accept them as friends despite the appallingly ruthless cruelty necessary for the pursuit of their evil trade, so frequently successfully masked under a veneer of good manners and individual kindness. They were after all men with whom it was possible to hold discussions on religious, cultural, historical or political issues in a manner which was quite impossible with almost all the Africans:

men such as Sechele and Sebitoane were rare indeed and the lack of experience of a world beyond that of the surrounding tribes inevitably restricted their perspective.

Zanzibar itself was an eye-opener to Livingstone: the filth, the stench, 'the old, old way of living – eating, drinking, sleeping; sleeping, drinking, eating . . . slave-dhows coming and slave-dhows going away'. More depressing still was the infamous slave market, where he could identify most of the 300 slaves as having come from the Nyassa region. 'All who have grown up seemed ashamed at being hawked about for sale. The teeth are examined, the cloth lifted up to examine the lower limbs, and a stick is thrown for the slave to bring and thus exhibit his paces. Some are dragged through the crowd by the hand, and the price called out incessantly . . .'[5]

He used the time too to enlist the rest of his team. In addition to Susi and Amoda he found another man who had served with him on the Zambesi expedition, a native of Johanna named Musa. Incredibly, Musa had already shown himself to be a liar and a thief, a reputation attributed generally to his countrymen, yet Livingstone enlisted nine others and placed Musa in charge of them. He added a further 24 porters from the mainland when he arrived there making a total of 60. He considered this sufficient though Burton and Speke had always had at least 130 men. Livingstone had always preferred small groups. He felt that it was not only cheaper but less provocative. Also, the more men taken, the more stores needed carrying to feed them all. But the 'currency' required for daily expenses was cloth and beads, both bulky items to transport. And on his previous journeys his men had been primarily Makololo, tribesmen uncorrupted by Western trading conditions, there not to make money for themselves but because the tribe under its chief had decided Livingstone should be supported and delegated those individuals to do the work. Such men did not desert. The mixed bag he had now collected had no such inhibitions.

Strangely too Livingstone's leadership abilities seemed to have disappeared. On his journey across Africa he had always been firm, positive and tough as well as inspiring. With the Europeans on the Zambesi he had been far too tough, treating them too much as he had treated the Makololo, giving orders without discussing principles. While he thought that he was allowing them freedom to use their own initiative, they were given no indication as to how he was thinking. When the result was not what he had envisaged, he unleashed his fury on them and was surprised to find this resented.

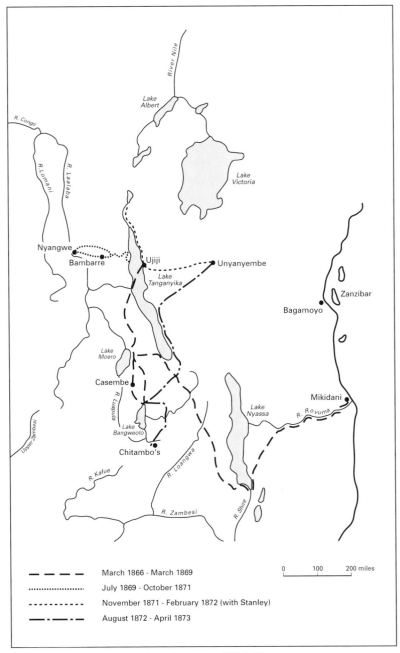

River Nile

Lake
Albert

R. Congo

R. Laalaba

R. Lomani

Lake
Victoria

Nyangwe
Bambarre
Ujiji
Lake
Tanganyika
Unyanyembe

Zanzibar

Bagamoyo

Lake
Moero

Casembe

R. Lapula

Lake
Nyassa

Mikidani

R. Rovuma

Upper Zambesi

Lake
Bangweolo

Chitambo's

R. Loangwa

R. Kafue

R. Zambesi

R. Shire

March 1866 - March 1869

July 1869 - October 1871

November 1871 - February 1872 (with Stanley)

August 1872 - April 1873

0   100   200 miles

Last journeys, 1866–73

Perhaps he had realized some of this during his rest in England and determined this time to be less dictatorial, regardless of the fact that he was now travelling with undisciplined Africans and Indians. If so, it was his greatest mistake. After several months of travel, he resolved on New Year's Day 1867 in his journal to be 'more gentle and loving'. A resolution to the opposite effect would have been more appropriate, amazing though that would have seemed to any member of the Zambesi expedition. When Oswell read his journals years later, he wrote to Agnes saying, 'The dear old fellow, how quiet and gentle he has grown.'[6] His men simply ran riot, ignoring him completely and frequently behaving appallingly. One of the earliest examples was in their treatment of the pack animals. He took with him three Indian buffaloes and a calf (the one allegedly taken by a tiger) and from Zanzibar six camels, two mules and four donkeys, hoping to establish which breeds were resilient to the tsetse fly. The experiment was nullified by all the animals dying at an early stage, perhaps through tsetse bites but equally probably as a consequence of their cruel treatment by the men, which Livingstone seemed quite unable to prevent.

The route Livingstone followed, while it was eventually dictated by circumstances, was originally supposed to prove or disprove the various theories concerning the possible sources of the Nile. He never approached the geographical issues with the necessary logical detachment, and his thinking became increasingly confused and obsessive.

Speke had believed, correctly as we now know, that Lake Victoria was the source of the Nile. He had not explored sufficiently far to prove his theory. Baker had discovered Lake Albert, north-west of Lake Victoria, and therefore, although it also flowed into the Nile, not that river's ultimate source. Murchison and Livingstone believed, incorrectly, that there was a river flowing from Lake Tanganyika into Lake Albert. Had this been the case either Lake Tanganyika or somewhere south of that lake would be the ultimate source. Murchison wanted Livingstone to start by confirming the existence of this river. Had he done this and discovered their mistake, much trouble would have been saved. But Livingstone, ostensibly because he was sure this was the case and wanted to jump to the next stage of investigating whether a river flowed into the south end of Lake Tanganyika so that he could trace this back to a much more southerly site, and in practice probably because he wished to start out in his own country around Lake Nyassa rather than the country which he thought of as belonging to Burton and Speke, refused to do so. When he approached Lakes Bangweolo and Moero from the south, he discovered that those two lakes were joined by the River Luapula, flowing from the former to the latter. The enormous River Lualaba flowed out of the north-west corner of Lake Moero. He soon convinced himself, and eventually reported back to England, that the Lualaba was the Nile. It could either flow into Lake Tanganyika then into Lake Albert and so into the Nile, or else perhaps it continued west of Lake Tanganyika. Even if the main Lualaba continued west of Lake Tanganyika and did not ultimately join the Nile, provided that there was a branch flowing from the north of Lake Moero into Lake Tanganyika, and provided that the latter lake then flowed into Lake Albert – both convictions which Livingstone came to hold, but both in fact fallacies – then Lake Bangweolo was in either case the ultimate source of the Nile.

The theory that the River Lualaba flowed into the Nile was an eminently reasonable one considering what was known at the time. An enormous river, Livingstone rightly deduced that it must become either the Nile or the Congo. Superficially, the Nile seemed much more plausible since it flowed predominantly from south to north, as did the Lualaba. What was known of the Congo on the other hand flowed from west, indeed north-west, to east. A massive turn of more than 90 degrees would be necessary to enable it to join up with the Lualaba. The Lualaba too is closer to the eastern coast of Africa than to the western. Livingstone, in concluding that it was the source of the Nile rather than the Congo (though he occasionally hedged his bets by suggesting that it could perhaps be the source of both) was selecting the more likely as well as the more attractive alternative. Unfortunately it was the wrong conclusion.

Livingstone developed these theories gradually as he made his discoveries, but from the start he was convinced that the source of the Nile was to be found to the south of Lake Tanganyika. For this reason, and perhaps personal ones too, he did not set off from the coast adjacent to Zanzibar, but was carried down to Mikidani close to the source of the Rovuma. As the *Penguin* sailed away on 24 March 1866 leaving Livingstone alone with his motley crowd of men and pathetic group of animals, his spirits were high. He wrote a lyrical passage in his journal extolling the joys of travel in Africa, the feelings of health and well-being it engenders. If he reread his journal during the coming years, the irony must have struck even Livingstone himself. Had he realized that in the seven years of life which remained to him he would only set eyes on one white man, even his indomitable spirits might have sunk.

The early weeks of his journey were filled with concern over the malicious cruelty of his team, and the sepoys in particular, to the animals, who died at an alarming rate. Livingstone seems curiously apathetic, unable to do anything about it and, despite threats to dismiss the men, constantly relenting and allowing them to stay, and frequently to carry lighter loads than was justified. In mid-June the hard-working African porters refused to continue and a week later one of the Nassick boys died. Livingstone's misery was increased as the route they followed became literally strewn with the dead bodies of women and children shot, stabbed or chained to trees by the neck and left to die by the slave traders. The country was devastated by raiders and famine affected the expedition as well as the tribesmen.

Here he met the first of the Arab slave traders who was to befriend him so incongruously. The kindness, to Livingstone at least, of Seph Rubea and the courage shown by one chief who insisted on the release of some captives taken by his men were rare shafts of light for the explorer.

Finally, late in July, he did dismiss the sepoys, who had been planning the murder of one of the Nassick boys. He allowed the havildar to remain, though the man deserted not long afterwards. The sight of Lake Nyassa cheered him, though the slaving dhows sailing there in place of the *Lady Nyassa* as he had once dreamed were depressing. Unable to cross the lake as he had hoped because of native suspicions and reluctance to supply a boat, he was forced to continue round the southern end of the lake. As he crossed the Shire River many sad reflections flooded his mind, of Mary, of Mackenzie and of all the failed hopes of earlier times. It was in this familiar country that Wikatani decided to go back to his roots.

In late September it was the turn of the Johanna men. Musa, terrified apparently by tales of the raiders awaiting them in the country ahead, announced that he and his nine colleagues were staying no longer. This left Livingstone with just 11 men. Despite all his anxieties, or perhaps secretly relieved by the departure of so many difficult men, his journal shows that, as in the past, he could happily enjoy the country, the villagers and the weather.

Unknown to him, Musa's departure sent ripples across the world. Keen to obtain payment rather than punishment from Livingstone's friends, the men returned to Zanzibar with a carefully rehearsed tale of an attack by raiders in which Livingstone and all the Nassick boys were killed and all their possessions stolen. So cleverly did they concoct this work of fiction that even Kirk was completely taken in. Long and sorrowful letters passed between him and Murchison, reports appeared in *The Times*, and all his friends started to grieve. But not everyone was convinced, and most sceptical of all was Lieut. E. D. Young, who had not only served with Livingstone on the Zambesi but also remembered how untrustworthy Musa had been. Backed by Murchison and the RGS, Young mounted an expedition to Lake Nyassa, eventually finding European items exchanged in villages beyond the alleged scene of the murder and meeting Africans whose descriptions of Livingstone were so vivid as to provide incontrovertible proof. Around the same time letters from Livingstone reached Zanzibar. The Consul there had wisely not paid Musa while his story remained unproven, and now the Sultan put him in irons for eight months.

After a happier autumn crossing Kirk's Range and continuing northwesterly, food again became so scarce that he dreamed of the meals he had so enjoyed at Newstead and his health started to deteriorate. When some men offered him dried elephant's meat, he commented 'It was high, and so were their prices.'[7] The year 1867 started badly. The boy carrying the chronometers so vital for calculating the longitude fell twice and the instruments were never reliably accurate again. His calculations were twenty miles out from that time on, and this affected him severely when he returned to the area just before his death.

A few days later, he suffered another loss. He had been accompanied for most of the journey by a little poodle-cross dog named Chitane. Full of personality, the dog had terrorized village dogs 'from their inability to distinguish his head from his tail' and raced up and down the line of march, his exuberance cheering everybody on. At a long river crossing of more than a mile, Livingstone forgot to help him and the little dog was drowned. His master grieved a long time for him, and the boys named the crossing Chitane's Water.

Early in December, he had taken on two additional porters who volunteered. In mid-January, these two men quite unexpectedly defected, taking with them many valuable supplies including the medicine chest. This was a devastating loss. 'I felt', wrote Livingstone 'as if I had now received the sentence of death, like poor Bishop Mackenzie.'[8] Although he lived another six years and eventually received new supplies, his death probably was attributable to the harm done to his health in the intervening years. Only a man of iron constitution and iron will would have survived in those conditions at all, though he may have been building up some immunity to malaria. He wrote to Zanzibar asking for supplies to be sent to await him at Ujiji on the east side of Lake Tanganyika: '. . . severe hunger. Don't think, please, that I make a moan over nothing but a little sharpness of appetite. I am a mere ruckle of bones.'[9] This from a man well known for understatement, particularly of his own problems.

Turning back, even to save his life, was not in his nature. On 1 April he reached Lake Tanganyika, though he did not at first know where he was. He lay seriously ill there for a month, cared for by Chuma and Susi, before travelling on in the company of the most famous of all the Arab slave traders, Tippu Tip, seeing at close quarters the suffering of the slaves, yet also profoundly grateful to Tippu Tip. After extensive delays, always a hazard of travelling with Arabs but in this case an opportunity for him to recuperate fully, and an earthquake which caused further damage to the chronometers, Livingstone eventually reached Lake Moero in November. He spent several months at Casembe, where the gates were decorated with human skulls and many of the inhabitants had lost ears or hands to the public executioner, indecisive himself as to whether he wished to go south to Lake Bangweolo or set out for Ujiji and his supplies before following the River Lualaba north. Constant fighting in the area made travel difficult. The Arabs too kept changing their minds and eventually he travelled 50 miles north of Casembe with them before resolving to travel south alone except for just four of his followers, the remaining five refusing to come. Soon after, he joined up with the Arab who became his closest friend, Bogharib, and they reached Lake Bangweolo on 18 July 1868. Unfortunately, due to various circumstances, his map of the lake was inaccurate since he was unaware that a large area of what he thought was lake was in fact only marsh.

With the New Year of 1869, he once again became seriously ill, suffering this time from pneumonia. Soon Bogharib was having him carried, delirious, in a litter. Eventually they reached the west side of Lake Tanganyika and after a month's delay crossed in a boat to Ujiji, his chosen base to which his supplies and mail were to be sent. He arrived to find virtually nothing there: everything had been stolen, and there were no letters. Of the 44 letters he now wrote, only two, those to the Sultan and to Kirk, ever reached their destinations. There was too much local suspicion of what he might report of happenings at Ujiji and elsewhere for anyone to wish to help him to communicate with the outside world.

He left Ujiji in July with Bogharib and set out for Manyuema to the north-west of Lake Tanganyika. It was unfortunate that they landed just north of a small river flowing out of the lake to the west. Had he seen this he would probably have realized that the river to the north of Lake Tanganyika flowed into that lake not out of it, and therefore the lake could not be a source of the Nile so that his only remaining hope was the Lualaba.

It was more than two years before he returned to Ujiji, two years during which he was frequently forced into long periods of inactivity either by health (tropical foot ulcers, which often proved fatal, were added to his list of intermittent complaints), by local wars or by the need to wait for Arab travelling companions to complete their negotiations. He spent seven full months at Bambarre. Yet even when things were at their worst he had an amazing capacity to observe, enjoy and record. Feeling ill and caught outside in the pouring rain, he would yet write a lyrical description of the activities of a tiny tree frog he had watched. He would also read for hours, the complete Bible four times through and a commentary on it, which he carried with him. This, together with earlier readings of Herodotus, first started him thinking about the legend that Moses had come to this part of Africa. He longed to find proof that there were remains of the city Moses possibly founded close by. He thought too, more and more obsessively, of the reference to four fountains which he convinced himself included the source of the Nile and, he believed, lay somewhere to the west of Lake Moero. These thoughts gradually acquired a mystical significance for him which overshadowed the last years of his life.

Eventually only Susi, Chuma and the Nassick boy Gardner remained with him. The three others who deserted included a boy called James. His decision proved unwise: soon after leaving Livingstone he was killed and eaten, for the local tribesmen were cannibals. When his murderer was subsequently caught, the villagers gathered in the hopes of being allowed to eat the murderer in retribution.

At last in February 1871 ten men reached him in Bambarre, sent to him by Kirk. They were mutinous and insisted that their orders were only to return with him to Zanzibar, but eventually, for a large pay rise, they consented to continue with him. More enjoyable company presented itself in the form of a pet baby monkey, which he described in a delightful passage of a letter to Agnes, but he was forced to leave it behind, in part because even without it he found himself constantly providing a spectacle to curious Africans who would embarrass him by staring at his every move. When he ate, his knife, fork and spoon caused endless mirth: he was forced to draw a circle in the dust around himself and persuade the audience at least to stay behind the line.

The next place where he stayed was Nyangwe, where he whiled away many happy hours wandering round the market, watching the people about their daily business, buying, selling, haggling, one man with a string of ten human jaw bones round his neck, swearing he had eaten the owners, little girls selling roasted white ants, all a happy diversion to the long wait for a canoe to continue his journey. The main Arab there at the time was a man named Dugumbe, rich, friendly and influential.

One morning Livingstone saw a group of Arabs from Dugumbe's party walking round the market carrying guns, haggling over the price of a fowl. Suddenly shots rang out. The three men started firing rapidly into the crowd. The terrified shoppers ran screaming to the creek, grabbing boats, paddling or swimming for the island. The Arabs continued to fire at them. Many others drowned in the confusion.

Dugumbe made a show of saving a few of them though Livingstone could not exonerate him in his own mind. The massacre was probably planned to instil terror in the neighbourhood in revenge for some earlier resistance. The Arab persuaded Livingstone not to shoot the murderers, as he first intended to do, and the explorer felt afterwards that this was a wise decision. Even the Arabs estimated that between 330 and 400 died that morning. The figure was probably considerably higher. Livingstone, in the vivid account he sent home, concluded that it gave him the impression of being in Hell. Sick at heart and unable longer to stomach the company of Arabs, even though the villagers asked him to stay and help to protect them, he left as soon as he was able, despite pleas from the Arabs to be allowed to help him, and started his lonely journey back to Ujiji.

His journey back was particularly dangerous, with raw nerves exposed everywhere, and on a single day he escaped an ambush which was temporarily unmanned but had a spear thrown at him from the bush which remarkably missed. A few minutes later a large tree, its roots destroyed by fire, came crashing down, landing where he had stood a second before.

At length he was back in Ujiji, hoping this time that supplies and letters awaited him. Once more all had been stolen, by the messenger who had brought them from Kirk and swore that he was convinced of Livingstone's death. The man showed no remorse and Livingstone knew that, almost bereft even of Arab support, his group was close to starvation with no means of replenishing supplies. On 24 October 1871 (it was actually rather later: his dates had become confused) he wrote in his diary: 'I felt in my destitution as if I were the man who went down from Jerusalem to Jericho and fell among thieves; but I could not hope for Priest, Levite or good Samaritan to come by on either side.'[10]

That was where he was wrong.

14
Ujiji and Unyanyembe: Scoop

The timing was remarkable. No wonder that Livingstone felt he led a charmed life, protected by Providence. Just four days later a volley of guns roared out in the distance.

> Susi came running at the top of his speed and gasped out, 'An Englishman! I see him!' and off he darted to meet him. The American flag at the head of a caravan told of the nationality of the stranger. Bales of goods, baths of tin, huge kettles, cooking pots, tents, &c., made me think 'This must be a luxurious traveller, and not one at his wits' end like me.'[1]

Susi and Chuma introduced themselves to the stranger, immaculate in a new flannel suit, his boots oiled, his helmet chalked, with a new puggaree folded around it. He pushed his way through the crowd of gawping villagers, past the curious Arab potentates towards the elderly white man.

> I noticed he was pale, looked wearied, had a grey beard, wore a bluish cap with a faded gold band round it, had on a red-sleeved waistcoat, and a pair of grey tweed trousers. I would have run to him, only I was a coward in the presence of such a mob – would have embraced him, only, he being an Englishman, I did not know how he would receive me; so I did what cowardice and false pride suggested was the best thing – walked deliberately to him, took off my hat, and said:
> 'Dr. Livingstone, I presume?'
> 'Yes,' said he, with a kind smile, lifting his cap slightly.
> I replace my hat on my head, and as he puts on his cap,

and we both grasp hands, and I then say aloud:
'I thank God, Doctor, I have been permitted to see you.'
He answered, 'I feel thankful that I am here to welcome you.'[2]

The friendship that developed between the two men during the months they spent together was remarkable. Henry Morton Stanley was not a man who made friends easily. The insecurity which bedevilled him meant that the slightest unfortunate word or gesture would always be interpreted by him as a sign of hostility or, worse still, mockery. One of his most loyal friends, Mrs Webb of Newstead, later told him that with strangers 'you are a perfect porcupine with all your quills out, and I can do nothing with you'.[3] He was hypersensitive, aggressive and conceited. Yet few men have achieved more from a start in life which made Livingstone by comparison appear to have been born with a silver spoon in his mouth. And no man travelled so far with Livingstone without an angry word passing between them.

John Rowlands, as he was christened, was rejected by his mother at birth. After the death of his grandfather, two uncles also spurned him and at the age of six he was sent to the workhouse. His time there reads in his own account like something out of Dickens. Indeed, it has been suggested that the resemblance between the schoolmaster James Francis and Wackford Squeers, between St Asaph's and Dotheboys Hall and between the manner in which John Rowlands and Nicholas Nickleby respectively departed from those establishments is not entire coincidence. Certainly Stanley, like many a good storyteller since, saw no reason to underplay the dramatic moments in his own life. But the fact remains that Francis ended his days in a lunatic asylum. Stanley's chilling account of the death of the best of his school friends and the secret nocturnal visit he paid to the mortuary to find the little body beneath the sheet horribly bruised and battered has been echoed too often since in the reports of civil servants on more recent equivalents of the workhouse to be disbelieved entirely.

He was then rejected by his remaining grandfather and everyone else to whom he turned for help. Eventually he found himself on board a ship crossing the Atlantic. In New Orleans for the first time fortune favoured the boy. He was befriended by a benevolent rich businessman whom he approached in his search for work. The businessman was so impressed by the boy's intelligence, initiative and capacity for hard work that he considered adopting him as his son, though the benefactor died before anything could be formalized. The businessman's name was Henry Stanley. He left the boy no money but he did give him his own name.

After a brief spell on a cotton plantation, terminated when he expressed his indignation at the treatment of the slaves, he enlisted in the Confederate army. Captured in battle, he took little persuading to exchange the appalling conditions of prison life for an equally brief spell in the Union forces. Discharged on grounds of health, he found work with a kindly farmer and eventually travelled back to Liverpool, only to be rejected once more by his mother. He went back to the sea as a sailor in the United States navy, but once again he eventually ran away.

A long succession of travels, adventures and jobs succeeded, but at some point Stanley realized that he was capable of earning his living with his pen. Soon his assignments ranged from interviews with Wild Bill Hickok and General Sherman to covering the British expedition to Abyssinia for the *New York Herald*, when he succeeded in telegraphing his story just before the cable broke so that no other reports could be sent.

Then he received a telegram summoning him to Paris to see James Gordon Bennett, son of the proprietor and himself the manager of the *New York Herald*. Stanley found him in bed in his hotel room.

'Who are you?' he asked.

'My name is Stanley!' I answered.

'Ah, yes! Sit down; I have important business on hand for you . . . Where do you think Livingstone is?'

'I really do not know, sir!'

'Do you think he is alive?'

'He may be, and he may not be!' I answered.

'Well, I think he is alive, and that he can be found, and I am going to send you to find him.'

'What!' said I, 'do you really think I can find Dr. Livingstone? Do you mean me to go to Central Africa?'

'Yes; I mean that you shall go, and find him wherever you may hear that he is, and to get what news you can of him, and perhaps' – delivering himself thoughtfully and deliberately – 'the old man may be in want: – take enough with you to help him should he require it. Of course you will act according to your own plans, and do what you think best – BUT FIND LIVINGSTONE!'

Stanley next raised the question of cost.

'Draw a thousand pounds now; and when you have gone through that, draw another thousand, and when that is spent, draw another thousand, and when you have finished that, draw another thousand, and so on; but, FIND LIVINGSTONE!'[4]

His next command superficially seems strange considering the priority attached to the search, for he told Stanley not to go straight to Central Africa but first to attend the opening of the Suez Canal, then cover the start of Baker's new expedition, then report from Egypt, Jerusalem, Constantinople, the Crimea, cross the Caspian Sea and go through Persia to India writing from Persepolis and Baghdad. Only then, if Livingstone was not already on his way back to Zanzibar, was he to find him, dead or alive. The 18-month intervening workload demonstrated Bennett's acute journalistic sense. For as they were talking in October 1869, Livingstone was not lost: the letters he wrote during his first stay at Ujiji were just arriving, and it may have been this which gave the newspaperman the idea. In around two years' time Livingstone would either be on his way home or lost, at least as far as the rest of the world was concerned, possibly dead or possibly in serious need. The timing was uncanny.

Throughout his life Stanley had needed to be hard to survive. His own account of his journey from Bagamoyo to Ujiji tells of repeated thrashings of villagers and expedition members, male and female, of his only two white companions attempting to shoot him and eventually being left at different points on the route never to be seen again and of active participation in Arab–African wars in which his men were killed.

This was not the manner in which Livingstone travelled. It was in part the discovery that matters could be handled so differently and yet with equal success which amazed and eventually entranced Stanley. He arrived, a brash journalist ready to file the greatest story of his career, and found perhaps the first man he had ever truly been able to admire who, and this was the part which truly astounded him, was genuinely pleased to see him, was grateful to him for coming and even seemed to like him.

Stanley had not been expecting this. In Zanzibar he had met Kirk and, in a manner which he hoped subtly concealed his real plan, told him a fictitious tale of an expedition he planned to make for his newspaper and asked with studied casualness what sort of reaction he was likely to meet with in the unlikely event of encountering Livingstone.

Kirk had not taken to the loud-mouthed young journalist and replied that Livingstone would 'put a hundred miles of swamp in a very short time between himself and [any pursuers]'.[5] This conversation was to have unfortunate repercussions later. For the moment, it accounted in part for Stanley's nerves when he first met Livingstone, and for the famous words about which he was to be so mocked, unreasonably, for the rest of his life. It also meant that when his dread of being rebuffed by Livingstone proved unfounded his relief and gratitude were unbounded.

The older man, lonely, longing for intelligent European company and for news of events in the outside world during the long years of his solitary travelling, as well as for stores and above all letters, was delighted with his visitor who brought him all these things. Livingstone longed passionately too for the company of his own children and it was inevitable that he should find in Stanley a substitute. This was a feeling which Stanley, whose whole life had been a desperate search for a father figure who would not reject him, could fully reciprocate.

Livingstone's long years of solitude had stripped him of his normal worldly cynicism. He was touchingly grateful to Gordon Bennett, seemingly unaware of the ulterior motives behind his saviour's arrival, and Stanley, embarrassed, did his best to pass over this aspect.

On one issue Livingstone was adamant. He would do anything he could to help his new young friend, including writing letters to Gordon Bennett for the latter to publish which were such a mixture of Livingstone's style and that recommended by the reporter as likely to appeal to the readers of his somewhat sensational newspaper that their authenticity was later to be questioned. But he would not contemplate a return to England. No inducement, neither the desire to see his family nor even the need for a new set of false teeth, would make him change his mind. He felt that he had not yet achieved any of the objectives for which he had come out and any return at this stage would be an admission of failure. As for his family, he recorded in his journal:

> My daughter Agnes says, 'Much as I wish you to come home, I had rather that you finished your work to your own satisfaction, than return merely to gratify me.' Rightly and nobly said, my

darling Nannie; vanity whispers pretty loudly, 'She is a chip of the old block.' My blessings on her and all the rest.[6]

The two men agreed instead that there was one important geographical question which needed resolving and they could investigate together. They made a joint expedition, at Stanley's expense, to the north of Lake Tanganyika where they established that the river at that end flowed into not out of the Lake. This meant that all hopes of a southern source for the Nile now rested on the Lualaba. Livingstone by this stage had come to expect this: indeed, he frequently confided to his journal his dread that the Lualaba would ultimately prove to be the source of the Congo and not of the Nile.

The combined expedition was a success. It was a revelation to Stanley to learn that brutal ways of dealing with Africans were neither necessary nor even particularly effective. So devoted had he become to Livingstone that it required only a glance from the older man to quell his violent reactions. When tribesmen stoned them, 'here again my hand was stayed from planting a couple of good shots, as a warning to them in future from molesting strangers, by the mere presence of the Doctor who, as I thought, if it were actually necessary, would not hesitate to give the word.' Time and again, Stanley watched astounded as Livingstone quietly talked to a belligerent group of drunken tribesmen, or resolved a dispute between Stanley and his cook, always achieving his aim. '"You bad fellow. You very wicked fellow. You blockhead. You fool of a man" – were the strongest terms he employed, where others would have clubbed or clouted, or banned and blasted. His manner was that of a cool, wise old man, who felt offended and looked grave.' Livingstone knew too precisely how to put Stanley himself in his place.

'What can he be thinking about?' I used to wonder, and once I ventured to break the silence with, 'A penny for your thoughts, Doctor.'
'They are not worth it, my young friend, and let me suggest that, if I had any, possibly I should wish to keep them.'
After which I invariably let him alone when in this mood.

Stanley, both personally and professionally, wanted to think of Livingstone as a saint and all his publications portray him in this light. Only his private journal reveals that the months spent in the older man's company did reveal certain flaws to him. 'I felt the faintest fear that his strong nature was opposed to forgiveness, and that he was not so perfect as at first blush of friendship I thought him'[7] is how he expressed it. For Livingstone in the last years of his life had forgiven and forgotten nothing. His mind was constantly occupied with all his old grievances and he would reiterate to himself, and sometimes, in his letters, to his friends, the ways in which he had been badly treated, by the government and Russell in particular (though he was somewhat mollified when he found from the post Stanley brought him that the Treasury had decided to allocate £1000 for his relief and pay him a salary), by the LMS, by the members of the Zambesi expedition, by the RGS and so on.

Most of this was ancient history to Stanley, who could listen impartially and reflect that it was one of his hero's few failings to keep on remembering every grievance. There was just one man who was known to both of them: John Kirk. While Kirk had had considerable reservations about his leader at the end of the Zambesi expedition, the two men had communicated cordially ever since, and, together with Waller in England, they were making a forceful coalition on the slavery issue. Admittedly, Livingstone had not been happy with the way in which the men Kirk sent to help him had tried to insist that he should return to Zanzibar, and the supply of his provisions at Ujiji had been extremely unsatisfactory, but up to this time he had realized the difficulties and not held Kirk personally responsible.

Kirk and Stanley had jarred on each other from their first meeting. Unfortunately, Stanley was unable to resist inflaming Livingstone against his old ally. All the problems which had beset Livingstone could be blamed on Kirk, for after all Stanley had succeeded in bringing him all that he needed. The fact that Kirk was fully employed at Zanzibar and had given such help as he could to Livingstone out of the goodness of his heart and his own free time, whereas Stanley was being paid to find and help Livingstone before all else, was forgotten. The only way to ensure that goods or men travelled intact and were delivered in perfect condition was to escort them personally. This it was possible for Stanley and impossible for Kirk to do. Once Livingstone had listened to Stanley, he wrote bitterly to Kirk, reproaching him for his many perceived failures. Stanley, on his return to England, broadcast his own version of Kirk's behaviour to all who would listen. At one banquet, the *Telegraph* reported, 'he spoke in very severe terms of Dr. Kirk, whom, he said, he had a mission from Livingstone to describe as a "traitor."'[8]

Everyone who knew Kirk and Livingstone was appalled. Frere wrote a report exonerating Kirk. Waller in particular realized that this breach jeopardized all the work that was being done on the Slave Trade. He wrote Livingstone a very strong letter which, perhaps fortunately, never reached him. The same message was conveyed to him by his son Oswell and he wrote letters making it clear that he had never intended personal criticism of Kirk. Stanley eventually realized that, while some minor criticisms of Kirk might have been valid, he had overstepped the mark. In subsequent editions of his book *How I Found Livingstone* the references to Kirk were removed.

During their travels together Stanley became seriously ill and Livingstone nursed him back to health. Once again Stanley was appreciative of a kindness he had never previously known: he wrote that his days seemed to have been spent in an Elysian field.

They agreed to continue beyond Ujiji together as far as Unyanyembe (now Tabora) where stores were waiting for both of them, although Livingstone's once again were somewhat depleted, this time by white ants. However, Stanley provided him with sufficient to last him for four years and he was pleased also to find that Agnes had sent him some shirts and Waller some boots.

The date 13 March 1872, the last night before Stanley's departure, was an emotional occasion. Even the usually detached Livingstone expressed his full gratitude and tried to encourage Stanley to stay until after the imminent rains, despite knowing that the men he needed to continue with him would not be despatched from Zanzibar until Stanley had returned there. Stanley, always an emotional man despite his hard exterior, wept bitterly that night and as they parted.

On the journey back, the man carrying on his head the box containing Livingstone's letters and journals fell while crossing a river. Stanley, without the gentle frown to remind him, 'shouted to him, with a loaded revolver pointed at his head, "Look out! Drop that box, and I'll shoot you."'

In Zanzibar, Stanley found that an expedition, financed by the RGS after the death of Murchison in October, was coming to relieve Livingstone. Lieutenant Dawson was in charge, with three other white men, Lieutenant Henn, the Reverend Charles New and young Oswell Livingstone. Hearing Stanley's news, the decision was taken to abandon it, a decision Stanley deplored, though Oswell was still keen to continue and see his father. However, the country was seriously flooded and Oswell in poor health and Kirk, probably wisely, persuaded him to abandon his quest. Oswell himself later regretted this and he received considerable criticism, much of it stirred up by Stanley. Livingstone himself, waiting impatiently at Unyanyembe from March to August for his men to come, once more overreacted and believed that Oswell had only been interested in finding him to persuade him to come home for the financial benefit of the rest of the family.

Stanley's story was the sensational scoop he had hoped, the press went wild and the public remembered its forgotten hero and celebrated the man who had found him. But then doubts started to arise. The English were mostly merely sad that help had reached him under the Stars and Stripes rather than the Union Jack, but for those who felt, with or without cause, that perhaps they should have done something themselves, guilt mingled with an uneasy jealousy. The quiet professionals were alienated by the tone of the brash journalist. Some people took it further and began to suggest that the whole business was a hoax.

Livingstone's friends were amazed. Mr and Mrs Webb, for example, had read their letters avidly, wondering at the explorer's recollection of every detail, the names of their animals and similar details which Stanley could not possibly have known. Sometimes he undoubtedly imagined or exaggerated insults or mockery where there was no malicious intention. Many claimed that this was the case when he was invited to speak at Brighton but walked out in the middle because he was being laughed at. Yet on that occasion both Cotton Oswell and Mr and Mrs Webb, who had not then even met Stanley, felt that his treatment had been disgraceful.

Livingstone no doubt would have felt had he ever known about it that the most important thing Stanley did after his return was to deliver Livingstone's long report on the massacre at Nyangwe at a critical moment. The House of Commons Select Committee on the East African slave trade had reported in the previous year recommending total abolition of the sea-borne trade. The government had yet to decide how to act. Livingstone's paper ensured that the recommendation of the Select Committee was accepted. The consequent threat of a naval blockade enabled Sir Bartle Frere to sign a treaty with the Sultan of Zanzibar.

Livingstone was never concerned about Stanley's commercial approach. When he heard people saying that Stanley would make his fortune out of him, he remarked, 'He is heartily welcome, for it is a great deal more than I could ever make out of myself.'[9]

15
To Chitambo's Village: the Dying Man

Livingstone found the months at Unyanyembe 'wearisome waiting', as he repeatedly wrote in his journal. He read much, thought much, sometimes of God, sometimes of his hopes and plans, sometimes bitter thoughts of all those who he believed had treated him badly – his sisters as well as his son he was convinced were interested only in his money – and wrote endlessly. Not only did he write long letters to almost all his regular correspondents but he also used the unusual amount of spare time for some superb passages on all that he saw around him. Whether he is describing the women pounding rice with pestles and mortars, the children playing at imitations of their parents' work or the activities of a pair of whydah birds and their eight young fledglings, he has the power to create a vivid, delightful picture, conveying all the pleasure he himself derived from observing what was going on. His grief, too, comes through powerfully when he learnt in a letter of the death of 'the best friend I ever had', Sir Roderick Murchison. It was at this time that he wrote the words, included in a letter for the *New York Herald*, which were eventually to be quoted, or rather misquoted, on his tombstone. 'All I can say in my loneliness is, may Heaven's rich blessing come down on everyone – American, English, Turk – who will help to heal this Open Sore of the World.' In Westminster Abbey 'solitude' is substituted for 'loneliness'. Those words were written on 1 May 1872, precisely a year before his death. His priorities remained unaltered: he repeated many times that the suppression of slavery was infinitely more important than all the sources of the Nile together.

The first of the men Stanley sent did not reach him until 9 August, the remainder following on the 14th, weeks after he had optimistically expected them. But Stanley had done him well in his selection. There were 57 in all, including 20 members of Stanley's own party and six Nassick boys, among whom were John and Jacob Wainwright, who had been taken on by the Relief Expedition. He still retained his five most loyal supporters: Susi, Chuma, Amoda and two original Nassick boys, Gardner and Mabruki, and some of their wives. There were also cattle, goats and two donkeys.

They were a better group that those who had left Mikidani with him, but his rest and perhaps the journey with Stanley had also revived his flagging talents of leadership. Although he was now much weaker physically, there was no longer any question as to who was in control. When the Nassick boys lost the best milking cow, they were punished. This was indeed a grave misfortune, for milk was vital for Livingstone's health and already a large container of powdered milk had been accidentally left behind. Two men who behaved badly he chastised personally, though with light blows rather than resorting to the punitive slave collar Stanley had so thoughtfully included among his goods. Although the best donkey died partly as a result of bad treatment, such episodes were rare on this journey, unlike 1866. He was firm too with tribesmen who made unreasonably excessive demands. Eventually he paid his own men the ultimate compliment in a letter to Maclear: 'They have behaved as well as Makololo. I cannot award them higher praise, though they have not the courage of that brave, kind-hearted people.'[1]

But conditions deteriorated fast, as did Livingstone's health. The country through which they were travelling was flooded, the weather cold and wet and Livingstone's constant anal haemorrhages meant that he was slowly bleeding to death. Food too was scarce. As they came closer to Lake Bangweolo he became convinced that the guides were intentionally leading them astray, unaware that his own maps were at fault, for they were made when the chronometers were seriously damaged and when he failed to obtain an accurate impression of the dimensions of the lake or to realize that much of what he believed to be water was in fact marshland. Even so he could write occasional lyrical passages inspired by the beauty of the wild flowers. But now he had sometimes to be carried by his men, no easy task for them. He described how 'the main stream came up to Susi's mouth, and wetted my seat and legs'.[2] A few days later he was attacked by an army of red ants: 'the larger ones swarmed over the foot and bit furiously, and made the blood start out. I then went out of the tent, and my whole person was instantly covered as close as small-pox . . . on a patient. Grass fires were lighted, and my men picked some off my limbs and tried to save me.' The attack lasted all night, yet Livingstone recorded a detailed scientific description of the activities of the ants.

There were battles too with a chief named Matipa who created endless delays. Livingstone spent the time in writing what were to be his last batch of letters, which were full of plans for his return to England, showing no presentiment of his coming death, and that to Waller was in the teasing style he always adopted with him. On 19 March, his 60th birthday, he lost patience with Matipa and fired a shot through his roof, which speeded matters up.

Despite his suffering, he still had eyes and ears for the world around him. In early April 'a lion had wandered into this world of water and ant-hills, and roared night and morning, as if very much disgusted: we could sympathise with him!' A few days later: 'the fish-eagle lifts up his remarkable voice . . . once heard, his weird, unearthly voice can never be forgotten – it sticks to one through life . . . It seems as if he were calling to someone in the other world.' Perhaps after all he knew what lay before him.

Weak, ill and in intense pain as he was, he retained his old habit of understatement. 'It is not all pleasure, this exploration,' he wrote. For a few days at the end he was unable to walk or sit on his donkey but insisted on going on, so they made a litter to carry him. He asked how much remained to pay for the journey home: they thought he was considering turning, but more likely he was thinking of how his men would manage without him. The final entry in his journal was made on 27 April, the 11th anniversary of Mary's death. 'Knocked up quite and remain – recover – sent to buy milch goats. We are on the banks of R. Molilamo.'

They carried him, in acute agony, to the village of Chitambo and built a grass hut for him there. On the 30th the chief came to visit him but he could not speak. That night Susi helped him take some calomel from his medicine chest before leaving him with a young boy named Majwara to watch. At 4 a.m. on 1 May the boy woke Susi. He had slept himself and found the 'master' unmoved, kneeling in an attitude of prayer 'by the side of his bed, his body stretched forward, his head buried in his hands upon the pillow'. He had been dead for some time.

On 5 June John Kirk and the Sultan of Zanzibar signed the Treaty prohibiting the export of slaves and the great slave market at Zanzibar was closed for ever.

16
From Africa to Westminster Abbey: Venerated Leader

Susi and Chuma never hesitated. They were determined to take him back to Zanzibar. When Chitambo, who realized what had happened although they had attempted to conceal the death because of the superstitious African dread of a corpse, heard, he said: '"Why not bury him here?" But Susi replied, "No, no – very big man."'[1]

Whether their decision was in fact based on an appreciation of his greatness and a feeling that dead men should be buried in their home countries, or whether, remembering Musa, they thought more of their own responsibility for the dead man and his possessions and papers is not clear. The suggestion that Livingstone himself had asked them to do this seems unlikely in the light of his journal entry in June 1868 when, commenting on a native grave, he wrote 'This is the sort of grave I should prefer: to lie in the still, still forest and no hand ever disturb my bones,' and when Mary died he had written, 'I have often wished that it might be in some far-off still deep forest, where I might sleep sweetly till the resurrection morn, when the trump of God will make all start up into glorious and active second existence.' He had, though, always emphasized the importance of taking his papers back to English hands. Perhaps they believed that if they returned without him they would be accused of desertion, though what they decided to do provided no proof that they had not murdered their leader. Whatever the motives, the decision seems to have been unanimous, despite the difficulties they must all have anticipated of travelling across Africa with a dead body. Nor was there any dispute as to who would now lead the party. The authority of Chuma and Susi was accepted unquestioningly.

First Jacob Wainwright, the most literate of the party, was asked to make an inventory of Livingstone's possessions, with all the men present so that all shared the responsibility. Wainwright did this in Livingstone's notebook.

Relieved by the helpful reaction of Chitambo, who had heard Livingstone was dead because two of the men talked in the village but who simply commented that death often happened to strangers in their journeys, they now had time and space to prepare the corpse for the return. One of the men had some knowledge of embalming from his previous employment with a doctor. After a day of lamentations, the body was moved to a specially built hut away from the village. The embalmer then removed the heart and viscera, noting that there was a clot of coagulated blood as large as a man's hand in his left side, which must have caused him excruciating pain. The parts removed were buried in a tin box while Jacob Wainwright read the burial service from the prayer book then engraved Livingstone's name and the date of the burial on the tree. Using salt and brandy, the only materials they had available, they embalmed the body to the best of their ability and exposed it to the sun for 14 days. The legs were then bent up and the body wrapped in calico, then bark and sailcloth and coated with tar. Fixed to a pole, it could be carried inconspicuously by two men.

In just five months the procession marched to Unyanyembe. They marched in grand style, so that people would not realize they were carrying a corpse, with Majwara at the front beating a drum when appropriate and the Union Jack and the scarlet flag of the Sultan of Zanzibar flying. There were delays at the start when they were affected by a mysterious illness. Livingstone's donkey was killed by a lion. Once they became embroiled in a fight with drunken villagers, two of whom were shot. Ten of the party died on the way of different causes.

In the previous year, the RGS, anxious to avoid any further charges of endangering a British hero's life, had sent out two separate rescue expeditions. One, financed by James Young, had gone to the mouth of the Congo on the assumption that that was where Livingstone might emerge if he followed the Lualaba to the sea. This was eventually recalled. The other was led by Lieutenant Cameron accompanied by Livingstone's nephew young Robert Moffat and two other men named Dillon and Murphy. Tragically Moffat died of fever in May. The others, with Cameron and Dillon also suffering severely from fever, met Susi and Chuma at Unyanyembe.

Cameron's advice to them was to bury the body forthwith. They ignored this but were unable to prevent the young officer taking possession of a number of Livingstone's geographical instruments for his party's own use. He then proceeded to Ujiji to collect a box of papers belonging to Livingstone. The other two Englishmen joined Susi's party, though they ended by making separate arrangements as Susi strictly adhered to Livingstone's wise custom of making a very early start each morning and this practice proved unacceptable to Murphy. Dillon was in no state to consider any such paltry issues. Unutterably depressed by his illness, he shot himself.

In the same place, for the first time on their long journey, superstitious objections were raised about the corpse being carried through. Equal now to any such emergency, the men pretended that they had agreed to bury it. The original packaging was secretly disposed of and the body repacked to resemble ordinary goods.

When they reached Zanzibar, Kirk was away on leave. His deputy, Captain Prideaux, was unable to decide on the most appropriate action. He arranged for the body to be shipped home but no money was available to him for such unexpected contingencies. Livingstone's funds had been exhausted by the journey. Prideaux finally paid off the men from his own pocket, and the fact that he was not refunded for several years justified his parsimony. There was no one else there to pay for a passage to England for Susi or Chuma, and although the RGS later struck a commemorative medal for all members of the expedition, most of them could not by then be traced. Susi and Chuma did come to England, for as soon as James Young heard what had happened he paid their fares, but by then it was too late for them to attend the funeral.

Only one of the Africans did attend. Jacob Wainwright, as a Nassick boy, was selected by the Church Missionary Society, which ran Nassick, to become the token African at the service. The Society paid for him to accompany the body home and used him afterwards for publicity purposes.

The coffin in which the body now lay was received in Southampton on 15 April 1874 with all the pomp and ceremony of a Victorian state funeral. The coffin, draped in a Union Jack, was borne ashore to the strains of a band playing the Dead March from Saul. Next it was necessary for the body to be positively identified as Livingstone's, a duty which fell on some of his closest friends, including his father-in-law, Oswell, Waller, Kirk and Webb as well as the doctors. The examination as well as the lying in state took place at the Royal

Geographical Society. A junior doctor who assisted Sir William Fergusson told many years later how the coffin was opened to reveal a parcel just four feet long surrounded with sawdust and packed with a horse rug. The leg bones had been removed and tucked inside the body,[2] presumably when the pretended burial had taken place, in a manner which impressed Sir William. There was no difficulty over a positive identification, for the ununited fracture of the arm from the attack by the lion, which Sir William had examined for Livingstone when he was in London, could be clearly seen. Webb found the whole experience shattering as both the face and features were perfectly recognizable.[3]

Livingstone's bones now lie, not in the quiet forest he dreamed of, but in the centre of the main aisle in Westminster Abbey, in front of the Tomb of the Unknown Soldier. The eight pall-bearers at the funeral on 18 April were Cotton Oswell, who had journeyed so far with him, Webb, his host at Newstead, Steele, his first friend among the big game hunters who had since had a distinguished military career, Waller, who first met him on the Zambesi expedition, Kirk, Stanley, Lieutenant E. D. ('Gunner') Young who had led the expedition to prove he had not been murdered and the Nassick boy Jacob Wainwright. Livingstone's two sons and Moffat walked in front. Behind came a young black boy named Kalulu who was Stanley's protégé and, incongruously, Roger Price, surviving missionary to the Makololo, so much abused by Livingstone.

Livingstone's sisters were there: it was the first time they had been to England. Anna Mary, who on her own initiative had started up a correspondence with Hans Christian Andersen, told him that the vergers had not seen so many people in the Abbey since the funeral of the Prince Consort. Those who were there never forgot the crowds filling the Abbey and lining the streets, nor how moving the service was. The hymn 'O God of Bethel' was sung and the preacher commented that the Abbey was not only his last resting place but also his first.

Tributes poured in. Florence Nightingale told Agnes that he was the greatest man of his generation, Lord Curzon declared: 'As a missionary he was the sincere and zealous servant of God. As an explorer he was the indefatigable servant of Science. As a denouncer of the slave trade he was the fiery servant of humanity.'

The task of editing his final papers eventually fell to Waller, who was so cautious of Livingstone's reputation that he pruned much which was revealing if not entirely flattering. Tom Livingstone tried to do the job himself, but was forced to admit that the task was beyond his capabilities. Cotton Oswell had been asked first, but declined, telling Agnes in a gentle, affectionate letter that he did not feel he was fit for it, and that John Murray the publisher had made him feel it would be impertinent to do so.

When Susi and Chuma came to England they met all Livingstone's friends and family and spent long hours at Newstead and elsewhere helping with the editing of the papers and telling all that they knew, including making models of the hut in which Livingstone had died. Both made themselves extremely popular, unlike Jacob Wainwright, who appeared to be more interested in alcohol and women and to have become thoroughly spoilt by all the attention thrust upon him and the adulation of the Church Missionary Society for their fund raiser.

17
From Blantyre to Westminster Abbey: neither Saint nor Failure

Livingstone's funeral brought popular feeling for the great British Victorian hero to fever pitch. The 'missionary, traveller (and) philanthropist' had, in the words of his tombstone in Westminster Abbey, been 'brought by faithful hands over land and sea . . . for 30 years his life was spent in an unwearied effort to evangelise the native races, to explore the undiscovered secrets, to abolish the desolating slave trade of Central Africa.' The feeling in the country was comparable to that for Winston Churchill at the time of his death.

Livingstone had become the national hero in 1856 when he returned to England after his crossing of the African continent, embodying in the popular mind all the virtues most highly esteemed at the time. He was brave, determined, had achieved everything by self-help (Samuel Smiles used him as the prime example for his book on that subject); he was an intelligent scientific thinker, he had been to places never reached by white man before. He was also, as far as the public was concerned, a communicator. He brought back thrilling tales of encounters with lions and of the biggest, most spectacular waterfall in the world, which he named after his Queen. Above all he had a burning determination to help the underdog, in this case the African at risk of being enslaved.

Admittedly, the public had forgotten about him for some years, even showing only limited enthusiasm when last he came to England in 1864. There had been some questions asked over the way in which he had handled his expedition to the Zambesi, and he had been blamed when other white men, attempting to follow in his footsteps and no doubt lacking the skills he so conspicuously displayed, unfortunately died. By 1874 that all seemed a very long time ago.

After that, once again he had been forgotten, not, as it seemed to the public, by the public but by those, members of the Royal Geographical Society and of the government, who should have ensured that all was well with him and given him the support he so eminently deserved. Only the American press had been there to rescue him. Shameful as this reflection was on the irresponsibility of the British establishment, this had somehow enabled Stanley to become almost a popular British hero himself, albeit a somewhat farcical one, largely because of those four unfortunate, unforgettable words. More important, it meant that, since Stanley was a capable journalist, the image he chose to project was permanently latched onto the public mind.

Stanley wrote that 'Livingstone's was a character that I venerated, that called forth all my enthusiasm, that evoked nothing but sincerest admiration.'[1] A saintly figure for a hero made his story all the better, but he also happened to believe it. This was partly because, having found in Livingstone the father figure he had been searching for all his life, Stanley wished to preserve his perfect image to himself as well as to have the best possible story to tell the world. Consciously or unconsciously, he contrived to forget all the indications which emerged during the time they spent together of imperfections of character. He confined any comments on these to his diary and published nothing which did not reflect to Livingstone's credit. He started by telling of the unfavourable reports he had had before he met the man:

> I was led to believe that Livingstone possessed a splenetic, misanthropic temper; some have said that he is garrulous, that he is demented; that he has utterly changed from the David Livingstone whom people knew as the reverend missionary; that he takes no notes or observations but such as those which no other person could read but himself; and it was reported, before I proceeded to Central Africa, that he was married to an African princess.
>
> I respectfully beg to differ with all and each of the above statements. I grant he is not an angel, but he approaches to that being as near as the nature of a living man will allow.

Stanley goes on to describe him as humble-souled and to speak of his 'many amiable traits. His gentleness never forsakes him; his hopefulness never deserts him.' He writes too of 'innumerable jokes and pleasant anecdotes . . . joviality, humor, and abundant animal spirits' and his 'wonderfully retentive memory' (he could recite reams of poetry by heart despite the long separation from books) and of his 'quiet, practical religion'.

Stanley was not the first, nor the last, to build up Livingstone's image through a combination of genuine admiration and ulterior motives. The process had started with Tidman on behalf of the London Missionary Society and Murchison for the Royal Geographical Society. Tidman and his colleagues realized early in Livingstone's career that he was not as other missionaries, and that while this would inevitably create enormous problems there were benefits to be reaped. As early as 1852, when Mary and the children were leaving Cape Town, Tidman wrote asking that 'in order to give additional attractions to your reports, we would suggest that you keep a regular journal recording any remarkable events, notices of the manners & customs of the different tribes, the natural history of the country, & other topics';[2] already Tidman was assessing the public relations potential. Tidman was delighted to receive the RGS Gold Medal on Livingstone's behalf and longed to see him tour the country, telling of his great deeds while avoiding too much discussion of the rate at which African converts were made and allowing an LMS collecting box to be rattled close to his elbow. Livingstone declined to take any part in such a performance but Tidman and his colleagues did all they could to publicize his achievements.

For Murchison and his Society, the RGS, just as for Tidman and his LMS, publicity was important in the quest for more members. While Tidman needed to have Livingstone portrayed as a successful missionary, Murchison needed to have him widely admired and talked about as a successful explorer. Both men did their utmost on his return to England after crossing Africa to ensure that he received as many honours and invitations to speak as possible.

For these three men, Tidman, Murchison and Stanley, the decision to promote Livingstone was deliberately taken with a specific aim in view, but two of the three also admired him deeply and believed in principle in all that they said and wrote about his qualities and achievements, even if they took care not to broadcast so widely any failings they perceived in him. Had they had no reason for wishing to promote his image, as close personal friends they would not in any case have publicly stressed his shortcomings. Tidman did not share their affection, nor probably their admiration, for

Livingstone. Ultimately such responsibility as Livingstone bore for the disastrous mission to the Makololo proved professionally damaging to Tidman. He probably regretted any trouble he had taken to boost Livingstone's image but in any event his contribution was a small one.

The next of Livingstone's genuine admirers to play a positive role in the creation of the Livingstone legend in order to further his own agenda was Horace Waller in his editing of Livingstone's *Last Journals*. His object in so doing was one which would have met with more whole-hearted support from Livingstone than any other. Waller's first priority was the abolition of the slave trade.

Waller had been on the Zambesi with Livingstone, so had known him well and become a close friend at the time in his life when Livingstone was making enemies considerably faster than he was making friends. Waller went out as one of the younger members of the Universities' Mission: he was a contemporary of Kirk. He shared Livingstone's disgust at Bishop Tozer's decision to retreat from the mission and was responsible for rescuing the women and children left without protection as a result. Livingstone's letters to him were full of light-hearted, teasing banter: he once jokingly referred to Waller as a Tozerite, knowing full well how little love was lost between the two men. Their relationship was sufficiently good for Livingstone, unusually, to be prepared to apologize to Waller for a disagreement which he conceded was his own fault. After Young's expedition to establish that Livingstone had not been murdered, Waller was well aware of the benefit to the anti-slavery campaign in having Livingstone's name constantly before the public, and wrote delightedly to tell him that the Geographical Society might at that time be called the Livingstone Society. He told him 'I have not missed many opportunities of keeping the matter open & your name before the Public.'[3]

The question of who should edit the last journals was contentious. Apart from Cotton Oswell, the main contenders were Stanley, who was not available at the relevant time, Waller and Tom Livingstone. Although the latter finally admitted that he was not capable of the task, he did not relinquish the undertaking without considerable reluctance, making life difficult for Waller. Waller once wrote of Livingstone: 'he's the bravest man I ever saw or ever expect to see . . . so I always stick up for him tho' I confess with more tact in dealing with his companions he might make a much greater and more lasting mark.'[4] It was this want of tact he was determined to overcome in his editorial task. He was resolved so far as was possible to remove anything at all contentious from the finished product.

It is impossible at this distance in time to assess the rights and wrongs of the disputes in which Livingstone was involved in the last years of his life. His rancour against Kirk was certainly excessive against a man as balanced, sensible, helpful and reasonable as Kirk showed himself to be in all his other dealings. Livingstone when depressed at this time was very given to nursing any grievance that he could recall or imagine, and in the case of Kirk there seems little doubt that Stanley fanned the flames. On the other hand Agnes, who inherited so much from her father but did not in general share his unreasoned aggression, was bitter with Kirk, considering that he had not exerted himself for her father as he should have done. Kirk himself believed that peace was made between him and his old friend before the latter's death: in his copy of the *Last Journals* he wrote in pencil: '26th June, friendly letter from Livingstone. This shews he had received the Quinine from me.'[5] Whatever the rights and wrongs of the matter, Waller was determined to smooth all such elements of dispute out of the material to be published. It is equally difficult to know whether any of the hard feelings Livingstone developed for his son Oswell were justified: neither Oswell nor Tom appear to have been easy men to deal with. But any sharply critical comments from Livingstone, whether about his family or anyone else, disturbed the image of the gentle, saintly old man so dear to Waller's heart and was expunged if possible.

Waller longed also to portray Livingstone's relationships with the Africans in his team as perfect examples of a benign and gentle master deeply loved by his devoted followers: he was so successful that this image of Chuma and Susi survives after one and a quarter centuries. In fact, Chuma and Susi continued to be troublesome long after 1868, when both were smoking marijuana and womanizing to such a degree that Livingstone was forced to fire a pistol at Susi, intentionally missing him, to overcome his obstinacy. In 1871 Livingstone recorded that two of the other men, having been bundled out of the camp, impudently followed him till he told them to be off 'or I would certainly shoot them'.[6] Waller omitted these words. When the book was reviewed in *The Times*, the reviewer was impressed with Livingstone's 'simple, faithful and noble character' and his 'sweetness and serenity'.[7] Waller had achieved his objective.

Livingstone's first biographer, W. G. Blaikie, was more than happy to follow the route marked out by Waller. Blaikie declared in his Preface that Livingstone's 'modesty led him to say little in [his own books] of himself, and those who knew him best feel that little is known of the strength of his affections, the depth and purity of his devotion, or the intensity of his aspirations as a Christian missionary.'[8] Alice Spinner of Newstead, who appreciated the light-hearted side of Livingstone's character, points out that Blaikie did not know Livingstone personally but was determined to fit him into a preconceived ideal, omitting anyone or anything he considered 'wanting in earnestness'.[9] Many of Livingstone's earlier biographers persisted in adhering to the pious, saintly theme.

A century after Livingstone's death the tendency to hagiography was reversed. Tim Jeal's biography opened with the declaration that Livingstone

> appears to have failed in all he most wished to achieve. He failed as a conventional missionary, making but one convert, who subsequently lapsed. He failed as the promoter of other men's missionary efforts (the two missions that went to Africa at his behest ended in fiasco and heavy loss of life). . . . failure as a husband and a father, failure to persuade the British government to advance into Africa.

Jeal concludes too that the Portuguese had probably reached most of the places he is alleged to have discovered before him and that the Zambesi expedition was disastrous.

While Jeal's final chapter gives a more balanced assessment of his achievements and the long-term consequences for Africa of his thinking, the overall impression of his book is that of failure as conveyed in the opening pages. Livingstone's alleged failure as a missionary is emphasized the more by the chapter heading 'The Only Convert'. Even Seaver, whose much more sympathetic account was published in 1957, 16 years before Jeal's, concludes that at the time of his death 'it must have seemed that all he had striven for had been failure', as a husband, a father, a missionary, a geographer and a liberator. 'It is true,' Seaver adds, 'that he accomplished far more by his death than by his life.'

Jeal's catalogue of failures does make one important modification. Livingstone did indeed fail as a *conventional* missionary. He decided early in his career that the conventional approach was certainly not for him and perhaps was not the right way forward at all. Conventional missionaries established themselves in a small native community and remained there sometimes for the rest of their lives, establishing a church and preaching Christianity. Converts were supposed only to be admitted to the Church when they had an understanding and acceptance of the basic tenets of Christianity and were living what the missionaries would accept as a Christian life. In some ways much more was asked of a convert than of a parishioner in an English village, even without taking into account the different moral principles on which each had been reared. Livingstone had a deeper sympathy than any of the other missionaries with the Africans for whom embracing Christianity meant abandoning much which they had been brought up to believe was right. Sechele, for example, was seriously worried, and with reason, that if he put away any of the wives whom he had married quite legitimately within the terms of his own culture, considerable suffering would be caused to the wife thus rejected. Yet, when he returned to one of his former wives, he was regarded as a lapsed convert, branding both himself and Livingstone who had converted him with failure. Sechele in fact lived his final years in full church membership: his 'lapse' was only temporary. Livingstone accepted that this was the rule for 'counting' conversions, but he had reservations concerning the system, which would be shared by many modern Christians. Other principles of Victorian Christianity conflicted with correct behaviour within the social structure of an African tribe. Much which appeared sinful to the missionaries was seen in an altogether different light by the tribesmen. Even ways of expressing themselves which were merely figurative to the Africans and well understood between them could be interpreted as dishonest by the Europeans. Ownership of land and possessions was understood quite differently, again leading to moral confusion.

Livingstone, in common with most Englishmen at the time, had not appreciated before he reached Africa what a minute number of converts was actually made by the missionaries. Any missionary who could legitimately claim that his converts in a lifetime ran into double figures was outstandingly successful.

The relationship between missionaries and Africans was one of constant bargaining. The Africans in general wanted the powers the missionaries could give them without the discipline the missionaries sought to impose. They were particularly interested in 'gun magic' and the technical skills which the missionaries brought, and in the diplomatic advantages to be obtained in their dealings with other tribes or with the Boers. Livingstone's chief value to the Makololo originally lay in his relationship to Moffat and the influence exercised by Moffat over Mosilikatse. Even negotiations with the missionaries over such issues were in themselves an education to the tribesmen about Western political thought processes: discussion for example on the best system of rainmaking taught them much about rational thought. They resisted the reconstruction of their everyday lives and of the structure of tribal society. They also resented the religious element which they tended to associate with any natural misfortunes or disasters to hit the tribe. Livingstone was unfortunate: his attempts to convert Sechele coincided with a time of drought, and the Africans inevitably linked the two.

Livingstone's religious outlook was considerably in advance of his time. Personally he was a deeply religious man with a powerful faith which was at the centre of his existence. He deplored an overt show of religious behaviour: Bedingfeld in particular irritated him by parading his religion publicly. The fact that Livingstone kept his devotions as unobtrusive as possible probably accounted for some of the criticism during the Zambesi expedition of his failure to celebrate the Sabbath appropriately.

At a time when religious tolerance was rare, Livingstone's determination to embrace the whole of Christendom was exceptional. He first illustrated this by his decision to join the London Missionary Society, one of the few such societies to accept missionaries of all Protestant denominations. Agnes was confirmed into the Church of England while she and her father were both at Newstead with his enthusiastic support, although he was a Presbyterian minister. His remark that he would 'much prefer to see the Africans good Roman Catholics than idolatrous heathens' was seen as courageous.[10]

Since the rivalry between different denominations meant so little to Livingstone, inevitably as he grew older he lost interest in what was fast becoming a rigorously controlled, rule-bound competition between missionaries for the maximum number of converts. He longed for all Africa to share in the joy which he derived from his religion and to accept the broad principles of Christianity, which he saw as inseparable from the best elements of civilized life in Europe. He hoped too, above all, even though history did not support him, that this would prove incompatible with the practice of slavery. He saw it as best achieved not by the slow traditional missionary methods but by travelling through country 'beyond other men's lines' preaching Christianity increasingly by example rather than by intensive education and a demand for compliance with those aspects of the faith which were incompatible with the local way of life. Ultimately he hoped to see the breakdown of those aspects of the tribal system which were at variance with Christianity, but he was content at first at least to sow the seed without expecting total compliance. That this approach accorded well with his own preferred way of life is indisputable, but it is likely that he genuinely also felt that it was the best way forward. This was summed up by *The Times'* leader writer after his death. 'He was not a missionary who abandoned his proper vocation for that of a Traveller,' declared the paper, perhaps optimistically, on 14 April 1874, 'but he was the first missionary who fully realised that travel and the mutual intercourse which it promotes are the first conditions requisite for the successful introduction of Livingstone's message among uncivilised tribes.'

To describe Sechele as the only convert demands strict adherence to the letter of the law in defining converts. Two interesting examples are Chuma and Susi. Livingstone was responsible for baptizing neither of them. Chuma rejoined him in India having been baptized during his education there. In his early days with Livingstone, he could at best have been described as a lapsed convert. By the time of Livingstone's death he had become a true Christian in almost every sense of the word. The same could be said of Susi, and when the two men came to England, 'without making any ostentatious profession of religion, they showed themselves sincere Christians, both in conversation and conduct. On Sunday, as a matter of course, they attended morning and evening service in the Chapel, where their reverent demeanour was remarked by all to be an example to many English churchgoers.'[11] Susi was not baptized until 13 years after the death of Livingstone. Technically, neither of these two count among Livingstone's conversions. The technical rules seem to have little meaning.

Jeal names two fields in which he failed, which Livingstone might perhaps have conceded at the time of his death. Yet 30 years later none could question his success, and with his foresight and his optimism he would probably not have been surprised. As a promoter of other men's missionary efforts, failure soon turned to success. The two missions which had come out to Africa on his recommendation had both to be abandoned with considerable loss of life. The extent of his responsibility has already been considered. After his death Roger Price, the sole adult survivor of the Linyanti mission who had been so castigated by Livingstone, returned to Africa for the LMS. Within a few years of his death James Stewart, the young man who had been so disillusioned by the discovery that his boyhood idol had feet of clay that he had flung his copy of *Missionary Travels* in the Zambesi, had established a mission centre near Lake Nyassa: he named it Livingstonia. E. D. Young, who led the expedition to establish that Livingstone had not been murdered, brought a steamer to control Lake Nyassa: he called it the *Ilala*, after the region where Livingstone died. A group of Scottish missionaries built a town to house the mission they established in the Shire Highlands: they named it Blantyre. Bishop Tozer's successor, Bishop Steere, brought the Universities Mission back to a settlement on the shore of Lake Nyassa.

If in his lifetime he failed to persuade the British government to advance into Africa, no such reluctance was shown in the years after his death, in the time known to history as the Scramble for Africa. Livingstone would not have been pleased to know of the part played by Stanley in creating the Congo Free State for King Leopold II of Belgium, where some of the worst atrocities committed by Europeans in Africa were perpetrated. On the other hand he would have admired many of Stanley's successes, if not always the manner in which he achieved them. Perhaps the bitter pill of proving that the Lualaba was after all the Congo, as he had for so long feared, would have been sweetened by the knowledge that it was Stanley who proved this.

The consequences, good and bad, of the establishment of British rule over so much of Africa can hardly be laid at Livingstone's door, even though it was he, more than anyone, who had persistently drawn the attention of his fellow countrymen to that continent. A large part too was played by the missions he had done so much to inspire. Yet before ever Livingstone reached Africa it was evident that the continent would be dragged into playing its part in the world at large. The possibility, whatever its merits, of Africa remaining dark, hidden and isolated had long vanished. Since that was the case, and Livingstone had done all that he could to further this, he would have delighted in the knowledge that Britain was to play a full part. For his enthusiasm for colonization had always been based on the belief that his fellow countrymen had more to offer than other nationalities. His characteristically optimistic dream was to see the best of England and the best of Africa merged in a mutually beneficial symbiosis. Yet he appreciated too that this was but a transitory stage. He wrote in 1852:

> With colonies it is the same as with children – they receive protection for a time and obey from a feeling of weakness and attachment; but beyond the time at which they require a right to think for themselves, the attempt to perpetuate subordination necessarily engenders a hatred which effectually extinguishes the feeble gratitude that man in any condition is capable of cherishing.[12]

Other modern writers have had different criticisms of Livingstone. Timothy Holmes declares that 'Many Africans today, and with good reason, regard Livingstone as having been a spy. But he was more than merely that; he was the forward, and far from secret agent, of a new culture.'[13] Holmes's criticism is of the British Empire in Africa rather than of Livingstone, though he sees Livingstone as being in some measure responsible for, or used by others to appear responsible for, all that occurred after his death.

As an explorer too Livingstone's achievements are questioned by Jeal and other modern writers. If the only question is whether Livingstone was the first white man to see a particular lake or set foot in a particular place, the precise extent of the travels of Portuguese explorers before him becomes the paramount issue. Judith Listowel, writing a year after Jeal, states that Lake Bangweolo was Livingstone's only undisputed discovery, while Jeal concedes that he was probably the first to complete the crossing of the continent. The dictionary gives two relevant definitions of 'discover': to be the first to find or find out about, and to reveal or make known. Both definitions have usually been considered relevant to the world of exploring: were it now to be conclusively proved that Mallory and Irving did reach the summit of Everest, the effect on the reputation of Hillary and Tenzing would be minimal. For example, Jeal discounts any claim Livingstone may have had, and it was not something which interested him greatly, to the 'discovery' of Lake Moero on grounds that one Portuguese explorer died just south of there and three subsequent Portuguese expeditions reached that area. There is no clear proof that any of these actually reached the lake. Even if they did, since this fact was not made known to the rest of the world, the 'discovery' in one sense remained incomplete.

For much of Livingstone's success as an explorer lay in the way in which he revealed Africa to the world. Whether or not he was the first European to reach the Victoria Falls or Lakes Ngami, Shirwa and Nyassa, or to travel the full length of Lake Tanganyika, he was the first to reveal their existence to the world, to enable the 'armchair geographers' about whom Stanley wrote so bitterly to include them on their maps. By the time of Livingstone's death Jonathan Swift's verse was no longer applicable:

> So Geographers, in Afric-maps
> With Savage-Pictures fill their Gaps,
> And o'er uninhabitable Downs,
> Place Elephants for want of Towns.

As a geographer, however, Livingstone made two disastrous mistakes, both of which had far-reaching consequences. The first was his failure to explore the Zambesi thoroughly before his first return to England, so that he never realized that the Kebrabasa Gorge made it impossible to take a boat through. Since the whole existence of the Zambesi expedition was based on the concept of 'God's Highway' providing a navigable route from the sea to the heart of Africa, this was probably the most serious mistake Livingstone ever made, as he eventually realized, reluctant though he was to acknowledge it at the time.

The effect on his final expedition of his false conviction that the source of the Nile was to be found to the south of Lake Tanganyika was serious but not quite so devastating. For finding the source of the Nile was not the only objective although Jeal argues that it was the primary goal. While Livingstone's own views are expressed differently according to his mood and to his audience, his contention that the sources of the Nile were of no importance at all beside the need to destroy the slave trade holds more conviction. From a purely geographical viewpoint, the sources of the Congo may have held less romantic allure at the time, yet in the end they too had yet to be discovered. The work he put in was not wasted.

Yet Livingstone thought that his failure to find the source of the Nile was disastrous because he had convinced himself of the vital importance of this quest, not as an end in itself but as the only way he could think of, through the publicity it would engender, to achieve his real aim of putting an end to the slave trade. He did not realize in the last months of his life that he had already achieved the necessary publicity for this, not through a geographical discovery, but through the report he had sent home with Stanley on the Nyangwe massacre. His reports were always particularly effective because he never allowed them to become emotional. On this occasion, giving a factual account of the event which continued to fill his sleeping hours with nightmares for as long as he lived, he stirred all who read it in England so deeply that the signing of the treaty and the closing of the slave market in Zanzibar became inevitable. That did not complete the work, but from then on his two old associates, Waller, using Livingstone's name after his death, and especially Kirk, whom Livingstone had abused so bitterly, ensured that the transport of slaves by land as well as by sea was outlawed everywhere. A treaty to this effect was drafted by Kirk and signed by the Sultan on 13 April 1875. Livingstone had inspired the men who finally achieved his ambition. Like Moses, he did not live to see the promised land himself, but others only reached it when they did because of his leadership. He would have been pleased too, despite all that had happened, that the Universities Mission, which he had inspired, built the cathedral on the site of the old slave market in Zanzibar.

Livingstone's failure in his private life, as a father and as a husband, was a source of considerable grief to him in his last years. Few great men do become good family men: the best husbands and fathers are those who devote a high proportion of their thoughts, if not their time, to the welfare of wives and children. Time, energy and even concern are finite concepts, and Livingstone, like other great men, expected his wife and children to be as devoted to all he believed in as he himself was, and to accept without question the secondary, sacrificial part. Not for Mary the heroic role, the leadership, the opportunity to achieve. He would have liked her by his side throughout his life, but her mother eventually forced him to accept the impracticality of that. But even when she was with him, and fulfilling the role for which he had selected her admirably, he still saw her as secondary, secondary in importance to the aims he had set himself, and secondary too to himself. Probably when she agreed to marry him she had no idea of the calibre of man to whom she was promising to devote her life. For both it was a marriage of convenience, but they were also very fond of each other, although his letters to her never had the teasing wit which was so evident in many of his letters to friends. With Mary the tone was more often dictatorial, almost threatening.

When the children were small they too received letters with more of the authoritarian tone of a schoolmaster than either the wit or the delightful descriptions of things he had seen that he bestowed on other people. He soon lost touch with their interests and seemed to have no idea of the appropriate level for communication when away from them. He realized afterwards how much he had missed, and wrote to Cotton Oswell begging him to make time to play with his children before it was too late.

The main victim of his lack of care was Robert, though the others suffered too, both mentally and physically. Tom's constant ill health and early death have been blamed on his African childhood, though it is more likely that the problem started in Britain. Yet had Livingstone sent them away from him earlier Mary's life would have been even more wretched. The way of life Livingstone chose for himself was not suitable for a wife and children.

One of his children did love him deeply and became a source of great joy to him. The brief time he spent with Agnes was sufficient for them to develop a very special relationship. He was not overall a successful father, but he had a daughter whose love for and pride in him he fully reciprocated. It is more than many men can say of any of their children.

His relationship with his parents-in-law too was better than many men can boast. Despite Mrs Moffat's fury over his treatment of Mary and the children, the correspondence between them is friendly and reveals many shared interests as well as mutual admiration. Robert Moffat was for many years his closest confidant. They were involved in the same world, shared the same point of view on most issues and had a healthy respect for each other's opinions where they differed. The younger man was ready and willing to accept guidance and advice as well as practical help from the experienced missionary, and Robert Moffat was probably the first to appreciate what an exceptional man he had as a son-in-law.

As he got older and his reputation went before him, people meeting him for the first time would often have preconceived ideas. Perhaps it is an indication of the contradictions of his character that time after time they would reverse their original ideas. Many men when they met him for the first time had unrealistic expectations. Those who came expecting to find a saint were often so disappointed that they could never forgive him for his shortcomings. James Stewart was an extreme example of this, but others involved in the Zambesi expedition were similarly affected.

The converse was also true. Stanley had heard dreadful stories and found them so inaccurate that he swung to the opposite extreme and was soon convinced of Livingstone's close approach to sanctity. Before he ever met Stanley, Livingstone was aware that this was a common reaction.

At Zanzibar he found that a naval gentleman, who had been lately there, had not spoken of him in the most complimentary terms. But it had not hurt him with his best friends. 'Indeed, I find that evil-speaking against me has, by the good providence of my God, turned rather to my benefit. I got two of my best friends by being spoken ill of, for they found me so different from what they had been led to expect that they befriended me more than they otherwise would have done.'[14]

He did not always have any idea of the way in which people reacted to him. This was not so much insensitivity as a lack of experience with people. Although he could be vindictively bitter about declared enemies, others felt antagonized by him while he remained blissfully ignorant that he had said anything to indicate any cooling in his friendship with a person. After the Zambesi expedition he spoke in a kindly fashion to other people about Kirk and more especially Stewart, quite unaware that Stewart felt they had parted on extremely bad terms and Kirk had reservations about their friendship.

His experience of working and socializing with other people was quite exceptionally limited. As a boy, his burning ambition and determination set him apart from his contemporaries. They laughed at him and he despised them. As he grew older, up to the time when he sailed to Africa, he was a driven man, constantly working to earn enough money to pay his way and to acquire all the knowledge he was determined to absorb. At university a common interest in the topics they were studying and a shared determination to excel made him a few friends who would remain loyal for the rest of their lives. James Young is the outstanding example. His attempts to build satisfactory relationships with his contemporaries, both male and female, at Ongar were less successful. Once he reached Africa he saw himself, with some justification, as set apart from all those of similar age, most of whom he despised, sometimes with insufficient cause. He wrote to Moffat 'There is no more Christian affection between most if not all the "bretheren" & me than between my riding ox & his grandmother.'[15] He related well only to the older, more outstanding, men, Moffat and Philip in particular. Once his course was set in Africa he was determined to plough a lone furrow. The need to associate once more with men who saw themselves as his equals provoked the crisis of the Zambesi expedition.

His best friends throughout life might be divided into different categories. There were men such as James Young and Risdon Bennett whom he admired for their skills in a world where he had no wish to compete and, it must be admitted, whom he might correspond with regularly but spent little actual time with.

Then there were those rare and special people of whom Oswell is the outstanding example who were so generous spirited themselves that they could travel and work with Livingstone, contributing in equal measure to a true partnership, without ever provoking his impatience or his jealousy. Oswell brought out all Livingstone's best qualities and liked the man thus revealed to him. He wrote after Livingstone's death:

> He was pre-eminently a man, patient, all-enduring under hardships, content to win his way by inches but never swerving from it; gentle, kindly, brotherly to the children of the land; absolutely calm and unruffled amidst danger and difficulty, and well satisfied to see but one step in advance. If ever a man carried out the Scriptural injunction to take no thought for the morrow – that was David Livingstone.[16]

Judith Listowel, who accepts that Oswell was determined to claim no share of the credit for their joint discovery of Lake Ngami but blames Livingstone for failing to insist on this, feels that even Oswell eventually felt some resentment. The only evidence she offers for this is Oswell's refusal to edit the *Last Journals* and the fact that he did not visit Newstead while Livingstone was there. Yet his wife was unable to travel for health reasons at the time, he did not know Mr and Mrs Webb and did meet Livingstone in London and communicate constantly with him while helping him with his book.

Finally there were those men, including Webb, Waller and Stanley, usually considerably younger than him, whose genuine admiration survived a close acquaintanceship with him. For all his gruff, downright approach and lack of social polish, Livingstone must have possessed considerable charm. The Portuguese and the Arabs with whom he became friendly had every reason for avoiding his company, but in most cases he established excellent relations. Livingstone became a missionary originally because he had been brought up to see the propagation of the Christian gospel as the only worthwhile aim for any man. Yet this did not attract him personally. Much as he ached for the whole world to be converted to Christianity, his own religion was an intensely private affair, and preaching was not an art at which he excelled. He did long, though, to travel and explore, and he had a deep and abiding interest in scientific issues. Unusually for his generation, he regarded science and religion as complementary. It was not surprising that as soon as he heard of medical missionaries he should see this as the answer to all his needs, nor that, having experienced the life of the missionary in practice, he should find it unsatisfyingly restricted.

He lacked social and diplomatic skills and this failing was the cause of most of the problems in his life. An incorrigible optimist, his tendency to minimize difficulties arose from this, though other people frequently assumed that he was being devious. He has been accused of loving glory, yet any man for whom that was important would have returned more frequently to England.

Perhaps in a literal sense he was less than a successful missionary or explorer. He was so much more than either. A gifted doctor, scientist, linguist and writer, he travelled more extensively in Africa than anyone before him and told the world of all that he had found there. Through him, the centre of Africa ceased to be a dark, unknown space on the map and became a real place, full of interesting human beings, wonderful wildlife, with potential for businessmen, somewhere where in the not-too-distant future Englishmen might choose to go and live.

Even while he fought with many of those with whom he came in contact, he yet inspired men to carry on with his lifetime's real work: the abolition of the slave trade. His only interest in publicity was to use it to achieve this aim. Yet so effective was the campaign to promote him that he remains a part of our collective memory. A millennium poll to select our 50 top countrymen of all time placed him in 44th place. Even those who denigrate his achievements pay him the compliment of finding him still of interest more than a century and a quarter after his death.

The image so carefully created after his death of the gentle, saintly old man wandering round Africa still persists against all logic. No quiet and gentle innocent wraith could have destroyed the slave trade nor transformed a continent. The journey from factory boy at ten to Westminster Abbey at sixty is only made by an exceptional man. Livingstone was exceptional, a complex man of extraordinary contradictions. The kind and gentle doctor was also so single-minded in his pursuit of his own objectives that he could callously ignore everyone else's feelings. The optimist could be overtaken by deep depression. The logical thinker could be totally unreasonable. The teasing, witty letter writer could chill his wife and children with a cutting, dictatorial epistle. The peaceful man of God could hold a pistol to the head of his most loyal servant. The dreamer of dreams was also above all the man of action. He was so determined that men called it obsession, so courageous that he came close to insanity. Men would follow him unquestioningly to the ends of the earth, yet he was unable to quell a mutiny led by a handful of teenagers. He would do everything in his power to destroy the Arab slave traders, while continuing to travel in their company. He would wait patiently for weeks on the whim of an African villager, yet impatiently demand instant obedience from English colleagues.

Bishop Mackenzie wrote of Livingstone 'tramping along with a steady, heavy tread which kept one in mind that he had walked across Africa'.[17] He was an exceptional man, but neither saint nor failure.

Appendix
Livingstone's Alleged Love Child

In 1936 three elderly Africans, including Chief Chitambo, nephew of the Chief Chitambo in whose village Livingstone died, testified to the British authorities in Northern Rhodesia, including the District Commissioner, that Livingstone was accompanied on his last journey by a half-caste son. Chitambo claimed to have seen 'a man with red skin and everyone said it was the bwana's son.' His cousin stated that '[Livingstone] was riding on a donkey. Someone else was being carried in the machila [hammock]. The capitaos said the man in the machila was the bwana's son. He went in a machila because he was a chief's son, not because he was ill.'

These statements have recently been discussed in the press (*Sunday Telegraph*, 27 February 2000). The story was mentioned in a footnote by Oliver Ransford in his 1978 biography but no writer since then has considered it worthy of further discussion. Details of the statements are not consistent with each other or the known facts and when Livingstone's grandson visited Chitambo's village years before these statements were made he found that the oral account he was given there closely matched that given in the *Last Journals*. Sixty-three years is a long delay for the giving of reliable evidence.

None of Livingstone's most severe contemporary critics ever questioned his blameless reputation in respect of African women. From a practical point of view too it is almost impossible. On his last journey, the only district which he was revisiting was the Rovuma River and the southern point of Lake Nyassa. He first approached these regions in September 1859 and passed through for the last time in the spring of 1867. If, despite his previous unhappy experiences when travelling with children, he decided to take a child of six or less with him for the remainder of his expedition, the boy would only have been 12 when Livingstone died.

It is inconceivable that the existence of such a boy should never have been mentioned. Even if Stanley, Chuma and Susi adhered to a conspiracy of silence, others would have been less careful. Jacob Wainwright often spoke and acted unguardedly. Cameron showed scant respect for Livingstone's memory. All the Africans met many Europeans on their return. Some would inevitably have talked. It is unlikely that the Africans, including Chuma and Susi, would have seen anything wrong in Livingstone having a son by an African woman so they would have seen no reason to attempt concealment, at least until they met such Englishmen as Waller.

Two questions remain. What happened to the boy when they reached the coast? Did he make no attempt to accompany his father's remains to England? And why would a healthy young man be carried in a litter 'because he was a chief's son not because he was ill'? If anything is certain, it is that no son of David Livingstone's would have contemplated doing any such thing, at least while his father was there to see him do it.

Notes

Chapter 1 Blantyre: the Boy

1 David Livingstone Centre, Blantyre – original documents at the Centre.
2 David Livingstone Centre, Blantyre – original documents at the Centre.
3 Livingstone, *Missionary Travels*.
4 Jeal (1973).
5 Seaver (1957).
6 Livingstone, *Missionary Travels*.
7 Livingstone, *Missionary Travels*.
8 Livingstone, *Missionary Travels*.
9 Livingstone, *Missionary Travels*.
10 Livingstone, *Missionary Travels*.

Chapter 2 Glasgow, Chipping Ongar and London: the Student

1 Livingstone, *Missionary Travels*.
2 Gelfand (1957).
3 Gelfand (1957).
4 Livingstone, *Missionary Travels*.
5 Seaver (1957).
6 Seaver (1957).
7 Livingstone, *Missionary Travels*.
8 Seaver (1957).
9 Seaver (1957).
10 Blaikie (1880).
11 Jeal (1973).
12 Seaver (1957).
13 Seaver (1957).
14 Jeal (1973).
15 Jeal (1973).
16 Blaikie (1880).
17 Blaikie (1880).
18 Blaikie (1880).
19 Blaikie (1880).
20 Gelfand (1957).
21 Livingstone, *Missionary Travels*.
22 Livingstone, *Missionary Travels*.

Chapter 3 Kuruman and Mabotsa: the Newcomer

1 Blaikie (1880).
2 Holmes, *Letters*: to T. L. Prentice, 27 January 1841.
3 Holmes, *Letters*: to T. L. Prentice, 5 March 1841.
4 Jeal (1973).
5 Holmes, *Letters*: to T. L. Prentice, 5 March 1841.
6 Seaver (1957).
7 Blaikie (1880).
8 Holmes, *Letters*: to T. L. Prentice, 2 December 1841.
9 Chamberlin (1940): to Henry Drummond, 4 August 1841.
10 Chamberlin (1940): to the Rev. J. J. Freeman, 3 July 1842.
11 Schapera, *Family Letters I*: to Mr and Mrs N. Livingston, 26 September 1842.
12 Chamberlin (1940): to the Rev. Arthur Tidman, 30 October 1843.
13 Jeal (1973).
14 Many authorities, including Jeal (1973), follow Moffat's letter to the Directors in stating that the attack took place on 16 February. In fact Livingstone wrote to tell Moffat on the 15th, a Thursday, stating that it had happened 'last Wednesday' (Schapera, *Family Letters I*).
15 Livingstone, *Missionary Travels*.
16 Gelfand (1957).
17 Schapera, *Family Letters I*: to Mary Moffat, 1 August 1844.

Chapter 4 Chonuane and Kolobeng: the Missionary

1 School of Oriental and African Studies library: to Watt, 23 May 1845.
2 Schapera, *Family Letters I*, p. 121.
3 Schapera, *Missionary Correspondence*: to Arthur Tidman, 17 October 1846.
4 Schapera, *Family Letters I*: to Mr and Mrs Livingstone, 16 December 1843.
5 Schapera, *Family Letters I*: to Robert Moffat, 18 July 1845.
6 Seaver (1957).
7 Schapera, *Family Letters I*: to Mrs Livingstone, 4 May 1847.
8 Chamberlin (1940): to Charles Whish, 9 October 1846.
9 Chamberlin (1940): to Charles Whish, 9 October 1846.
10 Schapera, *Family Letters I*: to Robert Moffat, 27 October 1846.
11 Schapera, *Family Letters I*: to Mr and Mrs Livingstone, 5 July 1848.
12 Holmes, *Letters*: to Dr J. R. Bennett, 23 June 1848.
13 Chamberlin (1940): to Rev. Arthur Tidman, 17 March 1847.
14 Schapera, *Family Letters I*: to Robert Moffat, 5 October 1846.
15 To J. H. Parker, 11 May 1844 (quoted by Jeal, 1973).
16 Schapera, *Family Letters I*: to Robert Moffat, 12 May 1845.
17 Jeal (1973).

Chapter 5 Lake Ngami, the River Zouga and Cape Town: the Traveller

1 Schapera, *Family Letters I*: to Mrs Livingstone, 4 May 1847.
2 Holmes, *Letters*: to Miss Ingraham, 20 May 1849.
3 Listowel (1974), p. 56.
4 Phillips-Wolley et al., *Big Game Shooting*, pp. 27–31.
5 Schapera, *Missionary Correspondence*: to Arthur Tidman, 3 September 1849.
6 Schapera, *Family Letters II*: to Robert Moffat, 18 September 1850.
7 Quoted by Jeal (1973), p. 97.
8 Quoted by Jeal (1973), p. 101.
9 Seaver (1957), p. 160.

Chapter 6 To the West Coast of Africa: the Pioneer

1 Schapera, *Family Letters II*: to Robert Moffat, 16 September 1853.
2 Schapera, *Missionary Correspondence*: to William Thompson, 17 September 1853.
3 Schapera, *Missionary Correspondence*: to William Thompson, 17 September 1853.
4 Livingstone, *Missionary Travels*.
5 Livingstone, *Missionary Travels*.
6 Livingstone, *Missionary Travels*.
7 Chamberlin (1940): to William Thompson, 14 May 1854.
8 Jeal (1973).
9 Ransford (1978).
10 Chamberlin (1940): to Charles Livingstone, 6 February 1853.

Chapter 7 Across Africa from West to East: Great Leader of Africans

1 Schapera, *Family Letters II*: to Charles Livingston, 8 November 1854.
2 Seaver (1957).
3 Chamberlin (1940): to Tidman, 12 October 1855.
4 Livingstone, *Missionary Travels*.
5 Livingstone, *Missionary Travels*.
6 Schapera, *Family Letters II*: to Mary Livingstone, 14 September 1855.
7 Schapera, *Family Letters II*: to Robert Moffat, 12 September 1855.
8 Seaver (1957).
9 Schapera, *Family Letters II*: to Mary Livingstone, 14 September 1855.
10 Schapera, *Missionary Correspondence*: to Tidman, 12 October 1855.
11 Seaver (1957).
12 Schapera, *Missionary Correspondence*: Tidman to Livingstone, 24 August 1855.
13 Schapera, *Missionary Correspondence*: to Tidman, 23 May 1856, number 63.

Chapter 8 Britain: National Hero

1 Schapera, *Family Letters II*: to Charles Livingston, 16 May 1849.
2 Seaver (1957).
3 Schapera, *Family Letters II*: to Mary Livingstone, 14 January 1853.
4 Seaver (1957).
5 The chronology and quotations relating to this episode are taken from Jeal.

Chapter 9 The Zambesi and Shire Rivers: Flawed Leader of Europeans

1 Unless otherwise stated, all quotations from Kirk in this and the next chapter are taken from Coupland, *Kirk*.
2 Seaver (1957).
3 Seaver (1957).
4 Seaver (1957).
5 Jeal (1973).
6 Holmes, *Letters*: to James Young, 1859.
7 Jeal (1973).
8 Ransford (1978).
9 Seaver (1957).

Chapter 10 The Shire and Rovuma Rivers: the Husband

1 Coupland, *Kirk*.
2 Chamberlin (1940): to J. W. Sturge, 11 December 1858.
3 Ransford (1978).
4 Holmes, *Letters*: to James Young, 19 February 1862.
5 Stewart
6 Seaver (1957).
7 Ransford (1978).
8 Foskett, *Doctors*: Livingstone to Kirk, 8 August 1863.

Chapter 11 The Indian Ocean: Ship's Captain

1 Blaikie (1880).
2 Seaver (1957).
3 Blaikie (1880).

Chapter 12 Britain: Author and Father

1 Holmes, *Letters*: to James Young, 14 May 1861.
2 Holmes, *Letters*: to Mrs James Young, 29 August 1864.
3 Seaver (1957).
4 Holmes, *Letters*: to James Young, 19 February 1862.
5 Seaver (1957).

6 Holmes, *Letters*: to James Young (July–August 1863?).
7 Foskett, *Doctors*: Letter 23 (28 July 1864).
8 Jeal (1973).
9 Holmes, *Journey*.
10 Spinner (1913).
11 Seaver (1957).

Chapter 13 Lakes Nyassa, Tanganyika and Moero: the Explorer

1 Foskett, *Doctors*: Letter 60 (2 November 1870).
2 Coupland, *Last Journey*.
3 Ransford (1978).
4 Seaver (1957).
5 Coupland, *Last Journey*.
6 Seaver (1957).
7 Seaver (1957).
8 Coupland, *Last Journey*.
9 Coupland, *Last Journey*.
10 Seaver (1957).

Chapter 14 Ujiji and Unyanyembe: Scoop

1 Livingstone, *Last Journals*.
2 Stanley, *How I Found Livingstone*.
3 Spinner (1913).
4 Stanley, *How I Found Livingstone*.
5 Stanley, *How I Found Livingstone*.
6 Blaikie (1880).
7 Ransford (1978).
8 Coupland, *Last Journey*.
9 Jeal (1973).

Chapter 15 To Chitambo's Village: the Dying Man

1 Seaver (1957).
2 In this chapter quotations not otherwise attributed come from Livingstone, *Last Journals*.

Chapter 16 From Africa to Westminster Abbey: Venerated Leader

1 Seaver (1957).
2 *Eastern Daily Press*, 19 March 1913 (newspaper).
3 Spinner (1913).

Chapter 17 From Blantyre to Westminster Abbey: neither Saint nor Failure

1 Stanley, *How I Found Livingstone*.
2 Schapera, *Missionary Correspondence*, Tidman to Livingston, 14 April 1852.
3 Helly (1987).
4 Helly (1987).
5 Foskett, *Doctors*.
6 Helly (1987).
7 Helly (1987).
8 Blaikie (1880).
9 Spinner (1913).
10 Spinner (1913).
11 Spinner (1913).
12 Jeal (1973).
13 Holmes, *Journey*.
14 Blaikie (1880).
15 Schapera, *Family Letters II*: to Robert Moffat, 8 July 1850.
16 Ransford (1978).
17 Coupland, *Last Journey*.

Bibliography

Bennett, Alan (1991) *A Working Life: Child Labour Through the Nineteenth Century*. Cornwall: Waterfront Publications Cornwall.

Bierman, John (1990) *Dark Safari: The Life Behind the Legend of Henry Morton Stanley*. Austin: University of Texas Press.

Blaikie, William Garden (1880) *Personal Life of David Livingstone*. London: John Murray.

Campbell, R. J. (1929) *Livingstone*, London: Ernest Benn.

Chamberlin, David (ed.) (1940) *Some Letters from Livingstone 1840–1872*. London: Oxford University Press.

Chambers Biographical Dictionary (1990) Edinburgh: Chambers.

Clendennen, G. W. and Cunningham, I. C. (1979) *David Livingstone: A Catalogue of Documents*. Edinburgh: National Library of Scotland for the David Livingstone Documentation Project, 1979 and *Supplement* (1985).

Clendennen, G. W. and Cunningham, I. C. (1985) *David Livingstone: A Catalogue of Documents, Supplement*. Edinburgh: National Library of Scotland for the David Livingstone Documentation Project, 1985.

Comaroff, John L. and Jean (1997) *Of Revelation and Revolution*, 2 vols. Chicago and London: University of Chicago Press.

Coupland, Reginald (1928) *Kirk on the Zambesi*. Oxford.

Coupland, Reginald (1945) *Livingstone's Last Journey*. London: Collins.

Farwell, Byron (1958) *The Man Who Presumed: A Biography of Henry M. Stanley*. London: Longmans, Green & Co.

Forbath, Peter (1978) *The River Congo*. London: Secker & Warburg.

Foskett, R. (ed. and Introduction) (1964) *The Zambesi Doctors: David Livingstone's Letters to John Kirk 1858–1872*. Edinburgh: Edinburgh University Press.

Gelfand, Michael (1957) *Livingstone the Doctor: His Life and Travels. A Study in Medical History*. Oxford: Basil Blackwell.

Healey, Edna (1986) *Wives of Fame*. London: Sidgwick & Jackson.

Helly, Dorothy O. (1987) *Livingstone's Legacy: Horace Waller and Victorian Mythmaking*. Columbus: Ohio University Press.

Holmes, Timothy (ed.) (1990) *David Livingstone Letters and Documents 1841–72*. London: James Currey.

Holmes, Timothy (1993) *Journey to Livingstone: Exploration of an Imperial Myth*. Edinburgh: Canongate Press.

Hughes, Thomas (1889) *David Livingstone*. London: Macmillan.

Huxley, Elspeth (1973) *Livingstone and His African Journeys*. London: Weidenfeld & Nicolson.

Jeal, Tim (1973) *Livingstone*. London: Heinemann.

Liebowitz, Daniel (1998) *The Physician and the Slave Trade: John Kirk, the Livingstone Expeditions and the Crusade against Slavery in East Africa*. New York: W. H. Freeman.

Listowel, Judith (1974) *The Other Livingstone*. Lewes, Suffolk: Julian Friedmann.

Livingstone, David (1857) *Missionary Travels in South Africa*. London: John Murray.

Livingstone, D. and C. (1865) *Narrative of an Expedition to the Zambesi and its Tributaries*. London.

Moorehead, Alan (1960) *The White Nile*. London: Hamish Hamilton.

National Portrait Gallery (1996) *David Livingstone and the Victorian Encounter with Africa*. London: National Portrait Gallery.

Nicholls, C. S. (1998) *David Livingstone*. Stroud: Sutton Publishing.

Northcott, Cecil (1973) *David Livingstone: His Triumph, Decline and Fall*. London: Lutterworth Press.

Pachai, Bridglal (ed.) (1973) *Livingstone: Man of Africa Memorial Essays 1873–1973*. London: Longman.

Pakenham, Thomas (1991) *The Scramble for Africa*. London: Weidenfeld & Nicolson.

Parsons, Janet Wagner (1997) *The Livingstones at Kolobeng 1847–1852*. Botswana: The Botswana Society and Pula Press.

Phillips-Wolley, C. et al. (1895) *Big Game Shooting*, The Badminton Library. London: Longmans, Green & Co. (Authors include W. Cotton Oswell.)

Ransford, Oliver (1978) *David Livingstone The Dark Interior*. London: John Murray.

Schapera, I. (ed. and Introduction) (1959) *David Livingstone Family Letters 1841–56, Volumes I and II*. London: Chatto & Windus.

Schapera, I. (ed. and Introduction) (1960) *Livingstone's Private Journals 1851–53*. London: Chatto & Windus.

Schapera, I. (ed. and Introduction) (1961) *Livingstone's Missionary Correspondence 1841–1856*. London: Chatto & Windus.

Seaver, George (1957) *David Livingstone: His Life and Letters*. London: Lutterworth Press.

Simmons, Jack (1955) *Livingstone and Africa*. London: The English Universities Press.

Somervell, D. C. (1936) *Livingstone*. London: Duckworth.

Spinner, Alice (1913) *Livingstone and Newstead*. London: John Murray.

Stanley, Henry M. (1872) *How I Found Livingstone*. London.

Waller, Horace (1874) *The Last Journals of David Livingstone in Central Africa from 1865 to his Death*. 2 vols. London: John Murray.

Wallis, J. P. R. (1952) *The Zambesi Journal of James Stewart, 1862–1863 with a selection from his Correspondence*. London: Chatto & Windus.

Waters, John (1996) *David Livingstone Trail Blazer*. Leicester: Inter-Varsity Press.

Wilson, Colum and Irwin, Aisling (1999) *In Quest of Livingstone: A Journey to the Four Fountains*. House of Lochar Argyll.

Index